YOU Kan Red This!

YOU Kan Red This!

*Spelling and Punctuation for
Whole Language Classrooms, K–6*

Sandra Wilde

HEINEMANN
Portsmouth, NH

Heinemann
A division of Reed Elsevier Inc.
361 Hanover Street
Portsmouth, NH 03801-3912
Offices and agents throughout the world

Library of Congress Cataloging-in-Publication Data
Wilde, Sandra.
    You kan red this! : spelling and punctuation for whole language classrooms, K-6 / Sandra Wilde.
        p. cm.
    Includes bibliographical references (p.   ) and index.
    ISBN 0-435-08595-6
    1. English language—Orthography and spelling—Study and teaching (Elementary)—United States.   2. English language—Punctuation—Study and teaching (Elementary)—United States.   I. Title.
    LB1574.W55   1992
    372.6'32—dc20   91-23922
                                                              CIP

Designed by Jenny Jensen Greenleaf
Printed in The United States of America
94 95 96 97 9 8 7 6 5 4

In memory of Dr. Paul Dempsey (1947–1991),
in honor of his work with children

It is possible to spell a word correctly by chance, or because someone prompts you, but you are a scholar only if you spell it correctly because you know how.

Aristotle

As our alphabet now stands, the bad spelling, or what is called so, is generally the best, as conforming to the sound of the letters and of the words.

Benjamin Franklin

My spelling is Wobbly. It's good spelling but it Wobbles, and letters get in the wrong places.

A. A. Milne

Interviewer: Why do you think words are spelled the way they are? Does it make sense to you?
Jason (age 8): Sometimes it seems normal, sometimes it seems strange.

CONTENTS

SPELLING CELEBRATIONS

MINI-LESSONS

ACKNOWLEDGMENTS

First of all, I would like to thank the children and teachers whose work informed this book, especially Claudia Rossi, Jo Henn, Sister Conchita Boyer, Jeanie Freshcorn, and Sherrill Coutourier (teachers) and Gabriel Cachora, Jr., Sarah Estes, Erin Fey, Enna Hendricks, Lindsay Hyatt, Max Krochmal, Heather Moore, Annie Norris, Dylan Robards, and Jacob Slingland (children). Also, the National Institute of Education (through a grant provided to Yetta Goodman) and the Research Foundation of the National Council of Teachers of English provided financial support for much of my classroom research in spelling and punctuation.

   Many professional colleagues have stimulated my work on spelling, particularly Yetta and Ken Goodman, who gave me my first opportunity to conduct research in children's spelling and are an ongoing source of inspiration and encouragement. Dick and Lois Hodges have also been important "spelling buddies" whose interest in my work I greatly appreciate. Other colleagues who have supported my work and provided many hours of discussion, laughter, and occasional tears include Myna Matlin, Debra Jacobson, Maria Yon, Sharon Cathey, Martha Combs, Chris Faltis, Steve Lafer, Patricia Marshall, Mike Warner, and the Bobs (especially Christine Chaillé, Barbara Kiefer, and Harry Wolcott). A special word of thanks to Lois Bird; she knows why. My students have also been valuable sources of dialogue and feedback about spelling. I'm especially grateful to those who provided writing samples for the book, including Nance Greenstein, Jayme Hunsberger, Cathy McCormick, Samantha Moffett, Debbie Morin, Tom Snow, Chris Thurber, and Lisa Watanabe. David Northway and Vaughn Huff are also much appreciated for all their help and support.

   Thanks also go to Toby Gordon for her enthusiasm about this project, which began with her suggesting it and continued through helpful feedback and cheerful patience about missed deadlines; the title is also her contribution. (The title is in Tommie Sue Silva's handwriting.) Cheryl Kimball has been an excellent production editor; it's great to know that the book has been in such competent hands. Linda Kelm and Linda Zimmerman have provided last-minute faxing and other secretarial support, as well as morale enhancement, and my sister Janet (JT) Axelson is always just a phone call away for computer support.

Finally, I would like to honor the memory of Dr. Paul Dempsey of Tucson, Arizona, to whom this book is dedicated. Dr. Dempsey performed five operations on my face between 1984 and 1989, correcting a serious deformity and thereby transforming my life. As a member of Interplast International, the Flying Samaritans, and other organizations, he was active in performing reconstructive surgery on needy children in South America and elsewhere. Dr. Dempsey died in an airplane crash on March 27, 1991, at the age of 43, and is greatly missed by his family and the many patients he helped over the years. A portion of the royalties from this book are being donated to the Dr. Paul D. Dempsey Memorial Fund to help carry on his work.

· 1 ·

Introduction

M ike, a first grader, was studying the human body with his class, and had learned the old gospel song *Dem Bones* ("The head bone's connected to the neck bone . . . "). Sitting down to write with me one morning, he talked about how the song should use the scientific names for bones. We got up and went over to a chart of the human skeleton, where he discovered that *metatarsus* would be a good synonym for *foot bone* and *patella* for *leg bone*. He eventually decided to rewrite *Dem Bones* (Figure 1–1).

FIGURE 1–1   *Mike: Dem Bones*

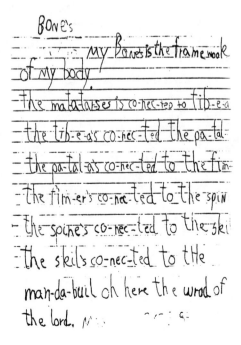

After writing MATATARSES[1], he commented that he had written the word "like in the dictionary" (i.e., by syllables), and then added dashes, saying they helped him write the words. He continued to use dashes as he wrote multisyllabic words. When he was about to write *spine,* he commented, "*Spine's* easy: *s-p-i-n-e*. And you don't have to put any dashes in." After he wrote *spine,* we returned to the skeleton chart to see if there was a word for neckbone, but there wasn't. Near the end of the story, he wrote WO as the first two letters of *word,* then commented, "W-o. That would be *ward,* right? Definitely," and changed the spelling to WROD.

Gordon, a fourth-grader, used quotation marks, hyphens, and capital letters as he wrote his piece "Avalanche in Bethlehem" (Figure 1–2).

FIGURE 1–2 *Gordon: Avalanche in Bethlehem*

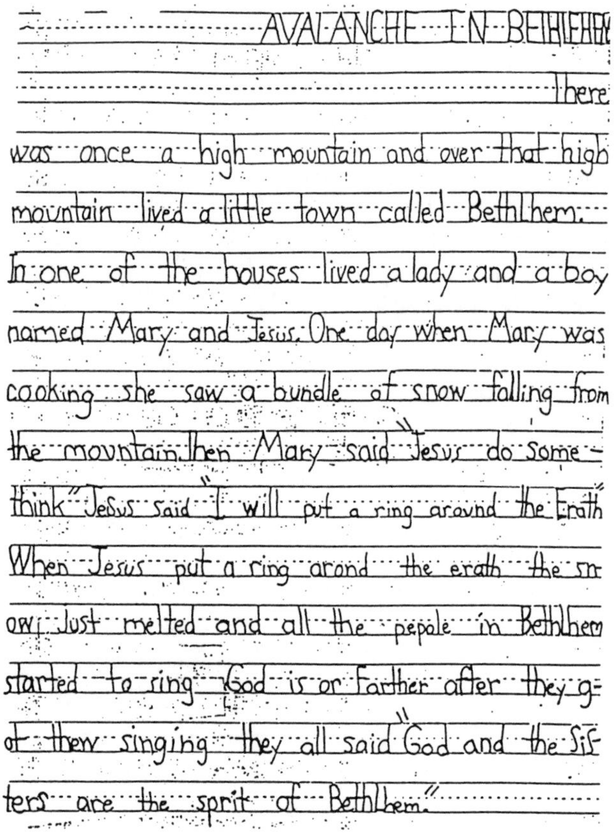
AVALANCHE IN BETHLEHEM
There
was once a high mountain and over that high
mountain lived a little town called Bethlhem.
In one of the houses lived a lady and a boy
named Mary and Jesus. One day when Mary was
cooking she saw a bundle of snow falling from
the mountain. Then Mary said "Jesus do some-
think" Jesus said "I will put a ring around the Erath
When Jesus put a ring arond the erath the sn
ow just melted and all the pepole in Bethlhem
started to ring "God is or Farther after they g-
ot thew singing they all said "God and the Sis-
ters are the sprit of Bethlhem."

[1] The usual convention of writing children's invented spellings in uppercase letters has been followed here.

Writing the first quotation mark of the piece (before *Jesus*), he originally angled it to the right, then erased it and angled it to the left. His second quotation mark, after *something,* was angled to the right. When asked how he knew where to place quotation marks, he responded that "it's after *said,*" and volunteered the information that "they use lines [i.e., as quotation marks] because when they talk it's like lines come out of their mouth." He used hyphens four times to divide words at the ends of lines: twice at syllable breaks (*some-think* and *sis-ters*) and twice in the middle of monosyllables (*sn-ow* and *g-ot*). He had previously volunteered the information that hyphens are used at the point where there is no more room on a line to finish a word; when asked why he had divided *something* after the *e* when there had been room for another letter, he was unsure, and stated that doing it the other way would have been just as good. When writing *Bethlehem* for the second time, he went to ask his teacher if it always needed to be capitalized. He answered his own question when he realized that it did because it's a place name, one of the categories his teacher had listed on a wall chart of words to be capitalized. He then went back and capitalized his first use of *earth* because "it's the name of a . . . a world!"

These two stories are typical of the many that teachers and researchers could tell about how children learn to spell and punctuate. They illustrate in microcosm the themes that will be developed throughout this book: the predictable kinds of developmental patterns that occur in young writers' spelling and punctuation, their active construction of knowledge, and the role of the classroom climate in contributing to growth in spelling and punctuation. But before discussing these, let's define some terms.

Invented spelling and developmental punctuation: Definitions

The term *invented spelling* first came into currency in 1971 (Chomsky, 1971; Read, 1971). Along with the less common synonyms *creative spelling* and *developmental spelling,* it is used to refer to writers' own spellings, which are recognized as being based on their underlying knowledge of language. Is invented spelling merely a euphemism for *misspelling*? No, for two reasons. First, "euphemism" means that an unpleasant truth is being glossed over, implying that the term "invented spelling" is an attempt to excuse error. But this is not the case. Instead, invented spelling appropriately implies that writers are actively involved in their own re-creation of written language. Insisting on a term like misspelling or spelling error suggests that the writer was aiming for the correct spelling but failed presumably through ignorance or carelessness. This does not accurately describe the process. Invented spelling is equivalent to the reading process term *miscue* instead of *error* (K. Goodman, 1982, Chapter 9). Invention is not a failure to achieve convention but a step on the road to reaching it.

Second, although the term invented spelling is sometimes used as a synonym for misspelling (i.e., a spelling other than the conventional or dictionary spelling), when the terms are used precisely, the former is more a description of process and the latter a description of product. The grid in Table 1–1 illustrates this point. Most commonly, we are used to thinking of spellings as being correct if the writer did not invent them and incorrect if they were invented. For in-

Spelling Celebration

Meaning relationships

Sheila, adult: "I was in EXCELLERATED classes all the way through school."

As adults, we often write words that are part of our oral vocabulary that we assume we know how to spell. If the word is one that we've seen in print and remembered, we may spell it correctly. If we haven't seen the word in print or haven't remembered its spelling, we may still spell it correctly as we use our knowledge about word meanings and analogies to other words. Sometimes we use the same knowledge base and come up with an incorrect but eminently logical spelling. This is what Sheila did here. EXCELLERATED classes are for those who excel, right? An important point to remember is that when spellings are constructed out of our knowledge about language rather than just remembered, the spelling is an invented one even if it happens to be correct. *Invention* refers to the process, not the product.

stance, Mike did not need to invent a spelling for *the* since he knew how to spell it and could just write it correctly, while he invented a spelling for *femur* and got the vowels wrong. However, the other two squares in the grid, though less common, are also possible. Mike's discussion of *spine* quoted earlier, where he named the letters before writing them, suggests that he was inventing the spelling (although of course any conclusions about process are necessarily inferences). In this case, however, the probable invention produced a correct spelling. Since English spelling is not completely regular, writers may or may not be successful in applying their knowledge of language to particular words. If Mike had followed the same vowel spelling pattern to write the word *fight,* he would have produced FITE, an incorrect spelling. Finally, writers may produce an incorrect spelling without inventing it. The spelling YAER (*year*), from another piece of Gordon's, came about because he miscopied the word from the dictionary. Noninvented incorrect spellings can also occur in other ways; for instance, when someone else tells the writer how to spell a word but

TABLE 1–1
Process and Product in Spelling

	PROCESS	
PRODUCT	Invented	Not Invented
Correct	SPINE	THE
Incorrect	FIMER (femur)	YAER (year)

gets it wrong. In that case it would still be an invented spelling but not the writer's.

The term *developmental punctuation* will be used in this book to describe a phenomenon parallel to invented spelling: children's use of punctuation that is based on their evolving knowledge of written language. The main reason that the word "invented" will not usually be used for punctuation is that the punctuation marks themselves are rarely invented in the same way that spellings are. Young writers do, however, use punctuation in ways that may differ from adult usage and that follow developmental patterns. In fact, children's punctuation can be seen as representing their gradually more sophisticated hypotheses about how this aspect of language works.

Looking at spelling and punctuation: "Dem Bones" and "Avalanche in Bethlehem"

One of the most important understandings coming out of recent studies of children's spelling and punctuation is that teachers can learn a great deal from looking at children's writing with an educated eye. We can use Mike's piece of writing (as we focus on spelling) and Gordon's (as we focus on punctuation) to explore some of this knowledge, which will be discussed and developed at greater length later on.

First of all, the writing itself illustrates a variety of the patterns that typically occur, patterns that the knowledgeable teacher learns to recognize and to track over time in children's writing. The following observations can be made about Mike's piece, each of them related to an appropriate generalization derived from spelling research.

1. *Observation* Although he used many difficult words, Mike still spelled 29 out of 50 words (58 percent) correctly.

   Generalization Children typically spell most words correctly after a certain point in their development (e.g., 92 percent for nine year olds; Applebee, Langer, & Mullis, 1987), particularly high-frequency words like *the, of,* and *to* (Wilde, 1986/1987).

2. *Observation* With the exception of the omitted *r* in *framework* and the failure to double consonants in three words (*connected, patella,* and *skull*), Mike spelled all consonants correctly.

   Generalization Consonants are more consistent than vowels in their spelling (Hanna, Hanna, Hodges, & Rudorf, 1966) and are therefore easier than vowels for young writers to spell (e.g., Read, 1975).

3. *Observation* Mike's incorrect vowel spellings in many cases occurred for very understandable reasons:

   The *e* in TIB-*E*-A reflects pronunciation.

   The *a* for short *e* in MA T-A-TAR-SE'S and PA-TA L-A is an instance of using the letter whose name sounds most like the sound being represented (to be explained at greater length in Chapter 3).

   The schwa vowel found in the unaccented syllables of words like *metAtarsUs* and *mandIblE* was sometimes spelled incorrectly. (The schwa sound can be spelled with any vowel letter, depending on the word, and is therefore highly unpredictable.)

② Spelling Celebration

How did kids spell 60 years ago?

Spellings of *circus* by 49 children, grade 1: "SRCUS (20), SRKS (10), SRKUS (8), CIRCUS (6), CRCUS (5)."

Ernest Horn (1929a) took a look at children's own spellings back in 1929, before the concept of invented spelling had been developed. He asked 195 first and second graders to write the word *circus*. He received 148 different spellings, 61 of them (by 108 children) at least somewhat reasonable phonetically. The five most common spellings are those above. Two patterns explain all of the invented features of these spellings: *c* is often replaced by *s* when it sounds like /s/ and *k* when it sounds like /k/; vowels before *r* and schwa vowels tend to be omitted. I think we can draw two conclusions here. First, invented spelling is something children have been doing for a long time; it's just that nobody understood how to look at it 60 years ago. Second, children's spelling certainly hasn't deteriorated from some golden age in the past; I would guess that 195 first- and second-grade children in today's reading/writing classrooms would produce far more than 5 correct and 108 reasonable spellings of *circus*. Does anyone out there want to replicate Horn's study?

The vowel in *hear* was spelled in a way that produced a homophone of the word.

Generalization The vowel system of English is complex and often unpredictable (Hanna et al., 1966), but children cope with it in systematic and fairly consistent ways (e.g., Read, 1975; Wilde, 1986/ 1987).

Mike's writing and the comments he made as he wrote provide evidence that these spellings were not mere happenstance but rather a reflection of his developing system of knowledge. First of all, his breaking down of long, difficult words into syllables shows his use of "sounding out" and phonetic information for spelling. Young writers who don't yet have a broad familiarity with written language draw heavily on the sounds of words in order to produce spellings. Mike ingeniously made the task a little easier for himself by segmenting these long words. Second, his oral spelling of and comment about *spine* showed that he was able to articulate a spelling as a complete oral string of letters, rather than dealing with only one sound and one letter at a time and that he recognized the difference between monosyllabic and multisyllabic words (although he would have been unlikely to use those terms). Finally, in his rejection of *wo* as the first two letters of *word*, he showed that he was able to think about and evaluate spelling alternatives before writing them down. (Perhaps in this case he was using an analogy to another word, assuming that the spelling *word* would have to rhyme with *lord*, which occurred three words later in his sentence.)

This vignette of Mike's spelling also reveals something about the role that the classroom climate plays in the process of learning to spell. Perhaps most importantly, Mike knew he was allowed, in fact encouraged, to use his own spellings, rather than being required to spell correctly in a first draft. This freed him up to feel comfortable in using big words that were far beyond what one would normally ask first graders to use. He also was aware of resources that spellers could use: he was familiar with the dictionary and used an anatomy chart to find the names of several bones. Although he didn't spell the bones' names correctly, his brief visual exposure to them may have led him to spell them better than if he had only heard them.

Similarly, one can comment on Gordon's use of punctuation including capitalization. Three main features stand out:

1. Four of his sentences (the first three and the last one) end with periods and the other three don't. Periods only appear at the ends of sentences. He didn't use any commas, although they would have been appropriate before the quotations and between some of the clauses.
2. Four words were hyphenated at the ends of lines, two correctly and two not.
3. Three quotations were correctly punctuated (except for the omission of a preceding comma).
4. The words *Mary, Jesus, Bethlehem, Earth* (one of two times), *God, Father,* and *Sisters* were capitalized, as well as the first word after each period.

Although it is not possible to relate each of these observations to specific generalizations from previous research since so little work has been done on children's punctuation, they can each be explained in terms of Gordon's actions and statements relating to his ongoing hypothesis construction about punctuation.

Gordon didn't discuss periods or commas while writing "Avalanche in Bethlehem," but an interview with him at the end of that school year was revealing. He was able to describe appropriately when periods are used ("at the end of a sentence"), but he gave only a partial explanation of commas, which he said are used for writing dates and in words like *don't* (i.e., he confused the comma and apostrophe). He also was apparently unaware of the use of commas within sentences and before quotations. In all of Gordon's writing in fourth grade, he omitted periods about a third of the time. My sense is that he knew how to use them but sometimes forgot, particularly once he got involved in what he was writing, as in this piece.

Gordon enjoyed using hyphens, which his sister had recently taught him, and his use of them appeared to be in transition, as evidenced by his hyphenation of *something*. Although he had not yet learned that monosyllables cannot be hyphenated, and consciously theorized that the amount of room one has on the line is the sole basis for determining where a word should be divided, on some more intuitive level he was beginning to realize that syllable boundaries are the appropriate spot for hyphenation.

Gordon had a clear hypothesis for how to use quotation marks, as well as his own ideas about why they take the form of little "lines" and an awareness of which direction they slant. (This latter awareness could only have come from noticing handwritten text, since quotation marks take a different form in print.) Although his rule for the placement of quotation marks, placing the first one after *said* and the second one after the person is done talking, worked accurately here, it was less accurate when applied to indirect and divided quotations, as seen in excerpts from another piece:

> HIS FATHER SAID "THAT HE CAN CARRY THE DEER WITH HIM."
> LITTLE KNIFE SAID "HIS FATHER DON'T WORRY. . . ."
> "(Little Knife," said his father, "don't worry. . . . ")

Gordon's first approximation of the rule for using quotation marks would therefore need to be refined over time.

Finally, Gordon had begun to apply rules for using capital letters. His teacher had provided a list of such rules, but he still had to decide the cases for which they were relevant. Interestingly, whether to capitalize *earth,* as Gordon did, falls within the realm of stylistic variation. The editors of *Time* magazine ("Why Not Earth," 1989) had been asked by readers why they chose not to capitalize the name of our planet. The editors stated that they capitalize only "those celestial bodies named after mythological gods." Gordon did not mention why he had capitalized *Father* and *Sisters,* but if asked presumably would have said that they were names of people. Again, his hypothesis would eventually need further refinement (i.e., to distinguish more clearly between common and proper nouns), but it was a good first approximation.

In the same way as with Mike's spelling, the classroom climate contributed to Gordon's development in punctuation. His teacher encouraged her class to use punctuation as they wrote rather than saddling them with worksheets. She also provided informal instruction and reference materials (such as her chart about when to capitalize) in order to stimulate the students' learning.

What is perhaps most interesting about what we have discovered from looking at these two pieces of writing is the depth and breadth of knowledge that is available to teachers who take the time to look closely at their students' spelling and punctuation and who know what to look for. An amazing amount of information about children's thought processes is available to a teacher who sits down with students and watches them write and listen, to their reasoning.

The importance of invented spelling and developmental punctuation

Although children's own spelling and punctuation are certainly of intellectual interest, the elementary school teacher may wonder what relevance they have for the classroom. Isn't it the job of teachers to get children to spell and punctuate *correctly*? I would rephrase that goal slightly and suggest that the goal of curriculum and instruction is to produce competent and independent spellers and users of punctuation (Wilde, 1990a) and that a developmental perspective is a crucial part of attaining that goal. There are two major influences that our increasing knowledge in this area has had, and will continue to have, on the classroom: a new way of looking at spelling and punctuation in the writing process, and a reconsideration of curriculum and instruction in spelling and punctuation.

The new interest in children's spelling and punctuation has emerged simultaneously with a re-emergence of writing in the classroom, as exemplified by the work of Donald Graves (1983) and others. Spelling and punctuation have been placed in perspective, as tools that writers use to make their thoughts more understandable to an audience, not as ends in themselves. In the traditional view, learning to write was seen as a part-to-whole process: children were to begin with correctly spelled words, which they would then learn to put into proper sentences, gradually working their way up to structured paragraphs and eventually essays and term papers. It was an unquestioned assumption that each step in the process would be "mastered" before moving on. Unfortunately, children never did much writing under this system. They spent a good deal of time filling in blanks in workbooks, punctuating sample sentences, and so on (Fillion, 1983). If children ever got a chance to apply this knowledge, the results were often disappointing, mainly because they had never developed the habit of writing, but also because the pressure to always be correct is inhibiting. When students were given the chance to write freely (often during "Creative Writing" on Friday afternoons), they were expected to use the dictionary or ask the teacher if they didn't know how to spell a word. This focus on correctness produced, for the most part, nonwriters.

In many classrooms today, the situation has completely changed. Children are writing right from the beginning of school, at whatever level they are capable of. The focus is on the whole: the expression of ideas is primary and central, and there is an expectation that the parts—the shaping of a piece, the construction of sentences, and yes, correct spelling and punctuation—will gradually become refined over time. Parents, when their children learn to talk, focus on the expression of ideas, knowing that children will eventually pronounce their words better and produce more coherent sentences, that form follows function. Similarly, teachers have come to realize that not only will their students be better writers if the mechanics of writing are deemphasized but that the mechanics themselves develop best in the context of extensive, meaningful writing. Another way of saying this is that the best way to develop competent, independent spellers and users of punctuation is to focus first on independence, on letting writers rely on their own evolving knowledge base rather than on teacher-supplied rules, formulas, and spellings, and to trust that competence will evolve over time.

This leads directly into the other classroom implication of invented spelling and developmental punctuation: a new way of looking at how we help children to learn about spelling and punctuation. Traditional curriculum, again, went from part to whole. Children memorized lists of spelling words and rules for punctuation and practiced these in interminable exercises, in the hope that there would be a transfer effect to writing. Recent research has, however, made it clear that children's spelling and, by extension, their use of punctuation can best be described as the instantiation of increasingly sophisticated schemata, which are conceptualizations of the system as a whole (Zutell, 1979). Therefore, teachers and researchers have begun to rethink what curriculum and instruction for spelling and punctuation should look like. In addition to recognizing the powerful role of wide reading and writing, they have begun to question whether there is any continuing role for textbooks, as well as to consider what kinds of materials and activities will support the evolution of children's spelling and punctuation concepts.

A look ahead

This book will examine all of the themes touched on briefly in this introduction. Part I, Understanding Spelling and Punctuation, will help teachers to develop their own knowledge base. Chapter 2 explores spelling and punctuation themselves: how they work, their complexity, and why they are the way they are, as well as giving an overview of what we know about how children learn to spell and punctuate. Chapter 3 uses writing samples to illustrate what we know about the predictable developmental paths that young spellers and users of punctuation follow. Part II, Spelling and Punctuation in the Classroom, will help teachers apply that knowledge base to classroom practice, with individual chapters focusing on portraits of spelling and punctuation in the life of the classroom; how to help children use these written language conventions more effectively; strategy development; integrating spelling and punctuation into the broader curriculum; and evaluation, grading, and parent communication.

One special feature of this book which you may have already noticed is a series of anecdotes and meditations that I've called "Spelling Celebrations." These celebrations, many of which have also appeared in the *Whole Language Catalogue* (Goodman, Bird, & Goodman, 1991), both provide information about how to look at invented spellings and, it is hoped, model an attitude of curiosity and delight in children's language development. They are scattered throughout the book, with a list of them included after the table of contents. One other special feature is an annotated reading list, in Appendix F, which is a resource to help both teachers and students further extend their knowledge about various aspects of spelling and punctuation.

PART ONE

Understanding Spelling and Punctuation

· 2 ·

Spelling and Punctuation: How They Work and How They're Learned

Years of workbooks and drills have turned many of us away from spelling and punctuation; which seem to be dull and dry topics of study, superficial aspects of language that are of little interest to anyone but a scholar. But when one looks at spelling and punctuation not as lists of rules and examples but as *systems*, they are fascinating in their richness and complexity. This chapter focuses on providing the reader with information both about how spelling and punctuation work as written language systems and about how learners come to use and understand them. Since this is a complicated and somewhat technical subject, I've tried to be illustrative rather than comprehensive; the suggested readings in Appendix F are resources for those who would like to read further. Although I will discuss the English language, much of what is said applies, with appropriate modifications, to other languages as well. I've addressed various topics by posing and answering questions about those aspects of written language conventions of English and how they are learned that a teacher might wonder about.

Understanding English spelling and punctuation as systems of written language

Teachers might ask why it is valuable to know about spelling and punctuation in the first place and be tempted to skip ahead to ideas for classroom practice. This information is useful for two reasons: First, the more teachers develop their own knowledge base about the English language, the better equipped they will be to evaluate and develop curriculum. For instance, if one understands how complex the relationship between sounds and letters is in English, one is unlikely to try to teach children a set of rules for predicting spellings based on pronunciation. The teacher is also better able to appreciate how children often produce spellings that are incorrect but plausible. Second, as teachers discover how interesting the study of language can be, as they learn to appreciate linguistics as a field of study, they can begin to share some of this enthusiasm with their students. For instance, helping children to explore creatively all the ways that writers have used parentheses can help to develop their sense of ownership in and appreciation for language.

It may seem at first glance that spelling and punctuation can best be described as ways of representing spoken language: that spelling represents the sounds of words and punctuation represents features of intonation like the pauses between words. It's not that simple, however. Oral language and written language are two different ways of representing thought; they use different media and therefore have different constraints (K. Goodman, 1984). Although spelling and punctuation certainly have a relationship to oral language, they aren't a direct representation of it. Both oral and written language can perhaps be described as sets of rules for translating meaning into a surface representation. Therefore, learning to spell and punctuate isn't just a matter of learning a set of rules for translating sounds into writing. It's more appropriately conceptualized as learning to understand the workings of a system that expresses meaning in systematic but complex and subtle ways.

The English spelling system

Many writers over the years have complained about the complexity of English spelling. George Bernard Shaw is well known for his observation that the word *fish* could be spelled *ghoti: gh* as in lau*gh*, *o* as in w*o*men, and *ti* as in na*ti*on. This complexity has led educators to suggest that spelling should be learned either by the memorization of extensive lists of words or by the systematic study of a large number of rules about relationships between sounds and letters. Many users of written language over the years have wished that our spelling system were simple, logical, and rational.

Why is our spelling system so complicated, and how do the history and geography of English spelling influence the way it works? In order to answer these questions, we can make several statements that examine the system from a variety of angles, each one filling in one piece of the puzzle.

1. We don't have enough letters.

   English spelling is an alphabetic system, but only partially. If we had one letter for every sound, spelling would be easy, but we have about 40 sounds[1] (depending on dialect) and only 26 letters. The 21 consonant letters work fairly well for spelling 24 consonant sounds[2], but we have only 5 vowel letters (plus the help of *w* and *y*) to represent about 16 vowel sounds.[3] This is why, for instance, we need two letters to spell most vowel sounds.

2. Spellings vary according to a sound's position in the word and are affected by other letters in the word.

   If our spelling system were purely alphabetic, we'd spell the word *judge* as **juj*[4], but that looks funny, doesn't it? This is because we don't

---

[1] Appendix A summarizes the symbols I've used to represent each of these sounds.

[2] /b, ch, d, f, g, h, j, k, l, m, n, ng, p, r, s, sh, t, th(*th*in), TH (*th*is), v, w, y, z, zh(az ure)/

[3] Short and long *a, e, i, o,* and *u;* and the vowels of b*ou*t, b*ough*t, b*oy,* b*oo*k, b*oo*t, and *a*bout

[4] Following linguistic convention, I've used an asterisk to indicate illegitimate possible spellings.

 Spelling Celebration

Homophones

Elaine, fourth grade: "It was BRING (*brighting*) in *ARE* (*our*) eyes.... We ALMOTS (*almost*) went OF (*off*) the RODE (*road*).

Homophones are words that are pronounced the same and spelled differently. Spelling textbooks usually devote at least one lesson a year to studying homophone pairs, with the idea that if students' attention is drawn to them they are less likely to confuse them. I wonder about this, though. Frank Smith (1982) has said that often we misspell words not because we can't remember the right spelling but because we can't forget the wrong one. Before I became a teacher, I never confused the words *their* and *there*, but after a year or so of seeing one substituted for the other in student writing, I began to occasionally switch them myself. (I still knew the difference between them, but my pen would produce the wrong one.) Maybe we'd be better off not associating homophones with each other at all. Homophones that we don't think of as homophones (such as *prize* and *pries*) are probably not confused very often. As for Elaine, her class had studied homophones the week that she wrote these lines. (In her dialect, as in many, the words *are* and *our* are homophones.) I can't prove that there's a connection, but this is certainly something for teachers to think about!

---

use *j* at the ends of words. Why do we have a silent *u* in the word *guide*? Because otherwise the *g* would have the wrong sound since *g* followed by *i* is pronounced like *j*. Why do we have two *n*'s in *dinner* when we only hear one? To show that there's a short vowel in the first syllable.

3. We have some arbitrary rules that aren't even directly connected to pronunciation.

Egg, odd, bee, and *wee* are all three letters long when a two-letter spelling would have worked just as well because we don't usually have two-letter words that aren't function words (like *be* and *we*). *Basically* (from *basic*) isn't spelled **basicly*; instead, it looks the same as words like *radically* (from *radical*).

4. Spelling reflects meaning as well as pronunciation.

It might be more logical to spell *nation* as **nashun*, but then we wouldn't be able to see the connection to *native*. The different spellings of *frays* and *phrase* (both pronounced /frāz/) help the reader to keep their meanings straight.

5. English has adopted words from other languages.

Many adopted words that aren't spelled the way we'd expect (based on their pronunciation) reflect the spelling system of the language they come from, such as *Cello* (Italian), *troussEAU* (French), and *tortiLLa* (Spanish).

 Spelling Celebration

Silent letters

Kris, second grade: "RIST (*wrist*)" (on a labeled diagram of the body)

Gordon, fourth grade: "There was once a boy named Little NIFE (*Knife*)."

It's certainly not surprising that children sometimes omit silent letters when they spell. Words that begin with the sounds /n/, /h/, and /r/ sometimes begin with the letters *gn* (*gnash*), *kn* (*knock*), *wh* (*whole*), and *wr* (*write*). But the only way that a writer can know if a silent letter appears is by knowing the word. The vast majority of words that begin with the sound /n/ begin with just the letter *n*, so the most reasonable strategy is to assume that a word does *not* begin with a silent letter. In my study of third and fourth graders (Wilde, 1986/1987), children omitted initial silent *k* and *w* about half of the time (37 out of 70 cases). Interestingly, they also occasionally added an unnecessary silent letter (e.g., KNOW for *now*). Omitting silent letters can be explained as phonetic spelling, but adding unnecessary ones grows out of an overgeneralization about the *visual* aspects of our spelling system.

6. Oral language changes over time more than spelling does.

The *p* in words like *psychology* used to be pronounced (as it was in the original Greek and still is in French). So were the *g* and *k* in words like *gnash* and *knife*. Although pronunciation changed, traces of the old version were preserved in the spelling.

7. Spoken dialects differ more than spelling does.

The spelling system in North America is pretty much the same for everyone, even though we don't all pronounce words the same. Those of us who pronounce *Mary, marry,* and *merry* alike need to learn that they're spelled differently; those of us who feel that the different spellings of *pen* and *pin* logically reflect their different pronunciations may not realize that they are homophones for other speakers of English. Also, don't forget about the British kids (and Bostonians), for whom the *r*'s in words like *park* are silent. (*Parks* in England is roughly a homophone of *pox*.) If spelling matched any one speaker's language perfectly, it would still be a mismatch for someone else living across the country (or someone from a different social class living two streets away).

So, going back to the original questions, English spelling is complicated because it *is* complicated; it carries a lot of information. (Also, it's harder to spell acceptably than it used to be, say five hundred years ago. More variation occurred in spelling back then, and even Shakespeare spelled his name several

 Spelling Celebration

How many ways could you spell "circumference"?

Ernest Horn, adult: "PSOLOKHOEGMPPHOURIADNZ (*circumference*)"

No, Ernest Horn (1929b) didn't really use this spelling of *circumference*, but he did invent it. In an exploration of the predictability of English spelling, Horn determined every possible spelling of each phoneme in *circumference* and then figured out how many possible combinations there would be. He came up with nearly a trillion! (Even using only relatively common spellings of each phoneme resulted in 396,900,000 possible spellings.) Of course, in practice not all combinations of spellings can go together, but there is enough unpredictability in the spelling system that every word has at least several reasonable spellings (e.g., SERCUMPHARANCE for *circumference*), if you're going mainly by phonetic information. This should make it very clear that sounding it out cannot possibly be an effective spelling strategy! Oh, by the way, *ps* as in *psychology*, *olo* as in *colonel*, *kh* as in *khaki*, *oe* as in *does*, *gm* as in *diaphragm*, *pph* as in *sapphire*, *our* as in *journey*, *ia* as in *parliament*, *dn* as in *Wednesday*, and *z* as in *quartz* equals PSOLOKHOEGMPPHOURIADNZ.

different ways.) On the negative side, it may take longer to learn to spell in English than it would take to learn a "purer" alphabetic system. But our system is an interesting one that reflects the history and meaning of our words as well as their pronunciation. At any rate, we're stuck with it; massive spelling reform isn't likely at any time in the near future (and a perfect system wouldn't remain that way anyway). English spelling is frustrating only when we expect it to be something it's not (i.e., a pure alphabetic system). If we see it for what it is, we can appreciate it for representing a lot of information about sound, a fair bit about meaning, and a little about etymology and history. Being aware of this can help teachers realize that it may take young writers a while to spell as competently as we would like, as well as suggest how we can support the learning process.

Punctuation

Most of us, if asked what punctuation does and how it works, would probably respond by saying it indicates pauses in speech, but it's really much more subtle and complicated. Examining two questions illuminates this: First, how do punctuation marks like the period, question mark, and comma mark off sentences and parts of sentences; and second, how do other punctuation marks act as meaning units?

In oral language, we use intonation (pauses, stress, and pitch changes) to signal where sentences end and what kinds of sentences they are; in writing we use punctuation (periods, question marks, exclamation points, and the capital letters that mark the beginnings of sentences). In speech, we have a lot more choices and can use intonation to mark fine shades of meaning; we can pronounce four words like "you're going to China" in ways that express attitudes ranging from excitement to curiosity to disapproval and so on. All punctuation can express is whether we're making a statement, asking a question, or exclaiming. But in most cases, of course, this simple information is all we need; when we read aloud we can add normal intonation. (If we need to say more in writing, we can do something like the following: " '*You're* going to *China*?!' she shouted incredulously.") In modern English, punctuation is primarily a signal of grammatical boundaries, although this hasn't always been the case; in ancient Greek and Hebrew, as well as in early English, punctuation marks were often used as pause markers for orators (Brown, 1985; Little, 1984). Their role now is more abstract. It isn't really true, as many of us were taught, that a comma marks a short pause and a period a longer one; instead, they mark grammatical units like sentences and clauses that sometimes are separated by pauses in speech. Learning to punctuate sentences is therefore a conceptual task that will reflect the writer's evolving sense (explicit and/or implicit) of what a sentence is. With more sophistication, writers will also learn to use punctuation marks like the colon, semicolon, and comma to signal grammatical division within sentences.

In addition to those uses of punctuation, there is also a grab bag of other punctuation marks that signal specific meanings and usually aren't represented orally at all, even indirectly. (For instance, the slash in *his/her* isn't pronounced; in oral language, *or* can replace the slash, or the sentence can be rephrased.) A few examples of how punctuation marks can be described in terms of the meaning they express are the apostrophe, capital letters, parentheses, and quotation marks.

Apostrophes can carry either of two messages: "This is a possessive noun," or "Two words have been joined." The apostrophe is perhaps the clearest example of a punctuation mark that has no corresponding form in speech. In oral language, only the context can clarify the different meanings of the following four phrases:

    a. The monkey's howling (and it's running around the cage).
    b. The monkey's howling (annoyed us; we wanted to kill it).
    c. The monkeys' howling (annoyed us; we wanted to kill them).
    d. (We listened all night to) the monkeys howling.

In written language, the only possible confusion is between the first two, which do require context to be distinguished.

Capital letters divide sentences but can also signal "This is a proper name," or "This is important." In marking proper names, they tell us something about meaning, providing a clear visual signal to the reader:

    a. They were going to the white house for dinner.
    b. They were going to the White house for dinner.
    c. They were going to the White House for dinner.

(In German they provide a different signal: all nouns are capitalized.)

Capital letters also, because they stand out visually, provide emphasis, which we see when they're used to facilitate text organization (as in titles or headings), as well as in dialogue to express loudness of speech or intensity of emotion.

Parentheses say "This is a parenthetical remark." They enclose material that is incidental to or explanatory of the main thrust of a sentence or text. Parentheses can also enclose material that only echoes, comments on, or clarifies the main text, and is often not read aloud at all, as in these examples:

   a. The budget is sixty million dollars ($60,000,000).
   b. I'm going to Moose Jaw (!) for the summer.
   c. Elaine's story read, "I went to the CORVLFAROV (carnival)." (In this case, the word inside the parentheses is read instead of what precedes it.)

Quotation marks usually say "Someone is speaking." But they can also, in a more sophisticated use, say "I disavow what I'm saying." or "I'm being ironic." Finnegan (1986) describes how in South Africa,

> mere quotation marks may call into question the entire society's legitimacy. Thus, one can say that 15 percent of the population owns 87 percent of the land, or that 15 percent of the population "owns" 87 percent of the land—impugning, in the latter case, the very idea of legal ownership in South Africa, and suggesting, perhaps, that this state of affairs is not only illegitimate but also temporary.(p. 28)

The varied and subtle shades of meaning that punctuation can help to express can be seen most clearly in literature, where unconventional uses are most likely to be explored. The French novelist Marcel Proust wrote sentences hundreds of words long, broken up by commas and semicolons; e. e. cummings wrote poetry with little or no punctuation and capitalization, sometimes even frequently putting one word in parentheses inside another; the journalist Tom Wolfe uses a variety of punctuation to suggest the rhythms of oral speech. As with spelling, the more punctuation is seen in all its complexity as a written language system, the more interesting it becomes.

Spelling, punctuation, and the learner

In recent years, our knowledge of how children learn spelling and punctuation has expanded tremendously. Where being a good speller was once seen only as a matter of having "mastered" the spellings of a large number of words (Hodges, 1987), today we realize that children's spelling is not only a reflection of their exposure to and knowledge of specific words but an indication of their understanding of spelling as a system made up of complex and varied patterns. This new understanding has grown not only out of research specifically related to spelling but out of our understanding of cognitive development in general and language development in particular. We do not yet know very much about how children learn to punctuate, but the research that exists suggests that it similarly involves an increasing understanding of language systems.

How does learning to spell and punctuate fit into a broader picture of learning?

Spelling and punctuation are learned not through brute memorization but as intellectual processes. Intellectual development generally can be seen as the generation of increasingly varied and sophisticated schemata, defined as mental processes or constructs that organize and structure experience (Neisser, 1976). For instance, our schema for bookstores helps us predict where we might find bestsellers, children's books, and the cashier. Any learner's knowledge of spelling is a high-level schema, containing simpler ones such as schemata for long and short vowel spellings. Learning to spell takes place primarily not by accumulating information but by elaborating one's schemata. Knowledge begins globally and develops through both greater differentiation and greater abstraction or integration (Gibson & Levin, 1975), as we can see in oral language development. For instance, a child learning to talk may at first refer to all small animals as "doggie" (a global category), then learn distinct terms like "cat" and "bunny" (differentiation), then learn that "animal" is a category that applies not only to these creatures but to others (integration). The child is not so much matching labels to objects in the world as he or she is learning a whole category system for classifying and making sense of experience. A similar process takes place with spelling. For instance, a child must learn to abstract out the category of past tense words that end in -ed even when the suffix's pronunciation varies (e.g., *missed, played, wanted*), yet also differentiate those words from others ending in the same sounds (*list, made, solid*) to avoid overgeneralization.

In this kind of conceptual or schematic development, much of our knowledge and learning exist tacitly, below the level of consciousness (Polanyi, 1966). Tacit knowledge is often a result of tacit learning. When children learn to speak, no one "teaches" them nor are they aware that they are learning; also, they learn far more than they could have learned through conscious effort. Estimates of how many new words children learn in early childhood range from about two per day (M. Smith, 1926) to about ten per day, 365 days a year (Templin, 1957; both cited in Lindfors, 1987). This is obviously far beyond what instruction or other explicit acquisition could account for and must therefore reflect a good deal of tacit and incidental learning.

Tacit learning, however, does not mean passive or only gradual learning. It occurs actively and sometimes by leaps and bounds rather than smoothly. Ferreiro and Teberosky (1982), taking a Piagetian perspective, suggest that language and other cognitive development takes place through an active process of assimilation and accommodation, where learners operate out of one conceptual schema as long as the available data can be made to fit it but eventually reach a point of cognitive dissonance where the schema itself must change. Thus periods of gradual growth are punctuated by discontinuous leaps.

One further important point about cognitive development is that it can't be separated from the social context where it occurs and indeed is grounded in that context. Language development moves from the universal to the culture-specific (Bissex, 1980). Parallel examples of this occur in oral and written language development. It is a myth that when children learn to talk they produce babbling noises that include all the sounds that occur in all the languages of the world (DeVilliers & DeVilliers, 1978). They do, however, produce a variety of sounds that gradually come to reflect the sounds heard in the language community that they are a part of. Similarly, children's scribbling, at first undifferentiated, soon begins to look like the print they see around them, even before they've learned any actual characters or letters (Harste, Woodward, & Burke, 1984). Vygotsky (1978) spoke of culture as providing the framework that enables humans to learn in a way that animals cannot: "human learning presupposes a specific social nature and a process by which children grow into the intellectual life of those around them"(p.88).

Spelling

There's been a great deal of research, especially in recent years, about spelling and the learner. The following only touches on some of the highlights of this work, those that will be of the most interest and value to classroom teachers. Four topics are covered: an overview of spelling growth and development in children; a characterization of what good spellers do and how they are different from less successful ones; the relationship between spelling and reading; and the effect of dialect on spelling.

What kind of developmental progression is seen in children learning to spell?   First of all, knowledge about spelling begins globally and becomes more specific. The child needs to learn how spelling systems work in general and how his or her own culture's particular system is organized. Children learn that letters are a special category of markings, that text represents meaning differently than pictures, and that letters combine and are arranged on the page in specific ways (Clay, 1975; Ferreiro & Teberosky, 1982). When children begin making their own marks on paper, they move from scribbling to alphabetic writing in fairly predictable ways (Heald-Taylor, 1984; Hildreth, 1936). Children's writing, even at the scribble stage, reflects the visual features of their culture's spelling system; French-speaking children's scribble may contain accent marks (K. Goodman, 1985), and Saudi Arabian and Israeli children produce scribbles that look like the writing systems used in those countries (Harste et al., 1984).

   Children's early writing focuses to some extent on the visual as it changes from scribble to letters, but there are also attempts to use writing as a way of transcribing sounds. Once the child has some knowledge of the alphabet and can conceive of writing as operating on a syllabic or alphabetic principle, invented spelling can be said to begin with *phonetic spelling*.[5] When letters are first used, writing often consists of varied combinations of whatever letters the child knows. Changing to a syllabic hypothesis involves a conceptual leap to thinking of a written string as being related to a word phonetically and in a linear way; that is, as corresponding to a string of sounds. (Before this, children are aware that readers can look at a text and produce an oral rendition, but this awareness may not include an understanding of the mechanism involved. For instance, a young child may fill a page with scribble and then ask an adult to "tell me what it says.") Writing where each letter represents a syllable is common at this point in development and is eventually followed by the further refinement of alphabetic writing, where letters more or less represent single sounds. This particular sequence is, of course, true only for cultures with alphabetic spelling systems; it's interesting to note that children's development reflects the history of those spelling systems, which evolved from logographic (representing whole words) and then syllabic systems (Gelb, 1952).

---

[5] *Phonetic spelling* is the usual term for this, but in most cases we are technically talking about *phonemic spelling,* where children represent their understanding of the phonemes of their language but aren't attempting a detailed phonetic transcription.

6 Spelling Celebration

Using one letter many ways

Tammy, first grade: "The BADE (*body*) has legs. Some PEEPLE (*people*) are MESEN (*missing*) one leg."

In three words here, Tammy had four "misuses" of the letter e. Yet look at what she has revealed about her knowledge of phonetics and language! In BADE, the e represents the long e sound that is so often spelled with the letter e. Tammy is just not yet aware that this sound is often spelled with a y at the ends of words. In PEEPLE, the double e also represents the long e sound, and she shows an awareness here that it's often spelled with two letters, particularly in the middle of a word. (If the word had been *steeple*, her *ee* spelling would have been correct.) Two e's occur in MESEN. The first one is a common children's spelling for the short i sound, which really sounds a lot like the letter name e. The second one may appear to be the same, but my hunch is otherwise. Don't a lot of us really pronounce the second syllable of *missing* not as *sing* but as *seen*? I think she's spelling long e again here! One final note: in addition to these four so-called misuses of the letter e, Tammy also used it correctly seven times here.

Read (1971, 1975) singlehandedly began the modern interest in invented spelling with his research into young children's attempts to represent the English sound system through spelling. His original intention was to explore children's phonological systems (i.e., their categorization of sounds) and how they differ from those of adults. He also succeeded in explaining features of preschool children's spellings that seem unusual to adults. Children produce spellings based on their analysis of sound/letter relationships, often representing phonetic properties that aren't represented in standard spelling. Precisely because many of these properties are not represented in written language, they may be below the level of awareness of adult speakers (such as the similarity between the vowels in *pen* and *pain,* and between the initial sounds of *truck* and *chuck*). Chomsky (1972) has also written about the process of preschool children's phonetic spelling, which is based primarily on the sounds contained in letter names. Through this process, the child "gets practice in thinking about how words really sound, gets practice in representing sounds accurately according to [his or her current] knowledge of letter names and sounds . . . and learns this way that the written word is for real and not arbitrary" (p. 121). (The specific kinds of spellings that children produce at various ages will be described in detail in the next chapter.)

During the earliest years of school, children explore, refine, and move beyond purely phonetic spellings. In a variety of ways, spelling becomes more sophisticated through becoming less phonetic. As children grow older, they begin using the correct letters for short vowels, learn to use more than one letter for long vowels, use double consonants, spell past tense endings consistently, and so on. (See Henderson & Beers, 1980, for several illustrations.) Children also grow as spellers by increasing the stock of words they know how to spell (Applebee, Langer, & Mullis, 1987; Milz, 1983). Growth continues through the high school years and beyond as spellers become aware of more subtle rules and continue to spell new words by analogy to familiar ones (Marsh, Friedman, Welch, & Desberg, 1980).

Spelling development, therefore, is a process that begins globally, perhaps with a scribble intended to represent a message as a whole, and eventually becomes far more complex, incorporating increasingly elaborated knowledge of the various linguistic levels represented in spelling. The integration of spelling strategies takes place gradually. Zutell (1978) has described the process as one of rule construction and hypothesis testing, in which the learning of individual spellings is replaced by rules that are at first overgeneralized but eventually internalized in a more mature form. Bissex (1980) describes the process in detail as she saw it in her son:

> He moved from associating letter forms in general with meaning . . . to associating specific letter forms with specific speech sounds. Once he mastered an invented spelling system that transcribed speech phonemically, he became aware of other bases for spelling, and focused on units larger than phonemes—on words and on morphemes. Before these differentiated aspects of spelling became integrated, there was some interference between concepts, as in Paul's spelling of "the" as TEH from visual recall after he had mastered the digraph *th* in invented spelling. Later, he was able to coordinate phonic principles, visual recall, and morphemic awareness to help determine spellings he was uncertain about or to correct misspellings . . . Paul seems to be asking himself not only, "What does this word *sound* like?" and "What does this word *look* like?" but "What does it *mean*?" As he grew aware of more variant spelling patterns, he also grew more aware of the conditions (such as position in word) governing the choice among these possibilities. Operationally, he was aware of the complex nature of our orthography. (p.206)

One other question to consider when looking at how children develop as spellers is how well they actually do spell at various ages. Sometimes teachers feel discouraged about their students and think that their spelling is quite poor, when actually they are spelling the vast majority of words correctly, particularly in their own writing rather than on spelling tests. We have data going back nearly a century: Rice (1897) found that scores on spelling tests he devised and administered to a large sample of students ranged from 64 percent for fourth graders to 84 percent for eighth graders. Eighth graders also showed 98 percent conventional spelling in written compositions. More recently, the latest National Assessment of Educational Progress studies (Applebee et al., 1987) found an average rate of conventional spelling (in written texts) of 92 percent in 9 year olds, 97 percent in 13 year olds, and 98 percent in 17 year olds, with growth occurring for writers at all levels of proficiency. (Even the worst spellers at age 9, those in the bottom 10 percent of the sample, averaged 80 percent correct spelling.) These studies and others strongly indicate that quantifiable spelling growth does occur throughout the years of schooling, and that by the end of elementary school, most students spell the vast majority of words correctly.

How do successful spellers differ from less successful ones? Good spellers have managed to integrate a wide variety of information about written language and how it works (Hodges, 1982); they must, for instance, be able to use both phonetic and visual knowledge, which sometimes conflict. Several researchers have looked at the spellings produced by good and poor spellers in an attempt to characterize the differences between them. We should remember, though, that this is to some extent an artificial dichotomy. It may be more useful to think of learners as spread out along a continuum of spelling knowledge than as divided into two groups. Even a continuum is an oversimplification since knowledge is multidimensional. For instance, one speller may spell a high percentage of words correctly, while another one may have a greater number of, but more sophisticated, invented spellings (Wilde, 1989a). When thinking about this line of research, therefore, the reader must consider that so-called good and poor spellers are artificial constructs abstracted out from data about real, complex people. Given this caution, we can make several statements about how good and poor spellers differ.

    1. Good spellers have moved beyond phonetic spelling. Spelling obviously involves the use of phonetic information, which is indeed the primary resource for young children's invented spelling. Tovey (1978) pointed out that first graders' spellings are often more phonetically precise than the standard ones (e.g., JEZUS for Jesus), and in most cases are phonetically acceptable or nearly so. But, as spellers mature, they eventually must move beyond a phonetic strategy to spell more conventionally. (In fact, children's misspellings tend to be phonetically acceptable, so that more phonics instruction isn't the way to improve it: Horn, 1954.) Similarly, Chomsky (1970) stated that children must abandon their early phonetic hypothesis to become successful spellers. That is indeed what happens; Nolen and McCartin (1984) found that as children grow older they are more likely to spell by analogy than phonetically.

    2. Good spellers have a good visual sense of words. Because of the obvious inadequacy of phonics as the sole strategy for effective spelling, research has begun to focus more and more on the role of visual factors. (Many of these studies appear in Frith, 1980a.) Barron (1980) believes that spellers use both a phonological strategy and a more direct visual/orthographic one, which consists of an internalized word list and is especially valuable for irregularly spelled words. He found that poor readers tended to use phonetic more than visual strategies for spelling, so that much of the reason they spelled worse than good readers did was because of phonetically accurate spellings of irregular words, including three times as many silent letter omissions as good readers. Several researchers have suggested that a visual sense is especially useful for checking spellings, seeing if a word "looks right." (Valmont, 1972, referred to this ability as "spelling consciousness.") Sloboda (1980) found evidence for the interaction of visual and phonological factors in the recognition process. It was harder for adults to choose the correct spelling from two alternatives if they were both phonetically acceptable; those who found the task difficult, in the sense of being

⑦ Spelling Celebration

One word spelled many ways

Spellings of *people* by various children, grades 3 and 4: "PEPOLE, POEPLE, PAPAGOLE"

These are examples from a set of eleven different spellings of *people* by seven children over two years. (Out of 69 uses of the word, 27 were invented spellings.) PEPOLE is probably the most phonetically reasonable of all the spellings, but POEPLE was the most common, occurring nine times. Both of these are also permutations, including all the right letters but in the wrong order. Why was *people* so tricky to spell? Probably because of the unusual eo vowel combination. Most of the eleven different spellings showed some visual awareness of the word; all but two of them (PAPAGOLE and PELANP) included various combinations of most or all of the four letters (*p, e, o,* and *l*) that actually occur in the word. Even PAPAGOLE is not as weird a spelling as it appears to be; the writer is a member of what was known at that time as the Papago tribe of Native Americans!

---

less able to tell which of the spellings "looked right," were more likely to consider themselves poor spellers.

This kind of internalized visual knowledge about spelling appears to be acquired over time. For instance, Rosinski and Wheeler (1972) found that first graders couldn't distinguish between pseudowords that followed normal English spelling patterns (e.g., *glox*) and those that didn't (e.g., *xogl*), while third graders for the most part could.

These studies and others strongly suggest, therefore, the importance of visual representations in spelling, and demonstrate that the use of phoneme/grapheme relationships can carry spellers only to a certain point and can only explain part of what successful spellers do.

3. Good spellers have integrated a variety of knowledge about words. Some researchers have found that knowledge of orthographic regularity (i.e., common spelling patterns), more than the effective representation of sounds, discriminates between more and less successful spellers. As Beers and Henderson (1977) commented:

> Clinical experience has . . . suggested that the poor speller is not one who is deficient in "phonics" for he [or she] typically spells words as they sound. . . . What has appeared to be wanting in his [or her] performance is an underlying concept about words that might make possible the classifying and efficient storage of orthographic elements. (p.134)

Good spellers don't just know more words than poor spellers; they have schemata that integrate a variety of knowledge about the spelling system generally. Manolakes (1975) found that the top third of elementary school spellers tended to produce the same invented spellings for words, often ones representing alternative acceptable spelling patterns, while the bottom third produced a wider variety of spellings, including some that were nonphonetic and many reflecting an incomplete understanding of English spelling regularity. Marino (1980) had sixth graders play the game Word Mastermind, where one tries to figure out an opponent's hidden word; good spellers were much better able to use knowledge of letter frequency, positional constraints, and common spelling patterns. Radebaugh (1985) found that good spellers' strategies included analogy, awareness of alternative spelling patterns, and visual imagery, while poor spellers tended to sound out spellings phoneme by phoneme. Some students are good readers but poor spellers, indicating that more than just general language proficiency contributes to spelling. Frith (1979, 1980b) found that while students who were poor at both reading and spelling tended to produce nonphonetic spellings of nonsense words, those students who were good readers but poor spellers were more likely to produce forms that were phonetically acceptable but not the most likely spelling. Frith suggested that such students are those who read effectively using a sampling strategy but don't pay detailed letter by letter attention to words. In my own informal polling of adults, I find that about half of them are the kind of readers who are immediately aware of misspelled words on menus; my hunch is that these are the people who have the visual awareness to be naturally good spellers, while others have to work harder at it.

Spelling bee contestants have, of course, reached the highest level of integrated knowledge about spelling. Hodges (1982) has described the wealth of knowledge that they draw on. They tend to be interested in words generally, not only their spellings, and knowledge of word meanings is a crucial part of their spelling ability. They also use knowledge about roots and affixes, and only rely on letter/sound relationships (usually with little success) when their other strategies don't work.

4. Poor spellers probably don't have a spelling disability. Sometimes teachers and researchers think that students who are particularly poor spellers may have some kind of learning disability that produces qualitatively different spellings than are seen in other children. A few important studies, however, suggest that this isn't the case. Holmes and Peper (1977) found that mentally retarded readers made more spelling errors than did normal readers, but with an almost identical profile of error types. Gerber (1984) described the spellings of students who had been defined as learning disabled as being like those of normal students three to four years younger, with similar developmental progressions. The learning disabled students also had a less sophisticated repertoire of spelling strategies. Moats (1983) found that students categorized as dyslexic had spelling profiles very similar to those of nondyslexic students a few years younger, except for somewhat more copying errors and letter formation problems. The author commented that previous studies may have identified dyslexics' spellings as not phonetically accurate when they were merely reflective of an early developmental stage of phonology, and suggested that the frequent recommendation of more phonics instruction for this group of students is not an appropriate one.

5. Good spellers can spell many words automatically. Perhaps, finally, becoming a good speller involves reaching a point where many words are spelled "automatically," in the sense that they can be written with little or no conscious attention to their spelling. Simon and Simon (1973) proposed a spelling process model in which words are if possible written by direct recall, with generation on the basis of sound/letter relationships used only when direct recall is not possible. F. Smith (1982) described the large memory load that remembering spellings involves as being no more difficult than learning oral vocabulary and as taking place through incidental learning, largely through reading. Kirk (1983) ingeniously described the achievement of automaticity in spelling as similar to learning telegraphy, with a focus on the process itself eventually able to be replaced by a focus on the message being represented. It appears, then, that becoming a good speller involves two processes: the ability to use all of the information contained in the spelling system, and the internalization of a large number of spellings.

What is the relationship between spelling and reading?   Spelling and reading are obviously related to each other. They're both written language processes, and one must certainly be a reader to become a good speller since in most cases it's only because we've seen a word in print that we know for sure how to spell it. But the connection isn't a simple one; as a result there have been several attempts to characterize how spelling and reading differ. First of all, relationships between sounds and letters aren't necessarily reversible, so spelling and reading can't be simple inverses of each other. For example, the letter *k* is usually pronounced /k/, but the sound /k/ can be spelled with *c, k,* or *q.* Also, spelling to some degree requires equal attention to all of the letters in a word in a way that reading doesn't (Shaughnessy, 1977). Read (1981) described how for very young children, writing involves a segment by segment construction that stays close to surface features and has little concern for standardization and audience. (We can see this in an invented spelling like HAPE for *happy,* where the child has logically represented each sound with a letter but ended up producing a spelling that most readers would see as rhyming with *cape.*) In its egocentricity, early invented spelling is very different from reading, which, although it also involves meaning construction, starts from another person's message. Bissex (1980) described how, for her son, reading began relatively globally with the whole message as the focus of attention and became more specific; his writing, on the other hand, began with the focus on small segments characteristic of early invented spelling but gradually became more concerned with meaning (i.e., he became better at spelling meaning-related features like *-tion* endings). Chomsky (1971, 1979) suggested that writing should precede reading because of children's natural ability to analyze and represent sounds; since reading always involves dealing with representations more abstract than phoneme/grapheme relationships but spelling can begin on a purely phonetic level, the latter is bound to be easier. For instance, a word like *one* isn't very predictable for reading and may thus be hard to identify, but it can be spelled phonetically as easily as *sun.* (Although a phonetic invented spelling of *one* won't be correct, this isn't a matter of concern in beginning writing.)

A few studies have illustrated some of the specific differences between reading and spelling. Goodman and Goodman's (1963) daughter, at the age of 6, could read all 65 words on a list but could spell only 50 percent of them conventionally, suggesting that spelling a word correctly is likely to be harder than reading it. This is borne out by the common sense observation that most adults can read many words that they can't spell. Similarly, young children can hear distinctions in oral language that they can't yet produce. Bryant and Bradley (1980) found that in most cases young children could read more words than they could spell, but there were exceptions, with some words (those with all short vowels and no consonant clusters) being easier to spell than to read. In another study (1983), they found that words that were easy to spell correctly were those that were phonically regular, while easily read ones were common and familiar ones. They suggested that spelling begins with a phonemic strategy and reading with a visual one, but after a few years of experience with written language, spelling and reading strategies become more alike.

The main implication of this research for teachers seems to be that although spelling and reading are related, they are certainly not just mirror images of each other. Also, children can write many words that are in their oral language vocabularies that they couldn't recognize in print, but this doesn't mean that they can spell them *correctly* yet. Put another way, children's reading vocabulary is bigger than their correct spelling vocabulary but smaller than their writing vocabulary (i.e., words they can come up with *some* possible spelling for), which is shown diagrammatically in Table 2–1. Of course, as children mature as writers, the boxes in the diagram will grow more equal in size, so that spelling, reading, and writing vocabulary will be very close to identical, as they are for adults.

How do writers' dialects affect their spelling?   Most teachers understand on some level that their students may speak a variety of dialects but may not have a clear sense of how this affects students' use of written language, including spelling. A dialect is a regional or social class variant of a language, such as Black English or a Georgia accent. Dialects differ in pronunciation, grammar, vocabulary, and social use, but it is the first of these that we'll mainly be concerned with here since pronunciation is so closely related to spelling. The misconception about dialect that causes the most problems in educational settings is the idea that there is one correct or best dialect that everyone should learn to speak and

TABLE 2–1
Vocabulary Relationships

that's embodied in written language. One part of this misconception, the position that some dialects are intrinsically better than others, is beyond the scope of this book, but the reader is encouraged to consult Labov (1970) and National Council of Teachers of English (1974) for discussions of the cultural and educational issues involved. What I will do here is to focus on the other part of the argument, the idea that written language represents one dialect more than others and therefore will present problems for speakers of those other dialects as they learn to spell.

Many of us (if we are North Americans) have had the experience of seeing a British movie, particularly one with Cockney-speaking characters, where the dialect was so unlike our own that we would have liked subtitles. Yet if we were to receive a letter from one of those characters, we would have no trouble understanding it and probably would hardly be able to tell that it was British, except for vocabulary differences. Although some British and American spellings differ, it isn't usually because of pronunciation. *Color* and *colour* are pronounced far more alike than are the American and British versions of *lieutenant* and *schedule*, which are spelled the same. Written language represents all dialects. (One interesting exception is the case of books that have been written specifically to represent a particular dialect, such as Lucille Clifton's children's books written in Black English. These are a special case since they are attempting to represent the rhythms of oral language and often use unusual spellings to do so.) The primary kinds of dialect differences that affect spelling are those that create homophones (words spelled differently but pronounced alike). Although *too/two* is a homophone pair for all speakers of English, the pairs *cot/caught, which/witch,* and *pen/pin* are homophones only for some dialects. Research on dialect and spelling has focused mainly on these kinds of features.

Black English is the dialect of American English that's most often been the subject of spelling research; it's generally been shown to have some effect on spelling, but the effect tends to be a small one that decreases over time. Kligman, Cronnell, and Verna (1972) found that second graders who were speakers of Black English had somewhat more dialect-related spelling errors, such as past tense deletion, than did so-called Standard English speakers, but the rates were only 19 percent and 12 percent of possible errors respectively. (Of course, if both speakers and nonspeakers of Black English produced such comparable numbers of these kinds of spellings, it is hard to see how it is fair to even call them dialect-related.) McCardle (1980) found that second-grade Blacks spelled more presumed Black English homophones alike than whites did (21 percent vs. 8 percent), with the difference most apparent on those pairs involving vowel similarity. Groff (1978), however, stated that although second-grade African Americans tend to use dialect spellings about 20 percent of the time, the frequency drops to about 5 percent by fifth grade, making any need for special instruction questionable. O'Neal and Trabasso (1976) also pointed out that the moderate Black dialect influence seen in third-grade spellers largely disappears by fifth grade.

Other studies have looked at the influence of various other dialects on spelling. The earliest of these is that of Rice (1897) who, in a large-scale study, found that students of foreign-born parents who heard a language other than English at home did as well as other students on a spelling test. Using a vocabulary reflecting the attitudes of his time, he declared that there was no difference in spelling between children of "cultured" parents and those from the "foreign laboring element." Other studies (Boiarsky, 1969; Graham & Rudorf, 1970; Walker, 1979) have found some influence of dialect on spelling in elementary school children, but it's never been found to be very large or persistent.

It's interesting to note that discussion of the presumed problems for spelling created by dialect virtually always refers to speakers of less prestigious dialects. There have been no considerations of the special spelling difficulties faced by Americans for whom *which* and *witch* are homophones, or indeed by British speakers who pronounce *pox* and *parks* alike. Stever (1980) sensibly pointed out that in a sense all young children are "dialect spellers," in that they produce relatively phonetic spellings of whatever dialect they speak. The task for spellers of every dialect group is, of course, to become more sophisticated by learning to use the other kinds of information contained in standard spelling.

The most reasonable approach for teachers seems to be one of considering children's dialect to be a nonissue for spelling. For young children, spelling is highly phonetic, and therefore not very accurate, regardless of dialect. As children get older and incorporate more visual and semantic information into their spelling, phonetic features of their dialect are less likely to be represented, and make up only a very small proportion of their invented spellings. This is true both of the African American child who discovers that *asked*, although a homophone of *axed*, is spelled differently from it, and the standard English speaker who learns to include a silent *h* in *why*, as well as the British speaker who learns that the *f* that she or he hears in *lieutenant* isn't included in its spelling.

Although dialect and spelling is a nonissue linguistically, it's an extremely important issue educationally. Suggesting that a low-status dialect will cause problems with spelling has potentially serious consequences for the self-esteem and academic achievement of minority students. A teacher can perhaps understand what this feels like by imagining moving to England and sending one's children to school there. A British teacher could conceivably say that an American child would be likely to have trouble learning to spell because written English represents British pronunciation since that's where the language began. According to such a teacher, American children might need special remedial coaching in spelling because of their "deviant" pronunciation. We would, of course, be shocked and offended by such an attitude, yet this is exactly how some groups of American children are viewed by some American educators. This issue is important enough, and attitudes about it are so deeply ingrained, that teachers who understand the issue of dialect can provide a valuable service by helping to educate their colleagues.

Punctuation

Children's punctuation has been studied far less than their spelling, yet it's potentially a very interesting topic because, like spelling, it has to do with children's evolving hypotheses about language. In fact, it's only through such hypotheses that we can use punctuation at all. With spelling we can look up a difficult word in the dictionary, but with punctuation even a detailed reference book can't always give a clear answer in difficult cases; we must instead rely on our intuitive sense of written language systems.

What do we know about children's developing concepts of punctuation? Traditionally, research about punctuation has focused on "mechanical errors," particularly in older students, and their correction. Cronnell (1980) provided a review of this work. Most recently, the National Assessment of Educational Progress studies (Applebee et al., 1987) documented punctuation errors occurring at a rate of 3.4 per hundred words for 9 year olds, 2.8 for 13 year olds, and 2.0 for 17 year olds. There has also been, however research that views the learning of punctuation as a developmental process and has observed its emergence in young children. Ferreiro and Teberosky (1982) discovered that preschool children gradually come to discriminate punctuation marks from numbers and letters. They described five stages in this process: not distinguishing punctuation marks from letters or numbers; identifying periods, colons, hyphens, and ellipsis marks as "not letters"; distinguishing all punctuation marks except those that look like letters (e.g., the question mark); stating clearly that punctuation marks are not letters; and attempting to label and assign functions to punctuation marks. Cordeiro, Giacobbe, and Cazden (1983) worked with first graders, who in some cases were given individualized instruction about punctuation. The researchers observed that even with instruction, punctuation marks were used conventionally only about half of the time and that progress was slower than it was for specific teaching of spelling rules. They also found evidence that progress isn't steady since children often appear to hold alternative hypotheses that eventually have to be reconciled. For instance, they may think that periods divide sentences and also that periods go at the end of a line. De Goes and Martlew (1983) also studied children of first-grade age, who were asked to copy passages and then asked about the spacing and punctuation in them. The more visually prominent marks like the question mark were copied most often, and more than 50 percent of the children ignored commas and periods. The children's conceptualizations of punctuation marks were described as "very diffuse"; most thought they weren't meant to be read like words but couldn't further define their purpose.

As children grow older and have more experience with writing, their use of punctuation becomes more sophisticated. Edelsky (1983) looked at segmentation and punctuation in the writing of first through third graders in a bilingual program and found that over time usage became less idiosyncratic and more conventionalized. Bissex (1980), in her case study of her son, found that he used the exclamation point, which is obviously expressive, before any other punctuation mark when he was just five, while he began to use more subtle marks like the colon, semicolon, and ellipsis only around age ten. Calkins (1980) interviewed third graders about punctuation and found that children who used it often in their writing were familiar with many more punctuation marks, such as the colon, asterisk, and semicolon, than a nonwriting class and were able to discuss it in functional terms; she saw them as "developing an intuitive sense for the nuances of punctuation" (p. 571). They were able to come to terms with its complexities without needing to be dependent on rules. Baldwin and Coady (1978) explored the role of punctuation and reading comprehension for fifth graders and adults and found that punctuation was useful for the adults but not the children in figuring out sentences with unusual word order. They suggested that punctuation isn't yet a fully active cueing system for fifth graders. Shaughnessy (1977), in her discussion of adult remedial writers, demonstrated that even older writers may not always have assimilated conventional punctuation and may still be operating with their own idiosyncratic rules. Her students for the most part used only periods, commas, and capitals, often in unconventional ways.

Like spelling, therefore, punctuation seems to develop from an early awareness through a period of exploration and gradual refinement and increasing conventionality. Although it involves fewer characters than spelling, it appears to be somewhat more difficult to learn since it's less clearly defined.

What do we know about how children use specific kinds of punctuation? In addition to providing a general picture of how punctuation usage develops in children, research on punctuation has looked at specific kinds of punctuation and how they're used. Spacing between words, also known as segmentation, often isn't thought about when considering punctuation since it doesn't involve actual punctuation marks, but it makes sense to consider it as part of the punctuation system. Edelsky (1983) provided the most detailed explanation of how segmentation emerges in young children's writing; she found primary school children, who were writing mainly in Spanish, segmenting conventionally a good deal of the time, while their unconventional segmentation was usually based on predictable patterns, such as not separating objects from verbs, or choosing to space between syllables. Bissex (1980) described how her son invented the use of periods as a separator between words or syllables, at around the age of five. Segmentation does develop relatively early in children's writing, even if it isn't always conventional. Milz (1983) found that five out of six children basically controlled word boundaries on entering first grade, while the sixth child developed control gradually throughout the year. By the middle of elementary school, children rarely have any problems with word boundaries; I found that six children during their third and fourth grade years joined or divided words inappropriately (e.g., THANKYOU or A SLEEP) only about once in every two hundred words (Wilde, 1986/1987). De Goes and Martlew (1983) asked first graders why there are spaces in writing; several of their responses indicated a good understanding of segmentation's purpose. Spaces were described as being used to keep the words from getting squashed or mixed up, or to signal the end of one word and the start of another. Increasingly successful use of spacing grows out of these early perceptions of its function.

Capital letters are another feature of writing that doesn't involve punctuation marks but is still a part of the punctuation system, either working with periods to define sentence boundaries or serving a semantic role, as in signalling proper nouns. Young children tend to begin writing with uppercase letters and gradually move to lowercase. Milz (1983) found that her first-grade subjects used mainly uppercase letters at first, then eventually switched to lowercase. Edelsky (1983) saw a variety of patterns of unconventional capitalization, including their use on certain letters or to start certain words. Odom (1962) found that children vary in their use of capitalization even at upper elementary school levels; students in grades four through six given a test were more likely to capitalize some items, such as names of countries, than others, such as the first word of a sentence. Growth was greatest over time for those forms that were easier to begin with; the author also suggested that some cases involved much more complex rules than others. I found that third and fourth graders capitalized words when they should have 86.3 percent of the time and that 89.9 percent of the capital letters they used were appropriate. *I* was most likely to be capitalized correctly, and proper names and headings least likely (Wilde, 1986/1987). Shaughnessy (1977) showed how capitalization problems can persist into adult life; the most common problem for the college students she worked with was overcapitalization, which appeared to be related to handwriting since it often occurred on the same letter at several points in a text.

The period is an important mark of punctuation that is difficult to learn because it doesn't stand out visually and its use can't be explained by simple rules. Edelsky (1983) found that in addition to complete omission of periods, common patterns were periods at the end of a piece but no internal punctuation, or periods at the end of each line. Cordeiro, Giacobbe, and Cazden (1983) found a variety of unconventional uses of periods in first graders' writing. Besides omission, periods were put between words, at the end of lines, at the end of pages, and after phrases or clauses. Conventional use tended to be about 50 percent whether children had received instruction about periods or not. Shaughnessy (1977) reported that her adult subjects tended to use only periods and commas and not other punctuation marks, and that they sometimes followed phrase structure patterns (e.g., punctuating clauses like sentences).

Other kinds of punctuation marks have occasionally been studied. Cordeiro, Giacobbe, and Cazden (1983) found that individualized instruction about possessive apostrophes and quotation marks resulted in their being used correctly about half of the time, with inappropriate use consisting mostly of overgeneralization and misplacement respectively. Calkins (1980) described how writers who did a good deal of editing became familiar with editing marks like the caret and paragraph sign. She also described the invention of features such as thickened or large letters for semantic purposes; Edelsky (1983) similarly found features such as stars and double bars used for end punctuation and elsewhere.

To summarize, then, these studies suggest that various types of punctuation gradually emerge in children's writing, reflecting a developing knowledge of syntactic and other linguistic structures.

How can teachers use research knowledge about spelling and punctuation?

As we've seen, we have a great deal of knowledge about how children learn to spell, as well as some sense of how they learn to punctuate. The sources of this knowledge range from psychological experiments to classroom stories, and all of it is potentially valuable for the teacher for several purposes: It makes the teacher an informed professional; classroom practice becomes consistent with research; it helps justify one's teaching to others; and it fosters new research.

First of all, professionalism in education as in other fields is a function of making decisions based on expert knowledge. A teacher who understands that spelling develops in a predictable fashion, and that error is a necessary part of growth, will be able to appreciate and celebrate children's invented spellings rather than being concerned about them. That teacher will also have the knowledge base to be a sophisticated kidwatcher (Y. Goodman, 1978) who can recognize the occasional speller who isn't progressing well enough and needs extra help.

Curriculum practices that are consistent with research also grow out of this informed professionalism. A simple example is that a teacher who realizes how strong a role visual knowledge plays in spelling is likely to suggest that children try writing a word to see if it looks right, rather than encouraging them to sound it out as their main strategy. On a wider scale, such a teacher will realize the importance of wide reading for developing visual knowledge about spelling and will understand that it's one of many reasons for prioritizing time for reading over other activities such as spelling exercises.

Teachers who make changes in the standard curriculum may meet resistance from administrators and parents, and knowledge about research can play a valuable role here as well. Although happy students who are obviously learning are the main way that new classroom practices become acceptable, it can't hurt to be able to cite research findings that support your curriculum model. This is suggested not in a spirit of trying to intimidate principals and parents by overwhelming them with your erudition but rather as a way of communicating to others that you do indeed know what you are doing, and that your practices are based on reading and reflection rather than caprice.

Finally, teachers who are comfortable with research, and who understand that some of the most interesting and relevant studies are those that are classroom based, can themselves become part of that research tradition. The teacher/researcher is an important part of the research community in education, and much work in spelling and punctuation remains to be done.

Patterns of Growth in Spelling and Punctuation: Young Writers Show Us What They Know

I believe that teachers can best understand children's knowledge and learning by becoming kidwatchers (Y. Goodman, 1978): informed observers of what children do in natural settings. I've chosen, therefore, to give you a kidwatcher's view of spelling and punctuation development in all its real-life complexity by sharing writing samples that illustrate common developmental trends. The writers' ages range from five to nine, with more samples from younger children since growth occurs more rapidly then. These samples have also all been chosen from writers whose spelling is average to good for their age, representing the kinds of patterns you'll probably see in about 80 percent of children, although not necessarily at the same ages. I'll share writing samples from less successful spellers in Chapter 9 when discussing evaluation.

In examining these writing samples, I have two purposes: first, that you'll come to understand typical kinds of progressions and variations that occur from year to year in children's writing; and second, that you'll start looking at your own students' writing with the same kind of exploratory and analytical eyes. Often the best teaching is responsive teaching, a direct outgrowth of what the teacher sees as children's existing knowledge base. Many of the curriculum ideas presented in the second part of this book will work best when they're geared to the unique needs of the particular children you work with. This chapter will help teach you how to discover more about what your own students know.

Nicole

Nicole, age five, was visiting my university language arts methods class with her mother, who didn't have a babysitter that day. When the class had broken up into small discussion groups about halfway through, Nicole came up and showed me what she'd been writing and drawing. When I saw her calendar (entitled "Springtime"; Figure 3–1), I realized I could use her emergent knowledge of numerals to conduct an on-the-spot demonstration for my students, who had been learning about the writing process and invented spelling.

I asked Nicole if she would write some numbers on the blackboard for us, and she eagerly set to work. As her writing began to spread across the bottom of

FIGURE 3–1   *Nicole: Springtime Calendar*

the blackboard, one of my students called me over; bothered by Nicole's reversals, she whispered, "Why don't you just show her the right way?" "Wait a bit," I said, "Watch what I'm going to do with her and then I'll come back to your question."

I pulled the class back together and asked Nicole to read us her numbers, which went up a bit past 20. Then I asked her if she'd answer some questions for us. On the blackboard, some of her numerals (2,3,4,7, and 9) were consistently reversed, while only the 5 and 6 were not. (The 1, 8, and 0 are of course symmetrical.) I picked one of her reversed numerals and asked her what number it was. After she replied correctly, I wrote an exact mirror image of her reversed numeral (i.e., wrote it correctly) and asked what number it was. She replied, "It's not a number." Her answer was the same each time I wrote the conventional version of one of her reversed numerals and, consistently, when I wrote a reversed version of one of her "normal" numbers. Next, I decided to introduce a little cognitive dissonance. I picked up a book and found page 13 and showed it to Nicole, asking if the 3 looked the same as her 3 or different. She immediately recognized it was different. (Although she added, "If you hold it like this [holding the 3 in the book up against her own 3], then they're the same" [i.e., they matched like a mirror image].) When she saw that numerals in a book faced the opposite direction from her own, she immediately and unquestioningly accepted the authority of the book and said that those versions were correct. As one further test, I drew a sketch of a cat and asked her what it was, then drew the same sketch facing the other direction, which she also recognized as a cat. On

FIGURE 3–2   *Nicole: Scribble Writing*

questioning, she stated very clearly that a cat is a cat no matter which way it faces, while a numeral can only face one way. This was the final piece of evidence I needed to explain to my students the significance of Nicole's demonstration.

Learning to write numerals correctly, and, of course, letters as well, involves three components: knowing the configuration (shape) of the character, knowing that its directionality matters, and knowing which direction it faces. Nicole had basically grasped the first two of these; only the third, relatively trivial piece of knowledge—knowing which way each number faced—remained to be firmly established. Why did she reverse the numerals she did? If you look at Figure 3–1, you'll see that she's written all her numbers (with the exception of the first 3) so that they "face right." Watt and Jacobs (1975) have pointed out that most of our letters do, in fact, face right, and that young writers' reversals understandably tend to follow this generalization. I then asked the class to answer my student's question of why I hadn't corrected Nicole; they realized that she would probably figure out the correct orientation of numbers for herself with more exposure to print, and I pointed out that my introduction of cognitive dissonance, getting her to think about it, would be more effective than just telling her she was wrong.

Nicole produced two other writing samples of interest that day. One of them (Figure 3–2) was written primarily in scribble. (It reproduced some of what I'd written on the blackboard: a grid explaining spelling as process and product (see Table 1–1), and illustrations of punctuation.) When I asked why she sometimes printed and sometimes scribbled, she replied that she scribbled when she wanted her writing to look like cursive. (She'd reproduced accurately, of course, the punctuation marks and the one familiar word in the grid.) Finally, I asked Nicole to write a few words for me, and she drew and labeled a bee and

FIGURE 3–3   *Nicole: Bee and Bear*

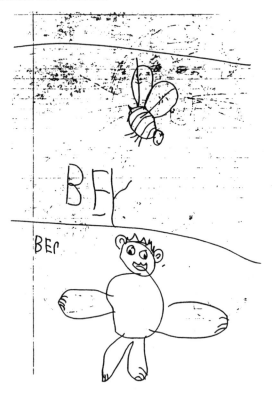

a bear (Figure 3–3). Her spellings show recognition of consonant sounds, including a /y / at the end of *bee* and a lower case *r* at the end of *bear*, and logical representation of vowel sounds, using *e* to represent both a long *e* and the *r*-controlled sound that's close to short *e*. All in all, Nicole showed an impressive array of knowledge for a five-year-old!

We can see this knowledge operating on at least three levels. First, Nicole understood something about text formats, creating writing with a variety of functions (calendar, imitation blackboard writing, and picture labels). Although young children often write scribbles that look like and are intended to be stories, they also reproduce other kinds of written language that they see around them. For instance, Baghban (1984) described how her daughter took make-believe restaurant orders and wrote letters to her grandmother, both in scribble writing, at the age of two. Second, Nicole knew how written language is laid out in sentences and words; she wrote from left to right and used a mixture of scribble writing, letter strings (SGROBAETI for *springtime*), invented spelling (BEY and BER), and standard spelling of a familiar word (*the*). Third, Nicole knew about the shapes of letters and their relationship to sound; she produced reasonably accurate renditions of letters, numerals, and punctuation marks; she also, with BEY, BER, and parts of SGROBAETI, related letters to sounds. Clay (1975) talks about how young writers come to understand left-to-right directionality, generativity (combining a set of characters in various ways), contrast (using different written forms for different meanings), and arrangement of characters on the page. Nicole had a good handle on all of these.

TABLE 3–1
Spellings by Jay, Brian, and Carol

	Word	Jay	Brian	Carol	"Predicted" spelling
1	meat	MET	MET	MET	MET
2	eyes	IA	IZ	EIYS	IS or IZ
3	knee	NEA	NE	KNEE	NE
4	bread	PRD	BAD	BERAD	BRAD
5	rib	REP	RAB	RABE	REB
6	intestines	ETASN	INTAST	ENTASTANS	ETASTNS
7	mouth	MAO	MOU	MALH	MOTH
8	esophagus	ASAFAK	OFGS	ASOFAGAS	ISOFIGS (possibly)
9	carbohydrate	KAPHRS	CRBAHIJAT	CARBANHIDRAT	CRBOHIJRAT
10	milk	MLK	MLC	MLCK	MLC or MLK

Jay, Brian, and Carol

Jay, Brian, and Carol were first graders who had been given a list of food words and body parts to spell. I've picked 10 words from that list (Table 3–1) to show you some common features found in the invented spelling of young children. The first ten features I describe are taken from the well-known work of Charles Read (1971, 1975), who was the first scholar to examine children's invented spellings in detail. (I've included a few spelling patterns that Read described but that these children didn't use.)

We saw Nicole, with her spellings of *bee* and *bear,* beginning to make the transition into realizing that the letters in words aren't random but are related to sounds. Children who have discovered this principle and who are encouraged to write independently will tend to produce spellings that follow characteristic patterns, although we can't necessarily predict precisely what spelling a particular child will produce at a particular time. In looking at writing from three children who are using phonetic knowledge to produce invented spellings, we can see how abstract linguistic principles may work out very differently in practice as they're filtered through idiosyncratic human beings. Put another way, the invented spelling features described here are abstractions that can be used to interpret what children have written but not to predict what their next spellings will look like. For comparison purposes, I've included a predicted spelling column in Table 3–1 to show what spellings would have been produced if the patterns described had been followed exactly.

Long vowels

Read found that preschool children using invented spelling usually spelled long vowels with the single letter that says the name of the vowel. This is an obvious,

TABLE 3–2
Short Vowels in Invented Spelling

SOUND	CHILDREN'S SPELLING	EXAMPLE		PHONETICALLY RELATED WORD
		Word	Spelling	
short e (ĕ)	A (ā)	pen	PAN	pane
short i (ĭ)	E (ē)	pill	PEL	peel
short o (ŏ)	I (ī)	pop	PIP	pipe
short u (ŭ)	O (ō)	pup	POP	pope

natural spelling pattern, documented repeatedly in other research, that Jay, Brian, and Carol all followed for *meat* (word #1). For the word *eyes* (word #2), however, they weren't so consistent. Brian's spelling, IZ, is what you'd expect, but the other two are less obvious. My hunch is that Jay overarticulated *eye,* creating an extra syllable (*eye*-uh, spelled IA; he also appears to have done the same thing with *knee*, word #3). My intuition about Carol is that she combined visual and phonetic knowledge, so that her spelling included the *i* that she heard as well as the *e* and *y* she'd probably seen in print. Visual knowledge probably also explains her double *e* in *knee*. These simple examples show the different factors that may be working to produce an invented spelling. I think it's important for teachers to look closely at invented spellings in order to develop the kinds of hunches and intuition I've used here, so that we can, when possible, give credit to the strategies that children are using.

Short vowels

One of Read's most fascinating findings was the way that young children tend to spell short vowels, as outlined in Table 3–2. It can be difficult for adults to understand where these spellings come from since we're so used to standard spellings of short vowels, but they are actually good phonetic letter-name spellings. Imagine a child deciding to write the vowel in the word *pen* and trying to decide what alphabet letter will best match it. Try saying *ĕ-ē* and then *ĕ-ā* out loud, noticing the position of your mouth as you do so. Can you hear and feel how the second pair is a closer match? *Pen* is much closer phonetically to *pane* than it is to *peen*. The same holds true for the rest of the table. (The match between ŭ and ō is the least close.) A diagram (somewhat simplified) of where these vowels occur in the mouth (see Table 3–3) can help you to feel the location of the vowels as you say them.

Looking back to Table 3–1, we can see that Brian and Carol followed this short vowel spelling pattern for *bread* (word #4, with Carol probably articulating it as *ber-ed*), Jay on *rib* (word #5), and all three of them on *intestines* (word #6: the initial short *i* for two of the children and the short *e* for all three). I can't explain the two *a*'s in spellings of *rib*; maybe they reflect pronunciation.

Rounded vowels

Read found that children spelling the rounded vowels found in *boot, book, bout, bought,* and *boat* tended to use either *o* or a two-letter spelling containing *o* a

TABLE 3—3
Position of Vowels in the Mouth

	Front	Middle	Back
High	ē ĭ		
Middle	ā ĕ	ŭ	ō
Low		ī*	ŏ

*ī starts mid-low and glides to high front

good deal of the time. We can see this in Jay's and Brian's spellings of *mouth* (word #7).

Schwa vowels

The schwa vowel (ə) is the one found in unaccented syllables like the first syllable of *about*. It's hard to spell correctly because it can be spelled with any of the vowel letters (e.g., *e*xist, penc*i*l, co*ll*ide, circ*u*s); you usually have to know the word or a related word to spell it correctly. Not surprisingly, Read found that young inventive spellers tend to omit schwas, since they don't stand out as much as accented vowels, or to spell them with any of the vowel letters, with *i* and *e* most common. We can see this in *esophagus* (word #8), where all vowels other than the *o* are likely to be pronounced as schwa. (See also Spelling Celebration #8.) All three children used *a* for the schwa vowels or omitted them. (Their spellings still look quite different from each other because of other omissions and substitutions.)

TR and DR

When *t* and *d* occur before *r*, they sound a little different than they do elsewhere. The linguistic term for this is "affrication"; it means that the *t* at the beginning of *truck* sounds as much like the *ch* in *chuck* as it does the *t* in *tuck*. You can hear this if you try pronouncing the made-up word **chruck*; it sounds pretty much like *truck*, doesn't it? The same holds true for *dr* and *j*; **jrum* sounds like *drum*. This pattern will sometimes turn up in children's spellings; Read found spellings like CHRAC for *truck* and JRAGIN for *dragon*; we can see it in the *j* of Brian's spelling of *carbohydrate* (word #9).

Preconsonantal nasals

When the nasal consonants *n*, *m*, and *ng* (the final sound in *sing*) occur before another consonant, they don't stand out as much as they do elsewhere in a word. You can feel this if you say *pan* and *pant* out loud. Described more technically, the main difference between *pant* and *pat* is in the nasalized vowel in the former. Read found that children tend to omit preconsonantal nasals; they can hear the difference between *pat* and *pant*, but hear it as a difference in the vowel, which they don't have any way of representing in spelling. We can see this in Jay's spelling of *intestines* (word #6).

8 Spelling Celebration

The schwa vowel

Spellings of *esophagus* by seven children, grades 1–3: "ASOPHEGESE, USOFUGES, ESOFIGIS, ASOFAGAS, OSOFUGOS, OSOFIGESS, ASOUGHAGUS"

Although these spellings of *esophagus* look unusual and are quite different from each other, they are all reasonably good invented spellings of the word. Aside from a bit of variation in consonant use (recognition, for instance, that /f/ may be spelled *ph* or *gh*, as in *phone* or *cough*), these spellings differ mainly in their vowels. Not all of the vowels, however: except for the last one, all of these writers spelled the second, short vowel as *o*. But the other three vowels in *esophagus* are the schwa vowel, the one found in unaccented syllables that can be spelled with any vowel letter (**a**bout, it**e**m, rig**i**d, parr**o**t, circ**u**s). Indeed, the schwa is spelled three different ways in *esophagus* alone! If one isn't familiar with a particular word, any vowel letter is a reasonable attempt to spell the schwa sound. Adults are able to spell schwa vowels reasonably successfully for two reasons. First, we have a large mental stock of words that we know how to spell, which don't look right to us if they're misspelled. Second, we're able to relate words to others with similar meanings where the vowel isn't a schwa. This is, of course, easier with common words. Most adults would be able to relate *medIcal* and *medIcinal*, while only a few will recognize that the root phag- (eat) in *esophagus* is related to *phagocyte* (a cell that eats other cells) and *anthropophagy* (cannibalism).

Vowel omission before L, M, N, and R

When a vowel occurs before *l, m, n,* or *r,* particularly in unaccented syllables, the consonant tends to swallow up the vowel. (Technically, the consonant becomes syllabic.) In the final syllable of the words *bottle, better, bottom,* and *button,* it's hard to hear a vowel sound separate from the consonant. Not surprisingly, Read found that children tend to omit these vowels; he saw spellings like LITL (*little*), FRM (*from*), and OPN (open). We can see this in *milk* (word #10), where all three children omitted the vowel.

Flap consonants

In some cases when *t* occurs between vowels, it sounds more like *d,* which is why *latter* sounds like *ladder.* This is called a flap consonant, because the tongue flaps against the roof of the mouth. Read found children using *d* instead of *t* (PREDE for *pretty*; LADR for *letter*), which reflects phonetic knowledge, as well as using *t* instead of *d* (MITL for *middle*), showing they'd begun to internalize standard spelling. (See also Spelling Celebration #9.)

9 Spelling Celebration

Flap consonants

Ellen, first grade: "It is *EVRY BUTEES* (everybody's) *BRTHTEY* (*birthday*)."

Hannah, second grade: "*EVREBUTEY* (everybody) is a *ANIMIL* (*animal*)."

Kris, second grade: "*BLATER* (*bladder*)" (on a labeled diagram of the body)

Isn't this strange? Three different children have used the letter *t* to represent a sound that clearly sounds like *d* and is spelled *d*. These examples, however, represent a special case of the letter *d*. When either a /d/ or a /t/ occurs between two vowels in English (as in the words *ladder* and *latter*), it turns into a sound called a "flap consonant," so called because the tongue flaps against the roof of the mouth. (Try it and see!) It sounds more like a /d/ than a /t/, but is actually not quite the same as the /d/ that occurs, for instance, at the beginning of a word. Many words that are familiar to children have flap consonants that are spelled with one or two *t*'s (*later*, *butter*, etc.) It is therefore not at all surprising that they would use t to represent the flap in a word whose spelling they don't know. It is important to remember that children's hypotheses about spelling grow out of their own experiences with words and their spellings and that they won't necessarily categorize language in the same way adults do.

Past tense spellings

Literate adults are so used to the constant spelling *-ed* for past tense endings that we may have forgotten that it actually has three different pronunciations. Read found that children's spellings of this ending were often phonetic, appearing in three forms: LIKT (*liked*), KILD (*killed*), and ADDID (*added*).

S/Z, C/K/CK, and other consonant variations

Most consonant spellings are straightforward; /b/ is almost always spelled *b*. Of the consonant sounds that can be spelled with a single letter, Read's subjects spelled most of them with the associated letter more than 70 percent of the time. (This, of course, doesn't always produce the accepted spelling, as we see in the spellings using *f* instead of *ph* in *esophagus*: word #8.) The only four exceptions were /j/ (often spelled with *g*), /y/ (often omitted), /z/, and /k/. The most interesting of these was /z/; the children spelled it with *z* only 3.7 percent of the time, mainly using *s* instead. What most adults may not realize is that, except for the beginnings of words, *s* is the usual spelling for /z/ in English (e.g., *is*, *easy*, *tries*). Brian's spelling of IZ for *eyes* (word #2) is therefore a fairly unusual invented spelling. Read also found children frequently spelled /k/ with *c* and sometimes

Spelling Celebration

Letter-name spelling

Dina, fourth grade: "One day .E.T. went to the .R.K. (arcade). He had some quarters he played pac-man."

When young children begin their first explorations with invented spelling, they use the names of letters to construct written representations of words. An example of such a spelling might be BKZ for *because*, where a spelling is made up from the letter names associated with consonant sounds in the word. (William Steig has written an entire children's book, *CDB!* (1968), or "See the Bee", in letter-name spelling.) For the most part, our spelling system reflects more complex rela- tionships between sounds and letters, but in the case of abbreviations, such as *NBC, FBI,* and of course *E.T.,* the word is spelled by writing the names of the letters heard in it. Dina merely extended this principle to the spelling of the video "R.K." where one can play Pac-Man. Notice also that she understood that periods may be used in such words; her overextension in this case involved also using a period *before* the word, bracketing it the way one does with quota- tion marks.

---

with *ck* or *q*, which are all common spellings of /k/ in English. We can see Jay, Brian, and Carol trying out different spellings for /k/ in their spellings of *milk* (word #10) and *carbohydrate* (word #9). Two other consonant patterns seen here that were rare or nonexistent in Read's data are the substitution of *p* for *b*, seen in Jay's spellings of *bread* and *rib* (words #4 and #5), and substitution of *k* for *g*, which Jay did in *esophagus* (word #9). These aren't random substitutions; most English consonants come in pairs that occur in the same part of the mouth and differ only in whether they are voiced (i.e., are produced with vocal cords vibrating) or unvoiced, as Table 3–4 shows. Try saying a word starting with each member of a pair with a finger placed on your vocal cords and see if you can feel the difference.

What Jay was doing, therefore, was substituting an unvoiced consonant for its voiced counterpart, a pattern that turns up occasionally in invented spelling.

Silent letters

Although Read didn't look at whether his subjects represented silent letters, in my own study of third and fourth graders (Wilde, 1986/1987), I found that initial silent letters were omitted about half of the time. This isn't surprising since the only way to know if a word starts with a silent letter is to know the word. Carol's inclusion of the *k* in *knee,* which the other two children omitted, suggests that she'd probably seen the word before.

Long words

One further observation that we can make about Jay, Brian, and Carol is that they differed in their approach to spelling long words. When a word is short, it's fairly easy for a beginning speller to hear and represent all the sounds in it, as we see in the children's spellings of the first four words on the chart. A larger word, however, may reveal some differences between children, with stronger spellers better able to handle a lengthier task. Table 3–5 breaks down the spelling of *carbohydrate* (word **#9**) into its eleven phonemes (sounds) and shows how the three children spelled those sounds. Not only did they vary in how close their spellings were to the standard one, there was a wide range in how many phonemes they included; Carol had a letter for every phoneme, while Jay represented less than half, including only one of the four vowels.

This exhaustive discussion of thirty first-grade spellings has, I hope, given you some sense of what patterns might turn up in young children's writing. This isn't to say that these spellings are necessarily to be expected in all children of any particular age; they were chosen from among other first-grade spellings from the same classroom that were both more and less sophisticated. The rest of the examples in this chapter will be discussed in less detail, highlighting some further features to look for at various developmental levels.

Daniel

Daniel, a six-year-old first grader, was asked by his student teacher Jayme to write about things he liked. His piece, seen in Figure 3–4, translates as, "I like Jayme. She is nice. She is my student teacher. Jimmy and Amber and Mario and Frankie are my friends. I like animals and whoever likes animals, they're sure to like Jayme." Writing on unlined paper, Daniel explored some of the visual properties of written language. He wrote consistently from left to right but varied the slant of his lines and size of his letters. He used mainly uppercase letters and consistently reversed *j* and *s*, using a *j* that faces right and an *s* that looks like a rounded *z*. (He also reversed *z* once.) In most cases, although Daniel

TABLE 3—4
English Consonant Phonemes

		stops		fricatives				affricates
voiced	b	d	g	z	zh	TH (<u>th</u>is)	v	j
unvoiced	p	t	k	s	sh	th (<u>th</u>in)	f	ch

TABLE 3—5
Three Spellings of Carbohydrate

phoneme	/k	ŏ	r	b	ō	h	ī	d	r	ā	t/		*	**
Spelling	C	A	R	B	O	H	Y	D	R	A–E	T		11	11
Jay	K	<u>A</u>		P	<u>H</u>			<u>R</u>				(S)	3	5
Brian	<u>C</u>		<u>R</u>	<u>B</u>	A	<u>H</u>	I	J		A	<u>T</u>		5	9
Carol	<u>C</u>	<u>A</u>	<u>R</u>	<u>B</u>	A(N)	<u>H</u>	I	<u>D</u>	<u>R</u>	A	<u>T</u>		8	11

  * Number of phonemes spelled correctly (underlined)
 ** Number of phonemes represented

FIGURE 3–4   *Daniel: I like Jayme*

didn't put spaces between words, his line divisions occurred between words, except for the division of STOODNT at the syllable break. The single punctuation mark he used was a period at the end of the entire piece. This is reminiscent of a child who said to Villiers (1989), "I put that dot there because it's the end. You always put a dot at the end of the story"(80). Daniel also included representations of writing in his picture, showing Jayme's name on her briefcase and a book filled with scribble writing.

Looking at Daniel's invented spellings, we can see many of the same patterns we did for Jay, Brian, and Carol: long vowels spelled with letter names (JAME/ *Jayme*); *o* used in spelling rounded vowels (STOODNT/*student*); misrepresentation of schwa vowels (ANEMLZ/*animals*); omission of preconsonantal nasals (FRAGKE/*Frankie*); omission of vowels before syllabic consonants (SHR/*sure*), using *z* for /z/ (AOMLZ/*animals*), and silent letter omission (HOO/*who*). He also, however, used more conventional spelling of vowels in a few cases (LIKE, IZ/*is*), and showed knowledge of the digraphs *ch* (TECHR/*teacher*), *sh* (SHR/*sure*), *th* (THAR/ *they're*), and *oo* (TOO/*to*). One aspect of Daniel's spelling that's particularly interesting is reinvention. He spelled the word *like(s)* four different ways in this piece: LIKE, LI, LIX, and LIK, and treated it as a new problem each time, rather than looking back at his earlier spellings. The spelling LIX suggests that he didn't yet understand -*s* as a verb marker; this is a purely phonetic spelling. (Jayme mentioned that he carefully sounded out each word as he wrote.) Daniel's response to two questions that Jayme asked him suggested that he was well on his way to being a confident, successful writer. When asked how he learned to write, he replied, "I concentrated and I watched other people. Mario helped me a long time ago; he concentrated and learned how to write and then he told me." He also felt he was a good writer because "I try my hardest and I don't give up."

FIGURE 3–5   *Johnny: Popcorn*

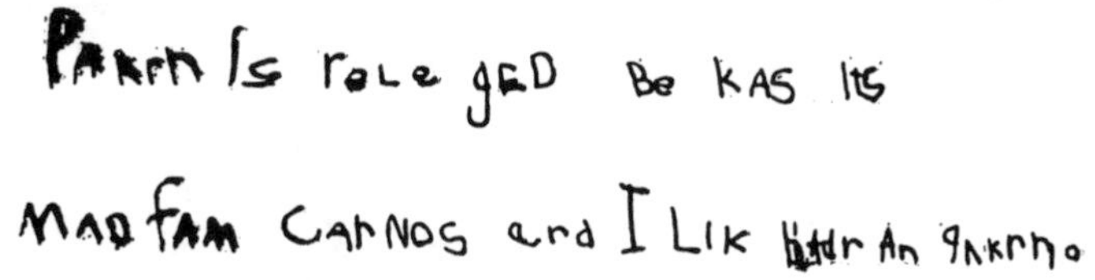

Pakrn Is roLe gɛD Be kAs Its

MAo fAm CaɲNos ɐnd I LIk butɐr An 9Ʌkɲɲo

Johnny

Johnny, like Daniel, was a first grader when he wrote his piece (Figure 3–5), which reads, "Popcorn is really good because it's made from kernels and I like butter on popcorn." Both boys used conventional spellings for only a few words at this point in their development. Both knew, or correctly invented, *I* and *and*, Daniel got *like* right once, and Johnny knew *is*. But we can see that Johnny's knowledge was already a bit beyond Daniel's in a few ways.[1] Most noticeably, he separated words from each other, in one case also splitting a word, *because*, between syllables. Johnny also used a period at the end of his piece but included a creative touch: He told me it was in the shape of a popcorn kernel! Like Daniel, Johnny mixed upper and lowercase, but his printing was neater and his only reversal was one backwards *p*. His invented spellings generally fit into the patterns we've already seen; I'd like to comment on just two examples. Johnny had learned that /k/ is sometimes represented by *c* and sometimes by *k*; unfortunately, he got it backwards most of the time. He used *k* in *popcorn* and *because*, and *c* in *kernels*. However, like Nicole learning about the directionality of numerals, Johnny knew the basic principle and merely needed to refine its application. Second, Johnny used the letter *a* exclusively to spell both short *o* (in *popcorn* and *on*) and short *u* (in *because, from,* and *butter*), which isn't easy to explain. Perhaps he was familiar with the *a* used to spell short *o* in *father,* and pronounced short *u* similarly. Or maybe he had a strategy of using *a* for short vowels he was unsure of. When a teacher sees a spelling pattern like this one whose explanation isn't obvious, the best way to figure it out is to sit down with the child as he or she writes, watching, listening, and questioning. Probably the least useful approach is to assume without further evidence that the spellings are merely "careless" or the result of some type of deficit.

Bennett and Carla

Bennett and Carla, both second graders, had begun to produce spellings that had moved beyond the purely phonetic.[2] Bennett made a personal shield (Figure 3–6) showing his favorite sport (*soccer*), person (*my Uncle Benny*), animal (*cheetah*), movie star (*Bruce Willis*), career (*bartender*), and book (*Scary stories to*

---

[1] Johnny's lines were straighter than Daniel's, but since he was writing on lined paper, no conclusions can be drawn from this.

[2] Henderson (1985) and others have referred to these kinds of developmental changes in children's spelling as "stages"; I prefer to avoid this terminology because it tends to oversimplify. Individual spellings can perhaps be categorized, but any one child's spelling taken as a whole is usually too varied to be pigeonholed.

FIGURE 3–6   *Bennett: Personal Shield*

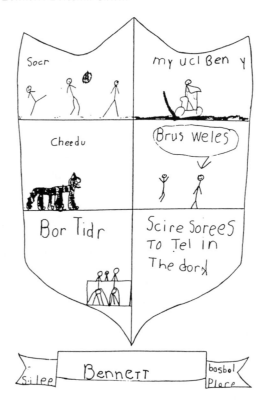

tell in the dark). He also described himself as *silly* and as a *baseball player*. Most of Bennett's spellings were invented ones, but many of his short vowel spellings were conventional, and a new feature appeared that was virtually absent in the younger children's writing: in some words, the use of more than one letter to spell long vowels. Bennett used double *e* in his spellings of *cheetah, stories,* and *silly,* and (perhaps) a silent final *e* on PLARE (*player,* if he pronounced it as a one-syllable word rhyming with *flare*). Notice also that he omitted preconsonantal nasals in UCL(*uncle*) and BOR TIDR(*bartender*) used a *d* for the flap consonant in *cheetah,* and hadn't yet discovered double consonants except in his own name.

Carla, a second grader who was a somewhat stronger speller than Bennett, also used two-letter vowel spellings in her description of uses for a tin can. Figure 3–7 reads: "You can paint it. You can put food in it. You can make it into a penny bank. You can break it. You can put food in it for catering. You can play with it. You can kick it. You can throw it. You can cut your finger. You can cut a hole in it and put a string on." Carla's two-letter vowel spellings included several silent final *e*'s (PANTE/*paint*, MACKE/*make*, BACE/*bank*, CATE/*cut*, and YORE/*your*) as well as a few words with two adjacent vowel letters (FOOD), CIEK/*kick*). These spellings represented both short and long vowels. Carla's spelling shows some other interesting features: she was still omitting some preconsonantal nasals (as in FEGER/*finger* and STEREG/*string* but not PANTE/*paint*), and in some cases she inserted an extra vowel before *r* (THEROW/*throw*, STEREG/

FIGURE 3–7   *Carla: Uses for a Tin Can*

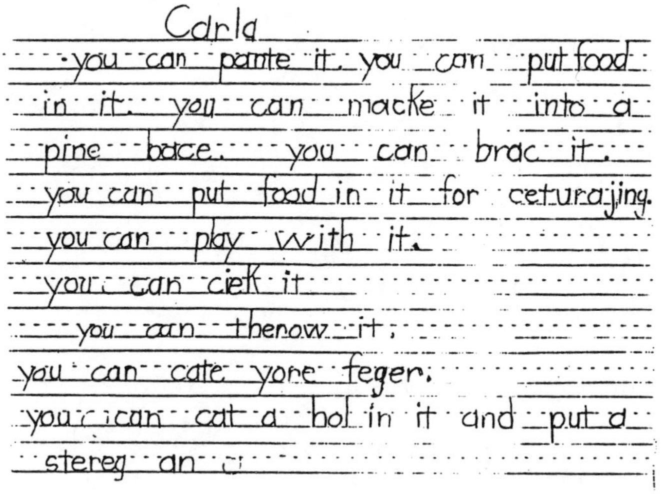

> Carla
> you can pante it. you can put food in it. you can macke it into a pine bace. you can brac it. you can put food in it for ceturajing. you can play with it. you can ciek it. you can thenow it; you can cate yore feger. you can cat a bol in it and put a stereg an c

string). In the latter, my hunch is that she'd taken the knowledge that sometimes vowels you can't hear appear before *r* (as in *finger*), and overgeneralized. She also used three different spellings for /k/: *c* (BRAC/*break*, CIEK/*kick*, and others); *k* (CIEK/*kick*); and *ck* (MACKE/*make*). This is also the first writing sample we've seen that includes punctuation other than at the end of the piece; most of her sentences end with periods.

Gordon and Anna

I've included two stories from fourth graders to illustrate what spelling and punctuation are likely to look like for most children by the middle of elementary school (Figures 3–8 and 3–9). The greatest difference between these two pieces of writing and those by younger children seen earlier is Anna's and Gordon's much greater proportion of correctly spelled words. Gordon and Anna had also

FIGURE 3–8   *Anna: The Day I Had 100,00*

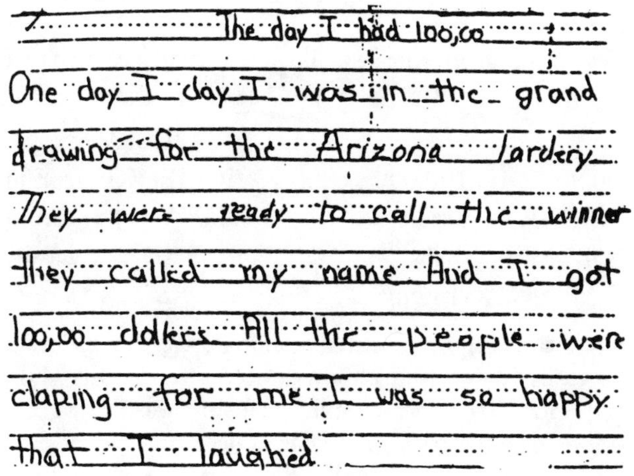

> The day I had 100,00
> One day I day I was in the grand drawing for the Arizona lardery. They wer ready to call the winner. They called my name. And I got 100,00 dolkes. All the people wer claping for me. I was so happy that I laughed.

FIGURE 3–9   *Gordon: One Night When I Was Coming Home*

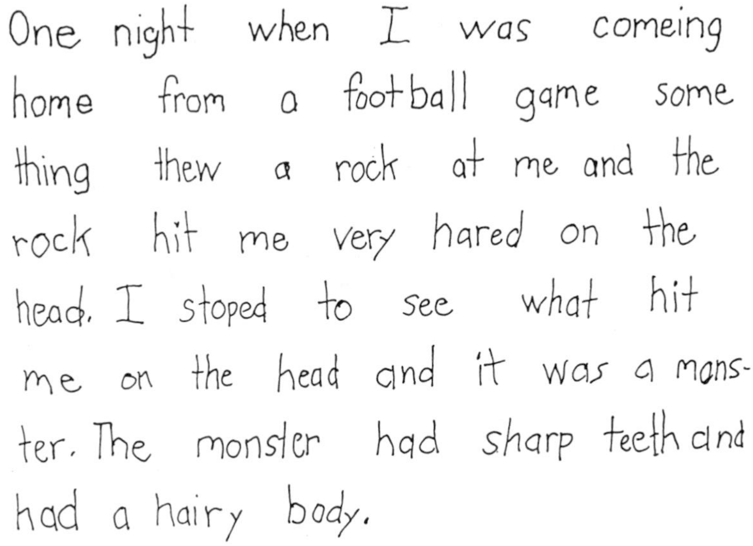

> One night when I was comeing home from a football game some thing thew a rock at me and the rock hit me very hared on the head. I stoped to see what hit me on the head and it was a monster. The monster had sharp teeth and had a hairy body.

almost completely understood how to use periods and capitals to divide sentences. Gordon's story was punctuated correctly, and Anna had only one run-on sentence. Her sentence starting with "And" may seem to be a fragment, but it falls within the acceptable realm of stylistic variation.

Children at this level have internalized a good deal of knowledge about how English spelling works; their ability to produce nonregular spellings correctly, as Anna did with *ready, people,* and *laughed* and Gordon did with *night* and *head*, shows that they have also learned the spellings of a lot of individual words. The invented spellings that do still exist provide insight into the knowledge that children have about the system itself and how it works. As always when we look at the expression of knowledge, error provides more insight into process than correct answers do. Gordon's correct spelling of *hairy* could have been created through knowledge of how to spell vowels before *r,* or he could have just known the word, but his invented spelling HARED (*hard*) couldn't have been produced by rote.

Each piece has four invented spellings that typify patterns seen at this age and beyond:

Anna		Gordon	
100,00	100,000	COMEING	coming
LARDERY	lottery	THEW	threw
DOLLERS	dollars	HARED	hard
CLAPING	clapping	STOPED	stopped

Looking at these eight invented spellings, we can see that they can be explained very easily: they fit into a few simple patterns. LARDERY is a phonetic spelling (Anna, like most people, probably wasn't aware that *lottery* is related to *lot*), with an extra *r* that may reflect pronunciation. THEW and 100,00 are very close to the intended spelling or numeral, and probably reflect

Spelling Celebration

Analogies

Gordon, fourth grade: "The rock hit me very HARED (*hard*) on the head."

After Gordon wrote the spelling HARED for *hard*, he noticed that it contained the word *are*, which confirmed for him that his spelling was right since *are* is contained in the pronunciation of *hard*. Writers frequently use analogies to other words if they are unsure about a spelling. This often successful strategy is commonly used by adult spellers and accounts for many of the few incorrect spellings that adults produce. Some of these unsuccessful spellings by analogy can be amusing. I have seen two cases where adults, unfamiliar with an ethnic surname that they had heard orally, translated it into a more familiar form: *Miguel* became *McGill* and *Segal* became *Seagull*!

---

visual knowledge that's just a little bit off. DOLLERS shows that the schwa vowel continues to be difficult to spell. HARED was written by analogy to the word *are*. Gordon stated this explicitly. And finally, CLAPING, COMEING, and STOPED show lack of knowledge of suffix rules. Gordon and Anna did, however, spell the suffixes themselves appropriately; this contrasts with Daniel (Figure 3–4), who, in spellings like ANEMLZ(*animals*) and LIX(*likes*), showed that he hadn't abstracted out the *-s* suffix.

These eight invented spellings are certainly far more developed than the thirty first-grade spellings in Table 3–1, which we needed a lot of linguistics to understand. As writers continue to mature, their spellings change in two ways: Children learn more words, so that their proportion of correct spellings is higher, and their invented spellings reflect increasingly sophisticated knowledge about our spelling system. When I talk to teachers about invented spelling, I often begin with a short spelling test of words whose spelling they are unlikely to know, like *syzygy, autochthonous,* and *Betelgeuse*. When we talk about how they came up with their spellings, we discover that they have used knowledge about how sounds are spelled, analogy to other words, and guesses about meaning. I then inform them that they have done exactly what children do: They have invented reasonable spellings based on their knowledge of our spelling system and how it works. The main difference is that adults have much more knowledge; the process itself is very similar. You might find it interesting to start noticing the invented spellings you see in the environmental print around you (menus, signs, and so on) and think about why they were produced. One of my students brought me a hand-lettered sign saying DIET SPRIGHT that had been taped onto a school soda machine; the person who wrote it was perhaps on some level thinking of SPRIGHT as a soft drink that's "light"!

PART TWO

Spelling and Punctuation in the Classroom

· 4 ·

Spelling and Punctuation in the Life of the Classroom

We turn now from language and learning to curriculum and instruction, as we consider the teacher's role in helping children come to understand the conventions of written language. In this chapter, I'll lay out a philosophy of classroom language learning and present a picture of how it might fit into the typical day, and then go on in the following chapters to flesh out that picture more fully, beginning in Chapter 5 with a discussion of learning about the spelling system itself through the use of mini-lessons and other focused instruction, then broadening the angle of view to examine strategy development in Chapter 6, punctuation in Chapter 7, and the role of spelling in the broader curriculum in Chapter 8. Finally, Chapter 9 provides some help with the very practical concerns of evaluation, grading, and communication with parents. The picture I'm painting here is very much an attempt to create an integrated vision of a whole-language approach (K. Goodman, 1986) to spelling and punctuation; it's meant to serve as an inspiration to teachers to find their own ways of integrating spelling and punctuation into their own individual, unique classrooms. Please see what I've written as an illustration, not as a prescription.

What purposes should curriculum and instruction for spelling and punctuation serve?

When I talk to teachers about what their spelling curriculum is like now, I usually hear one of two types of answers: either they follow a traditional spelling curriculum or some adaptation of it, or they have no formal spelling curriculum. The traditional spelling curriculum is the one most of us grew up with: textbooks with lists of 20 words to be learned each week, and enough related exercises to fill up about 15 minutes a day. I rarely meet teachers who are enthusiastic and excited about spelling books; they tend to use them because they're required or expected to, because they feel the programs are necessary even if they're boring, or because they're unsure of alternatives. I would guess that most teachers who use spelling textbooks think of them as, at best, a necessary evil. Some teachers, often those who have chosen to change their classrooms in a more holistic direction, have begun placing less emphasis on spelling books, often by assigning the activities in them as homework to free up class time for other activities. Others have eliminated spelling books but created alternative word lists based on words drawn from their science and social studies curriculum or from words students use in their writing. This is a step in the right direction, but it's an incomplete approach to spelling and one that is still locked into a list mentality. Finally, other teachers, probably those most dissatisfied with the traditional curriculum (and not mandated to use it) have eliminated spelling as a subject altogether, deciding that children will just pick up spelling on their own through reading and writing. (I've also met teachers from Canada who told me that their principals, having learned something about whole language, had completely banished spelling books from their schools.) Teachers who no longer have any spelling curriculum as such tend to feel a little nervous about it; they've eliminated programs they were justifiably unhappy with, but wonder, also justifiably, if there is a role for instruction in learning to spell.

Learning to punctuate is a smaller part of the curriculum but has also usually been textbook oriented, although I believe that many teachers using the writing process have developed punctuation mini-lessons based on children's writing; since punctuation seems like a smaller body of knowledge than spelling, it may seem like an easier one to develop one's own curriculum for.

Sometimes I think that whole-language teachers are particularly plagued by matters like spelling and punctuation; it's exciting and usually immediately rewarding to plunge into areas like the writing process and children's literature, but spelling and punctuation, the so-called mechanics of writing (often misleadingly referred to as the "basics"), carry all kinds of negative associations and bad memories. They're often part of what teachers would like to sweep aside to make room for more writing and literature. Whole-language teachers are usually comfortable with the role of invented spelling in the writing process, knowing that it permits independence and increases fluency, but in most cases they are only beginning to rethink how spelling as a school subject might be transformed. Such rethinking is what I intend to do here and in the following chapters; we need to go back to some basic questions of what children need to know about spelling and punctuation and how they are likely to learn it in the context of the larger question of what they need to know to be writers, and then to think through what this might look like in the classroom. To start with, it seems that a whole-language spelling and punctuation curriculum must be based on certain assumptions about goals for instruction and the learning process (Wilde, 1990a).

Independent, competent writers

One comment I've heard many times about the importance of spelling, usually from noneducators and usually in defense of traditional spelling programs, is that if we don't teach kids to spell, it does them a great disservice since misspellings on a job application never helped anyone's career. The intention behind this comment is a legitimate one—misspelling is still the single most egregious evidence of supposed illiteracy in the eyes of the general public and employers. But, traditional spelling curriculum, in its focus on knowledge to the exclusion of contextualized strategies, doesn't appear to be the answer. (If all the employers complaining about job applicants who can't spell are any indication, tradi-

Spelling Celebration

Awareness of spelling strategies

Elaine, October of third grade, when asked what she would do if she didn't know how to spell a word: "Ask the teacher . . . go talk to your group."

Elaine, April of fourth grade, same question: "Go get a dictionary and look it up . . . ask someone . . . try to sound it out . . . try to get it in your mind . . . write it on a piece of paper."

When I first met Elaine, early in her third-grade year, she was very concerned about correct spelling. If she didn't know how to spell a word, she would usually ask somebody, or if she knew that she could find it on a word list on the wall of her classroom, she would look there. During the next two school years, she not only became more relaxed about spelling, she grew more confident about relying on her own resources, which she could use for figuring out spelling on her own, mentally and in writing, and for using the dictionary. Her conscious awareness of spelling strategies reflected this growth in her practices. In helping children to become more adept and resourceful as spellers, we can encourage them to reflect on a variety of strategies as well as to use those strategies. A child who can recite a repertoire of resources—mental, textual, and human—for spelling is aware of all the choices that he or she has. Quite a change from the traditional single rule, "If you don't know how to spell a word, go look it up in the dictionary"!

---

tional spelling programs haven't been working anyway.) Spelling books focus on knowledge: learning to spell a large number of words (perhaps five thousand in grades one through eight) and probably learning something about spelling patterns as well. But they tend to ignore how learners apply that knowledge and move beyond it. (For a detailed critique of spelling books, see Wilde, 1990b.) I'd like to suggest a new goal for spelling and punctuation curriculum: the creation of independent, competent writers, with independence coming first.

Allowing children the freedom to write independently is the basic principle underlying the use of invented spelling in the classroom. Giacobbe (1981) phrased this nicely in the title of her article, "Kids *Can* Write the First Week of School." As children begin to express themselves through writing, they obviously aren't going to be highly competent writers right from the beginning—if by competence we mean expressing oneself cogently with perfect spelling, punctuation, and handwriting. Yet fortunately we don't have to be competent at an activity before attempting it; nobody would ever learn anything that way. Just as with learning to walk, talk, ride a bike, drive a car, and most other things we do, we start out by plunging in and doing our best, often with support from a coach, knowing that we'll get better at it as we go along. Fortunately, unlike riding a bike and driving a car, invented spelling isn't physically dangerous; we don't need pencils with training wheels or dual controls! Rather than focusing on children's mastering the parts before attempting the whole, insisting on competence from the start, and hoping that independence will follow, we need to start with independent writing and let competence evolve. Many teachers have, of course, already begun to do this.

Part of the competence we're aiming for involves helping children to develop the ability to produce perfectly spelled texts in situations such as applying for jobs. How do you go about proofreading a job application letter to make absolutely sure it contains no mistakes? What do you do when you're in a prospective employer's office, filling out a form, and need to use a word that you don't know how to spell? These kinds of real-world questions haven't usually been addressed in spelling curricula since they go beyond knowledge of spelling itself to deal with situational pragmatics, but they need to be. Memorizing spellings and punctuation rules only brings you to a certain level of competence; to achieve the close to 100 percent level of perfection that society expects in these matters,[1] you have to also know how to apply your knowledge in various contexts and have strategies for what to do when your knowledge isn't extensive enough. How many adults would feel comfortable writing the names of Russian republics like Azerbaijan and Tadzhikistan in a report without looking them up or asking someone?

Learning a system, little by little

Imagine moving to a new city and beginning to learn your way around. You probably get a map, ask people for directions, and do a lot of driving and maybe walking around. You find a few main streets to orient yourself by, you get a sense of where other streets are in relation to them, you start thinking of particular areas (downtown) or landmarks (a university, a shopping center) as reference points. If you're traveling with a spouse or friend, you help each other navigate. As your mental map of the community evolves, you may refer back to a paper map to fit your experience into an overall framework. You make wrong turns and get lost occasionally, especially during rush hour when you get rattled by the heavy traffic. Even so, you soon begin to feel comfortable enough to drive without referring to the map, though you still keep it in the car in case you go somewhere new. Eventually you feel enough at home in your new community, and have established enough of a routine, that you can go most places without paying much conscious attention to the process of driving. If the city is big enough, however, you still keep discovering new streets, even whole new parts of town, that you had never been aware of before, and continue to fit them into your now established, comfortable framework.

This type of everyday learning involves the development of a schema for your new city: a multilayered conceptualization, learned largely through direct experience, that becomes more elaborate and integrated over time. Does this

---

[1] These expectations are part of the problem, which I'll discuss later in the context of strategy development.

work as an analogy for learning to spell and punctuate? Let's try describing that process similarly and see if it has the same feel to it.

A beginning writer, knowing the names of the alphabet letters, begins to invent spellings that relate the sounds of words to those letters. As she begins to do more reading, she starts noticing how particular words are spelled, and this affects her writing. She starts spelling correctly (most of the time) the words she uses most often; she realizes and puts into practice patterns like the fact that long vowels are often spelled with two letters. She talks about spelling with her friends, and they enjoy trying to figure out together how a word might be spelled. She still has plenty of invented spellings, but they're more sophisticated than before. She becomes aware of punctuation marks in her reading, and starts using periods and capitals to divide sentences. She learns how to use a dictionary if she wants to be sure her spelling is correct. As her spelling and punctuation get better and better, she thinks about them less and less. As her knowledge of the world and the topics she chooses to write about expand, and as writing becomes more sophisticated, she continues to move into new areas as a writer, so that her first drafts continue to contain invented spelling and less-than-perfect punctuation. She has, however, gotten much better at proofreading.

In both of these descriptions, I've tried to communicate what learning a conceptual system little by little looks and feels like. One starts by forging into contextualized activity (driving around or writing), and gradually gets better at it (in a week or two for learning to get around a smallish city, years for spelling and punctuation). Mistakes are made but correct themselves eventually. Outside supports, both human and textual, are available. Some of the people helping you don't know much more than you do, but pooling your knowledge does help. Eventually the process becomes largely automatic (i. e., below the level of conscious awareness).

This model seems to be one that applies to many kinds of learning, particularly learning outside of school, which is likely to be very much under the control of the learner. In-school conditions for learning are often set up differently. Imagine moving to a new city and having formal daily lessons on the main streets, the layout of the city, and major landmarks, followed by worksheets and quizzes. You might or might not be allowed to drive on particular streets before you'd studied them. You get the idea.

Rather than trying to prove here that the first model is a more appropriate one for language learning (but see Wilde, 1990c), I'd like to treat it as an underlying assumption, suggesting that it's consistent with the model that others have suggested for whole-language instruction (see especially Weaver, 1988), and deserves a try in classrooms wanting to rethink spelling and punctuation curriculum.

Individualization of learning
All teachers know that their students are unique individuals, who come into their classrooms not as empty vessels (even in kindergarten) but with varied assortments of prior knowledge. Since classrooms don't provide an individual tutor for each child, teachers must find some way to address the needs of individuals in the context of a larger classroom community. Textbooks tend to overlook individual differences and provide a common curriculum for everyone, usually all at the

13 Spelling Celebration

Revision

Elaine, fourth grade, first version: "One day the SUWIX (*Sioux*) came to TMOW (*town*)." Second version: "One day the SUOIX came to TNOW."

Someone who didn't understand the meaning of invented spelling, who felt that you're either right or wrong and nothing else matters, would feel that Elaine had wasted her time in revising two of her spellings here. The revisions occurred as she was writing the words. In writing *Sioux*, she first wrote SUW, then changed the W to O and added the IX. Similarly, she wrote TM, changed M to N, and added OW. She did all of this without asking anyone for help or using a dictionary or other reference material. Why did she bother to revise if she wasn't going to spell the words correctly? My hunch is that although she wasn't a strong enough speller, nor did she want to take the time that day, to spell the words correctly, she did have enough sense of the words to change a letter that was obviously wrong. Sure enough, in both cases the spelling that she ended up with was a permutation, one which contains all of the right letters but in the wrong order, a fairly high-level type of invented spelling. The most important point about children's revisions of their spellings is not whether they're accurate or not but the process of aiming for a closer representation of the word. Greater accuracy will follow in time.

---

same time, although some provision may be made for ability grouping, a partial individualization that creates its own problems (see Allington, 1983). A more holistic program in spelling and punctuation starts with the learner rather than a set curriculum, and suggests that instruction can be most useful when targeted to individual development. Rather than spending fifteen minutes a day for a week doing lessons on long *e* vowels with a whole class, a teacher might look for a few children who have been exploring long *e* spellings in their writing and conduct a mini-lesson to help them be more consciously aware of the different spellings of that vowel. (Chapter 5 includes several examples of such mini-lessons.) Textbooks choose to teach everything to everyone; holistic programs are selective, recognizing that much learning takes place without formal instruction, and that small amounts of teaching, geared to the teachable moment, are far more effective than a lockstep approach for everyone.

Teachers who subscribe to these three principles—competent, independent writers as a goal, learning a system little by little, and individualization of learning—are likely to include two major components in their spelling and punctuation programs: opportunities to learn and support for learning, supplemented by appropriate evaluation. The remainder of this book will describe how to set up such programs.

Reading, writing, and inventing: Creating a classroom climate

Sometimes whole-language advocates are accused of wanting to ignore issues like spelling and punctuation, and it's certainly true that many teachers have no interest in teaching these topics the way they've always been taught. A true whole-language curriculum, however, is one that doesn't reject any area of learning as unworthy of study but instead contextualizes all learning. A large part of learning spelling and punctuation, which are part of written language communication, occurs through large amounts of exposure to written language as a reader and practice in written language as a writer. Reading and writing alone probably aren't sufficient experiences for most children to become good spellers and users of punctuation, since they also need to grapple more actively with their knowledge, but they are almost certainly necessary. Frank Smith (1982) has talked about how we learn to read like writers; we notice, whether consciously or not, how words are spelled and how language is punctuated, and begin to apply that knowledge in our own writing. This is the source for much of our instinctive knowledge about language: knowing from the way a word looks if it's spelled right, sensing how to best punctuate a sentence. (This kind of intuitive sense is probably especially important for punctuation since there is often not a clear-cut rule to apply.) It is important for teachers to remember that, although they may feel nervous about eliminating traditional curriculum components like spelling textbooks in order to free up time for reading and writing, this doesn't mean they're eliminating *learning* about areas like spelling.

So the first component of a good spelling and punctuation curriculum is extensive, daily reading and writing. Others have written at length about how to develop classroom reading and writing programs; two sources I'd recommend are *When Writers Read* (Hansen, 1987) for reading and *The Art of Teaching Writing* (Calkins, 1986) for writing. Spelling and punctuation development are, of course, just two of the many, many purposes that reading and writing serve. For writing to serve as a way of learning about spelling, writers need to be free to use invented spelling. Invented spelling in writing serves two purposes: First, children are able to write more freely, and second, they're able to explore the spelling system for themselves. Accepting the value of invented spelling may mean that students' writing will look worse than before if they've always previously assumed that

FIGURE 4–1   *Elaine: Rodeo Story*

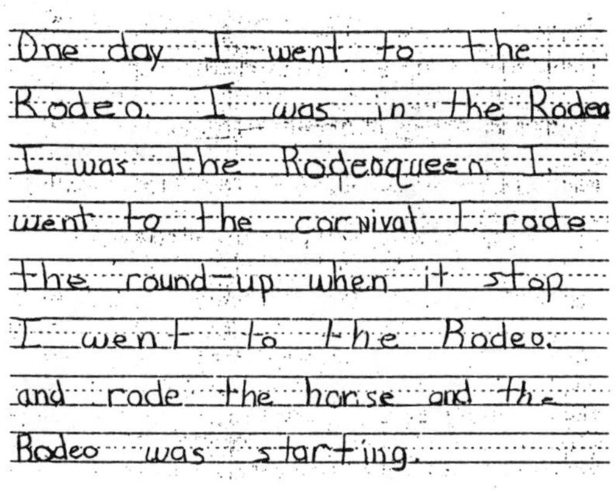

One day I went to the
Rodeo. I was in the Rodeo
I was the Rodeoqueen I
went to the carnival I rode
the round-up when it stop
I went to the Rodeo
and rode the horse and the
Rodeo was starting

FIGURE 4–2   *Elaine: Sioux Dancers*

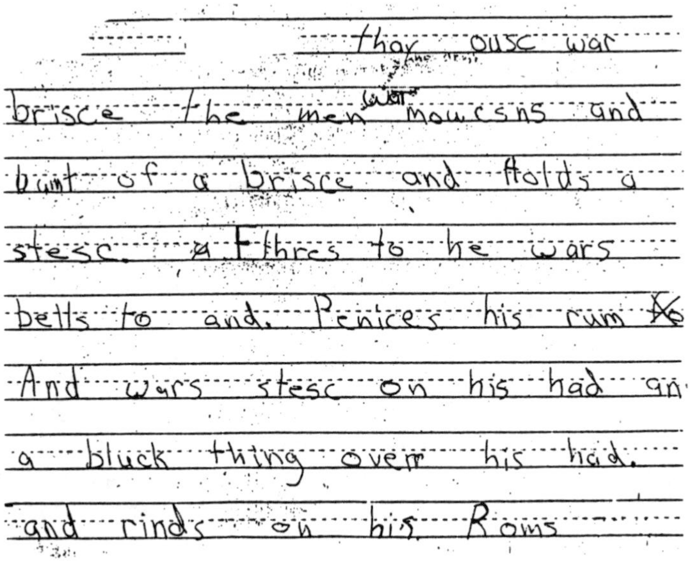

correct spelling was obligatory or nearly so. But there's a very positive trade off: writing will be freed up immensely if children aren't limited to writing words they can spell or asking for spellings. Two stories by Elaine (Figures 4–1 and 4–2) illustrate this.

The first piece, Elaine's rodeo story, is almost perfectly spelled, but it's dull and lifeless, with a very limited vocabulary. It was written on a day when more of her energy was going into interacting with her friends and trying to get spellings right than into developing the content of what she had to say. By contrast, the other piece, excerpted from a longer description of a picture of two Sioux dancers, is full of invented spelling. It reads: "They always wear dresses. The men wear moccasins and [the] bottom of a dress and hold a stick. Feathers too. He wears bells too, and paints his arms, and wears sticks on his head and a black thing over his head, and ribbons on his arms." She was tremendously excited about the picture (particularly since she herself was Native American) and wrote four rapid pages of description, realizing that it was all right to write so quickly that she didn't even take the time to produce "good," well-thought-out invented spellings, which explains why some of her invented spellings look so unusual.[2]

Teachers who are interested in having their students use invented spelling tend to have three major concerns: children's willingness to invent, the transition to conventional spelling, particularly for a final draft, and communication with parents. I'll deal with each of these in turn.

---

[2]The piece itself may not seem very impressive to the reader, but the important point is her active involvement in the process of meaning creation rather than the quality of the product.

Encouraging invented spelling

Children's willingness to use invented spelling depends to some extent on their previous experience. Children in kindergarten and first grade may plunge right in or, on the other hand, particularly if their parents have told them how to spell words before coming to school, may feel that it's not acceptable to write a word if they don't know how to spell it. Older children, similarly, may be relieved to know that it's all right to use their own spellings as they write, or their previous school experiences may have convinced them that it's better to get it right the first time. This is particularly true if their writing has mainly consisted of producing a single draft that is expected to be perfect. The best way to help children be active participants in invented spelling is to help them see the purpose for it. A mini-lesson early in the school year (see Mini-lesson #1) can serve this purpose.[3]

I would recommend *not* suggesting, as some teachers do, that children just put the beginning sound and/or a dash for words they don't know how to spell; this deprives them of the opportunity to think about and figure out spellings and gives them a subtle message that only correct spellings should appear on paper. Invented spellings *are* okay; they're a sign of linguistic and intellectual development that's every bit as legitimate as baby-talk for beginning speakers. I think that it's also important to be firm about not telling children how to spell words or telling them if their spellings are correct. It's far more important to help them develop their own resources in this area, as we'll see later when discussing strategies.

Most children are fairly quick to accept the value of invented spelling when they see how it increases their independence. I'm finding this to be true even for children working with teacher education students conducting a one-hour-a-week practicum lesson in classrooms where conventional spelling is expected the rest of the week. Some children who are insecure or perfectionistic, however, may feel that they don't want to write anything unless it's spelled right and may require a bit more patience. You might want to spend some extra one-on-one time with these children during writing time, helping them figure out possible spellings. Sometimes giving children the option of working with a writing partner, preceded by a mini-lesson on how to help each other think through spellings, can be helpful. But, particularly for older children who don't have much confidence in themselves as writers, it may take some time to help them loosen up. Perhaps the best impetus will be a whole classroom full of inventing spellers, which provides invaluable peer group modeling.

From invention to convention

Using invented spelling doesn't mean using only invented spelling at every point in the writing process; invented spelling is a convenience for the writer, but conventional spelling is a courtesy to the reader, and dealing with spelling is part of the editing process in writing. K. Goodman (1988) has talked about the tension and interplay between invention and convention in language learning. Invention is a centrifugal force (young learners go off in their own directions as they recreate oral and written language), while convention is a centripetal force, pulling

---

[3]Mini-lessons have been described by Calkins (1986) as brief episodes of instruction targeted to a single piece of knowledge or strategy.

MINI-LESSON #1
Introducing invented spelling

Goal: To help children understand how invented spelling will benefit them as writers.

Appropriate audience: Any class at the beginning of the school year, or students who haven't used invented spelling before.

Teacher background knowledge: None.

Major points to cover:

1. Ask[4] the children what it's like when they're writing and don't know how to spell a word. (They'll probably respond that it's frustrating: they have to wait for the teacher to come around, or look the word up.)

2. Tell them that their easiest and quickest choice is to write down the word the way it sounds or the way they think it might be spelled. (You might want to try group brainstorming of spellings for a word they know that's hard to spell, such as the name of a dinosaur.)

3. Tell the class that this is called "invented spelling," and that it's a way for young writers who aren't as good spellers as adults are to write more quickly.

4. Announce a classroom policy: you, and any other adults in the room, will no longer tell children how to spell words, although (particularly in the lower grades) you're willing to help them figure out how a word might be spelled.

5. Suggest that the children all try out invented spelling in their writing that day.

Follow-up: At the end of that day's writing time, ask the class what it was like using invented spelling, as well as asking for examples of spellings they produced.

---

everyone back to a common, shared communication system. As writers develop their sense of audience, they can learn to see the real importance of conventional spelling and punctuation: not to please the teacher or some external standard, but to make their writing more readable. Children reading each other's texts will soon discover this! In a classroom writing program that includes a publishing program, the role of spelling and punctuation in the editing process emerges very naturally. In this context, teachers and children also realize that editing spelling and punctuation is *only* important with pieces that are being polished into a final draft and that it's only part of a larger revision process that focuses on refinement of one's ideas and their expression.

---

4 Please forgive the imperative mood, reminiscent of a basal reader teachers' manual! I am attempting to show in detail what mini-lessons on different topics might look like but not to suggest a scripted lesson.

 Spelling Celebration

Multiple attempts

Gordon, fourth grade: "One day my rabbit ran away from me *because* I got mad at him."

Gordon spent several minutes coming up with what was eventually the correct spelling of *because*. He wrote B, then looked for the spelling in a few places: on a story starter, in an airplane book in his desk, and on a wall chart of common words. Not finding it, he said, "I think I know how to spell it," and added letters, coming up with BCESU. He erased SU, then walked around the room asking three people how to spell *because*, finally getting an answer. He erased all but the B, added EC, then said, "*Because* doesn't have an *o* in it, does it?" and got four or five classmates involved in a debate over it. He added letters to make BECUASE, erased the last four letters, and finally spelled it right.

I imagine that some teachers would say that this was a waste of time, that he should have just asked his teacher or looked up the word. Alternatively, some teachers would feel it was a waste of time because he should have just left the first spelling and focused on what he had to say. I disagree with both positions and feel that student choice needs to outweigh teacher shoulds. Here are my thoughts on this incident: Gordon was giving himself experience in using a variety of written language resources; Gordon's choice as a writer at that moment was to explore spelling while putting the composition process on hold; Some children have a hard time sitting still while writing and need regular social interaction!

One important point is that expectations need to be age-appropriate. For writers who are producing only about five to ten percent invented spellings in their first drafts, it's appropriate to ask for a final draft with *no* invented spellings. For a beginning writer whose spellings are mostly invented, editing might consist of choosing any three invented spellings to correct. I think the best way to accommodate the reader in such cases, whether in a published book or a bulletin-board display of children's writing, is to include both the child's handwritten text and a typewritten version with spelling and punctuation conventionalized. It's important to discuss this with the children, so that they realize that their age-appropriate writing is being honored, the reader is being considered, and they are getting a chance to see the standard spelling of their own text, which will help them increase their knowledge of spelling. In Chapter 6, I'll discuss how to develop strategies for editing.

What will parents think?

Concern for what parents, and to a lesser extent administrators, might think has kept some teachers from trying out invented spelling, envisioning hordes of irate moms and dads turning up at the classroom door with their children's writing (rich with invented spelling), yelling, "What the *&%# is this?! Don't you teach kids to spell anymore!?" Fortunately, parents can be your best ally if you can help them learn to celebrate invented spelling as a sign of learning. A useful analogy is to remind them of their child's learning to talk and the role of error in that growth. They were able to accept mistakes in oral language development (calling all men "Daddy," mispronouncing words, creating new forms like *goed*) because they realized that children learn to talk through trial and error or, more precisely, through developing and modifying hypotheses. Not only do parents accept error in speech but they see it as cute. They become excited about seeing their children gradually become talkers; error isn't a cause for worry because they know, through generations of human experience with language, that it's developmentally appropriate. If we can help parents see that written language works the same way, they can take part in celebrating that growth as well. I've included some sample letters to parents in Appendix B, as well as more ideas for communicating with parents in Chapter 9.

A day in the life

Let's take a look now at what a typical day might look like in a classroom with an integrated spelling and punctuation curriculum. In writing this, I've envisioned a second- or third-grade classroom, but the same basic format would apply at any grade level, with appropriate modification. I've described only those activities that relate directly and indirectly to spelling and punctuation; other classroom activity would of course also be going on. Later chapters flesh out what's been sketched in briefly here.

8:45 A.M.

As part of the morning class meeting, Kim Staples, the teacher, points to the word "mice" on the chalkboard, under the heading "Word of the Day," and asks the class what they think is special about it. After a few wrong guesses ("Are we getting pet mice for the classroom?"), Jacob realizes that *mice* is a special kind of plural ("We don't say *mouses,* we say *mice.*") Kim invites the class to think of other special plurals throughout the day, which they'll compile into a list later on. She also, during the class meeting, displays a new book on loan from the school library, *333 Word Book: Animals Everywhere* (Durham, 1987). This book has double-page spreads of animals and related pictures, all labeled, under headings like "In the ocean" and "In the pet shop." Kim suggests that the students can use it to get ideas for their animal reports, for help with spelling animal names, or just for the fun of browsing in it. She also mentions that she's spotted two misspellings in it, and challenges the class to keep an eye out for them.

9:45 A.M.

At the end of the class's half hour of silent reading, just before they begin oral sharing about what they've read, Kim reminds the students that if they've found a word in their reading that day that they'd like to learn how to spell, they should write it on the "Words to learn" list in the back of their personal dictionary.

10:00 A.M.

Kim begins the class's "Reading, Writing, and Language" time, which extends until lunch hour, with a group mini-lesson (Mini-lesson #2) on using visual

MINI-LESSON #2
Trying out three spellings

Goal: To help children develop the writing of three possible spellings of a word as a strategy.

Appropriate audience: Anyone.

Teacher background knowledge: None.

Major points to cover:

1. Mention that you're going to teach the class a new strategy for coming up with correct spellings of a word.

2. Demonstrate to the class how sometimes when you aren't sure of how to spell a word, you'll write three spellings and see which one looks right (e.g., **acommodate, *accomodate, accommodate*). Mention that you can use a dictionary to confirm your choice if you still aren't sure.

3. Suggest that anyone who's doing editing that day try this strategy out with a few words.

4. (Optional) Add "Try three spellings" to an ongoing chart of "Spelling Strategies."

Follow-up: At the next class meeting, discuss how the strategy worked.

---

knowledge to help them correct their spellings. Last week, the class discussed how to pick out which of their spellings might need to be changed for a final draft.

During the remaining time before noon, several activities related to spelling and punctuation are going on. Lindsey works on a piece of writing about moving into her new house, inventing spellings as she writes. Dylan is working on his final version of his story about two bank robbers. Following the item on the editing checklist in the back of his writing folder that says, "Find and circle words that might be invented spellings," he circles the spellings ROBER, POLECE, and ESCAPE, among others. Sarah has already circled her invented spellings and has begun correcting them. She finds *because* on a poster-size list of Dolch words (commonly used words, Dolch, 1941) posted on the wall, writes three possible spellings of *people* and chooses the one that looks right, and pulls a Disneyland coloring book out of her desk to check the spelling of *Matterhorn*. David and Liz meet at 10:30, as they've arranged previously, to help each other practice the five words they've chosen from their "Words to Learn" list for the week. On Friday, they'll give each other a quiz on them and add all the ones they've learned to their personal dictionaries.

Across the room, Kim Staples is meeting with Matthew for an editing conference on his book *Fluffy's Revenge*. She's noticed earlier that he almost always puts a period at the ends of his stories but rarely includes one elsewhere.

MINI-LESSON #3
Plural endings with -es

Goal: To help students realize that some plural endings are spelled with *-es*.

Appropriate audience: Students who use just an *s* to spell all plurals.

Teacher background knowledge: Words ending in the letters *(t)ch, sh, s, x,* and *z* usually spell their plurals with *-es,* which is pronounced as a separate syllable.

Major points to cover:

1. Ask the students what they usually do when they're writing a word that refers to more than one, such as "one bird, two _____ ." They'll almost certainly respond that they add an *s.*

2. Tell them that you're going to show them some words that this rule doesn't work for. After writing *watch, wish, kiss, box,* and *buzz* (or similar words of your choice) on the board, add-*es* to each one and read through the list.

3. Ask the students why they think these plurals are spelled differently. They'll probably realize, possibly with some leading questions, that they can hear a vowel sound in the plural. (Allow them to express this in their own words, without trying to overly formalize their generalization.) Suggest that they keep their ears open for these words when they write.

4. (Optional[5]) Mention that looking at a word as well as listening to it can tell you if its plural ends in *-es*; point out, or help them discover, that your words end in *ch, sh, s, x,* and *z,* and ask them to think of other examples.

5. (Optional) Point out that we hear an extra syllable in plurals like *spices* and *mazes,* and ask the students to hypothesize why we don't add *-es.*

Follow-up (optional): Ask students to circle any *-es* plurals they use in their writing over the next few days to be discussed at your next meeting.

She begins the conference by asking him to tell her what he knows about periods. He says that they go at the ends of sentences, but can't explain how to tell when a sentence ends. She then reads his story out loud, asking him to try to hear where the sentences end. He does pretty well, although he sometimes thinks clauses are separate sentences. ("When we got home. We couldn't find Fluffy anywhere.") Nonetheless, Kim is pleased at the level of knowledge Matthew reveals. She hands him back his piece and asks him to write in periods where he heard the sentences end. After they discuss how he can do this for himself all the

---

[5] Optional points in these mini-lessons should *only* be covered if the children seem eager to learn more and able to handle more information.

time now, they add "Put periods at the ends of sentences" to his editing checklist, and Matthew leaves the conference beaming at his newly found proficiency. Kim makes a note about Matthew's lesson in her anecdotal log book.

Around 11:00, Kim meets with a group of five students for a lesson on plural endings. (See Mini-lesson #3). These are all students who have produced spellings like AXS and MATCHS in their writing recently.

11:45 A.M.

As part of a class meeting discussing how the morning had gone, Kim asks the class how the "Try three spellings" strategy has worked. Most of those who tried it found it useful, but Brett says he tried three spellings for *boa constrictor* and none of them looked right. Franny says, "That was probably too hard a word to use that strategy with. Why don't you look in the new *333 Word* book on animals?"

1:30 P.M.

The students are working in small groups researching animals. Each group has a table and wall space in one section of the room. A large piece of chart paper in each area is being used to keep a running list of animals for that group ("Animals of Asia," " . . . of Africa," " . . . of Australia," " . . . of the Americas"). Since these are public displays, the children make sure of a word's spelling before adding it to the list. Each group's table has a wide range of books relating to their topic, including picture books, children's informational books, and profusely illustrated adult reference books. Although the children can't read the latter books in full, they love browsing through them, looking at the pictures and reading captions, and exploring charts and tables. They've learned to use indexes in books and realize that an index can be a quick place to check the spelling of an animal name.

2:45 P.M.

Kim calls the class together for the final class meeting of the day. Asking how many of them could think of funny plurals like *mice,* she gets a brief list: *children, men, feet, teeth.* She adds a few of her own: *geese, women,* and *oxen.* She says that tomorrow she would be willing to meet with anyone who would like to work on a picture counting book of funny plurals for the kindergarten class. Several hands go up eagerly.

3:10 P.M.

With all the children off safely on foot and on the bus, Kim thinks back over the last several hours, happy that the children have had another day of joyful immersion in literacy. In her plan book, she checks off successful whole-class encounters with funny plurals and a new spelling strategy, a small-group lesson on *-es* plurals, and Matthew's punctuation lesson. She thinks back to how often throughout the day she saw students using their knowledge from previous lessons and feels pleased that her students are growing so much as readers and writers. She is also pleased that they're learning about spelling and punctuation through both guided discovery and their own explorations with written language.

· 5 ·

Building a Knowledge Base
in Spelling

A s children write, inventing spellings as they go, they draw on their evolving knowledge base about the spelling system. Sometimes their knowledge is accurate and sometimes it isn't. Alison, a third grader, wrote about the
rock her friend Kathy found and mentioned that it had "a LITTEL TURQUOS
in it." When I asked her how she knew there was a *q* in *turquoise,* she responded,
"My dad knows how to spell it, and he spells it with a *q* and says whenever there's
a *q* there's a *u.*" From her father, she had learned both something about the
spelling of a particular word and something about a very regular English spelling
pattern. These two pieces of knowledge, both accurate, helped Alison produce
a spelling that, although not completely correct, did represent the /k/ phoneme
appropriately. Two weeks later, she spelled the word *language* as LAENG-
WIEG. When I asked her about it, she made two comments: that *a* and *e* (as seen
in the first part of her spelling) sometimes go together, so that when there's an
a there's an *e,* and that *i* and *e* (seen later in her spelling) sort of sound alike.
These comments, of course, make very little sense to an adult! Becoming a good
speller involves integrating a good deal of knowledge about written language:
knowledge about individual words, common spelling patterns, and relationships
between sounds and letters. Learning also usually involves misconceptions that
are eventually worked through.

When we go to write any individual word, our knowledge of the spelling
of that particular word is supplemented by our knowledge of how our alphabetic
system works. Take the word *guide,* for instance. It's not spelled purely phonetically, one letter for each sound, for that would give us **gid*. We know that for
the spelling to look right and to produce the right pronunciation, we need
something after the *g* so that it's not pronounced like *j,* and that we also need a
second, silent vowel letter to show that the *i* is long. Yet these rules still don't
necessarily produce the spelling *guide;* they could produce *guyed* (also a real
word). There's also no reason, except historically, why an *h* couldn't be used to
harden the *g* before *i,* producing **ghide*. When we spell *guide* correctly, therefore, our knowledge of English spelling patterns meshes with our knowledge of
that particular word. To spell Alison's words *turquoise* and *language* correctly,

Spelling Celebration

Easy and hard vowels

Ellen, first grade: "We UOS (use) MUSCLSE (muscles) for WOCING (walking). And GETING (getting) a shot. We UOS MUSCLSE for PICING (picking) up things. THER (there) is MUSLS in my MAWLTHE (mouth)."

Four invented spellings, involving four different vowels, have been highlighted here. In two of these words, GETING and PICING, the vowel has been spelled correctly, while in the other two, WOCING and MAWLTHE, it hasn't. Why is this the case? Some vowels are far easier to spell than others and are likely to be controlled by children at an earlier age. The main factor affecting how easy vowels are to spell is their predictability. The short vowels, like those in *getting* and *picking*, are usually spelled with the same single letter. There are exceptions (such as he**a**d for short e and wo**men** for short *i*), but not too many of them. Other vowels, such as those in *walking* and *mouth*, have a variety of spellings. The vowel that's spelled *a* (or *al*) in *walking* has a different spelling in l**o**st, g**au**dy, s**aw**, c**au**ght, and b**ou**ght. The vowel of *mouth* is also often spelled *ow* (*cow*). It's therefore not surprising that children take a little longer to become proficient with these vowels. What's interesting about Ellen's spelling here is that her vowel choices for *walking* and *mouth* are both reasonable ones.

---

knowledge about spelling patterns is useful to some extent (/kw/ is spelled *qu*; the /oi/ vowel is spelled *oi* when not at the end of a word; /g/ and /j/ can both be spelled *g* if the appropriate letters follow), but we need knowledge of these particular words to explain the first *u* in *turquoise* and the *ua* in *language*.

How can we help children build that extensive knowledge base that includes both patterns and words? On the one hand, we don't want to focus just on word memorization since we do have an alphabetic system with many regularities. On the other hand, these regularities can only narrow down alternatives, not predict spellings perfectly. Spelling textbooks for the most part use a model that groups words according to spelling patterns but also requires memorization of individual words. Spelling books have many drawbacks, however. They are decontextualized, treat learning as accumulative rather than evolving, and don't draw on learners' prior knowledge. (Later in the chapter, I'll discuss spelling books further: both their drawbacks and alternative ways to use them if you're required to.)

Nevertheless, there is a definite role for instruction in learning to spell. Although children will pick up a good deal of knowledge on their own, teachers have a very important role in getting children to think about spelling. If spelling instruction takes a discovery approach and builds on the teachable moment, it's valuable not just as a means to the end of producing better spellers but as an intellectual pursuit that's worthwhile for its own sake. When approached properly, language is an area of study fully as interesting as dinosaurs or geography. (These general comments apply as much to the learning of punctuation as to that of spelling, but I'll treat the specifics of learning punctuation separately, in Chapter 7.)

Knowledge, strategies, and "skills"

Much of American education has been stifled by an overemphasis on so-called "skills." Teachers worry that under a whole-language approach, skills might be neglected, and publishers even offer workbooks that use literature largely as a vehicle for teaching skills. Yet Frank Smith (1988) has talked about how the term "skills" is merely a metaphor, an inappropriate one, for most intellectual learning. Being able to chop onions is a skill: an ability that improves with practice and that can be applied in new situations. If one were to speak of a more abstract activity, such as being able to write a cogent book review, as a skill, it would surely be on a very different, more metaphorical level. Although one could to some extent write better book reviews through practice (i.e., through writing book reviews), the ability to do so comes largely from a broad background of reading and writing. It also isn't learned largely through the practice of related subskills, such as practicing writing summaries of books, practicing finding interesting quotations from books, practicing making lists of pros and cons, and so on. When I write a book review, the major activity I'm engaged in is *thinking;* the summarizing, quoting, and so on are merely ways of expressing my thinking to an audience, within the conventions of how book reviews are usually organized. I've learned these conventions through many years of reading and through working within them as I write real book reviews.

Although spelling is probably on a lower intellectual level than writing a book review, I still think it's more like a mental and cognitive ability of that type than it is like a skill such as onion chopping. Rather than talking about spelling *skills* that all children need to acquire, I prefer to talk about *knowledge* that it's useful for them to learn, partially through development and incidental learning and partially through instruction, as well as the application of that knowledge through *strategies,* to be discussed in the next chapter. In the area of spelling, I see five major realms of knowledge:

1. *Predictable relationships between sounds and letters.* The three sounds that appear in the word *bag* are generally spelled predictably[1] with the letters *b, a,* and *g.* Some of these predictable relationships, particularly those for consonants, are picked up quickly by children, while others, such as short vowel spellings, evolve more gradually.
2. *Variant spellings of sounds.* The words *frays* and *phrase* are pronounced identically (/frāz/), but *frays* uses *f* for the first consonant and *ay* for the vowel, while *phrase* uses *ph* and *a-e* respectively. These are all completely normal, acceptable spellings of the sounds involved. There usually aren't any hard-and-fast rules telling which spelling applies when; it

---

[1] Most of the time this is true although there are exceptions and special cases such as the short *a* of *plaid* and double consonants.

16 Spelling Celebration

Suffixes

Anna, third grade: "One day a queen and her prince got MARDIT (*married*) in a castle."

Anna, third grade: "Then we WACHT (*watched*) a little t.v."

Vincent, third grade: "We TRYED (*tried*) to shot (*shoot*) it."

Gordon, fourth grade: "The man *died*."

As children become more familiar with words, one of the ways that they begin to move beyond phonetic spelling is to abstract out features like suffixes; for instance, to understand that past tense words almost always end with -*ed*, even though the ending is pronounced three different ways in words like *jumped*, *played*, and *wanted*. The three invented spellings shown here suggest three different levels of evolution in the spelling of the -*ed* suffix. In MARDIT, Anna isn't even using a phonetic spelling but instead has created a fairly rough approximation of the word. WACHT, however, is a very phonetic spelling, including a *t* to represent the /t/ pronunciation of -*ed*. Vincent's spelling shows an understanding of the constant spelling of the suffix but no awareness of rules for changing the root word. The one correct spelling, *died*, doesn't tell us anything for sure. Gordon *might* understand the e-dropping rule, but could have just seen the spelling somewhere and remembered it, without understanding its underlying structure. Which child could benefit from instruction about rules for changing root words before suffixes (if, and only if, these spellings are typical ones for them)? Only Vincent! Anna is not yet ready, and Gordon probably already knows the rules, whether consciously or not.

depends on higher level orthographic or morphemic patterns, the history of the word, and so on. Spellers know what spellings are likely for a particular sound but can't necessarily narrow down the options definitively.

3. *Orthographic patterns.* Orthographic patterns are regularities in language where surrounding letters and sounds affect each other. For instance, the double *t* in *hatter* tells us about the vowel: It is different from the vowel in *hater*. Similarly, although we usually drop *e*'s before adding *able*, we don't in *knowledgeable* because we need to keep the *g* sounding like *j*.

4. *Morphemic patterns.* Our spellings often preserve meaning relationships, so that *electric* and *electricity* are spelled similarly despite differences in pronunciation, as are the -*ed* endings of *walked*, *prayed*, and *wanted*.

5. *Historical and arbitrary spellings.* Why does *gnash* have a *g*? Because it used to be pronounced with a *g* in Middle English. Why do some words

TABLE 5–1
Appropriate Curriculum for Spelling

	INFORMAL LEARNING	INSTRUCTION
SPELLING PATTERNS	Predictable patterns, morphemic patterns	Some developmental patterns, variants, orthographic patterns
WORDS	Historical and arbitrary spellings	Word lists (optional)

start with *ph*? Because in Latin *ph* was used to transliterate the Greek letter φ (phi, pronounced /f/). Why are *sale* and *sail* spelled differently? Aside from their different histories, it helps distinguish them from each other. In most cases, although a knowledge of historical roots can help you remember spellings, these arbitrary patterns are integrated unconsciously and spellings of particular words remembered individually.

Teachers might feel a little overwhelmed at seeing all of this, but with a focus on knowledge they will realize that curriculum in spelling doesn't have to be comprehensive. If spelling is seen as a collection of skills, then each of those skills is probably essential; if it's a realm of knowledge, we can stress certain basic ideas for all learners, supplemented with other topics that are not essential but enriching. For instance, all children should probably know that /b/ is usually spelled *b*, but explorations into the history of English spelling can be more selective, perhaps tied to learning about a particular region of the world in social studies. The building of a knowledge base in spelling can be seen as having two parts: learning individual words and learning spelling patterns. And it takes place in two ways: informally and through instruction. Table 5–1 suggests what mode of learning is most appropriate for different kinds of spelling knowledge. I'll deal with each of these domains in turn.

Informal learning of predictable and morphemic spelling patterns

One of the most important questions to deal with in spelling curriculum is how much time should be spent on instruction, as opposed to letting knowledge develop on its own. If children are encouraged to actively invent spellings, they very quickly learn certain predictable sound/spelling patterns, as Read's (1975) work demonstrated. This is particularly true for consonant spellings. Appendix C is a comprehensive list of spelling/sound relationships comparable to what might be reasonable to cover in grades 1 through 6 of a spelling textbook series.[2] I've marked the phonemes whose spellings are predictable enough that children, according to Read's work, will probably need no instruction in them. In kindergarten and first grade, with beginning writers, the normal kinds of

---

[2] Spelling series often include in their lists of skills rare spelling patterns, such as /z/ being spelled *thes* (as in *clothes*) and /u/ being spelled *iew* (as in *view*). These occur in only a few words and are probably better treated as arbitrary spellings than as rules.

contextualized instruction on the alphabet (e.g., making alphabet books with a page for pictures of things beginning with each letter, reading poetry with alliteration, and so on)[3] will be sufficient input for most children to begin internalizing these patterns. Once beginning writers are using the kind of invented spelling where they're trying to represent sounds, the teacher can begin a checklist to see if those predictable consonant patterns are being picked up. (The consonant sounds, including digraphs and single-letter clusters, that are almost always spelled consistently in English are /b/, /d/, /ks/(x), /l/, /p/, /t/, /th/, /TH/, /v/, and /y/. Others that are spelled consistently in most words are /f/, /g/, /h/, /m/, /n/, /r/, /sh/, and /w/. Short vowel spellings are also predictable but are learned more gradually and may therefore be suited to more instruction.)

At a different level of complexity, meaning-related (morphemic) spelling patterns are so word-specific (such as the words in which /f/ is spelled with *gh* or *ph*) that they're best learned informally. Particularly with older learners, there are two main ways for teachers to support this process. First, in discussing spelling strategies, students can be encouraged to think of a related word if they are stuck on a spelling. Second, when exploring an area like the history of the English language, students can learn about roots and prefixes. The focus would be not on memorizing lists of words and parts of words but on exploring patterns of students' own choice. (See Chapter 8.)

I'm suggesting, therefore, that a good deal of what is covered in beginning spelling books (basic, predictable sound/letter relationships), as well as some of what's covered in upper elementary books (lists and exercises for words with prefixes and suffixes) need not be taught formally but can be left to informal learning. There is one specific meaning-related spelling pattern that instruction probably would be useful for: the past tense *-ed* ending, which has three pronunciations but usually a single spelling. (Lessons aren't usually necessary for the *-s* ending since children tend to spell it correctly without instruction, or for the *-ing* ending since it's always pronounced the same.) I've included a writing sample from a student for whom this lesson (Mini-lesson #4) would be appropriate (Figure 5–1, with relevant past tense words circled).

Anna, a fourth grader, used two different words that should have ended with *-ed*. Of the three times she used *played,* she omitted the ending twice and used just a *d* the other time, as she did with *called.* Notice also that she didn't spell an irregular past tense verb, *made,* with an *-ed* either, though she ended up producing a homophone (spelled like *said*) instead of the right spelling.

Informal learning of words:
Historical and arbitrary spellings

As with predictable and morphemic spelling patterns, the spellings of many individual words can be picked up through reading. Most of us produce most of the words that we use in our writing without having to think about their spelling. This isn't because their spellings are totally consistent and regular because they aren't. English is famous for spellings like *though, through, bough, cough,* and *rough,* in which the same four letters are pronounced five different ways, or *ship, chef, sugar, schwa, notion, special,* and *mission,* which use seven

---

[3] See McGee and Richgels, 1989, for ideas about and suggestions for alphabet learning.

FIGURE 5–1   *Anna: A Cat and a Mouse*

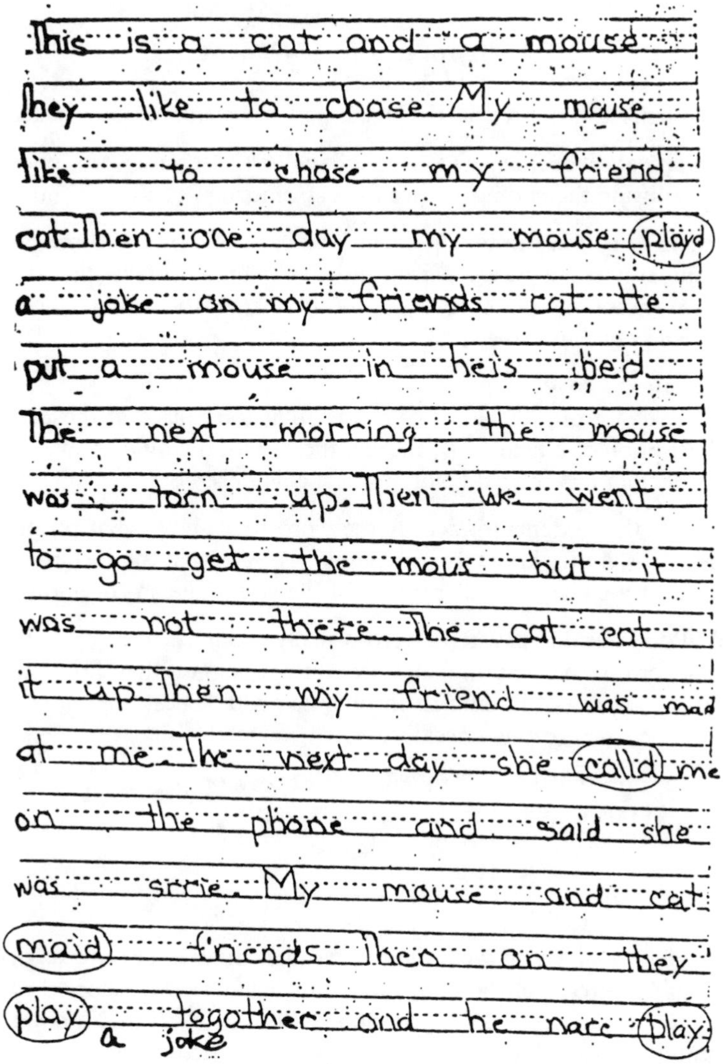

This is a cat and a mouse
They like to chase. My mouse
like to chase my friend
cat. Then one day my mouse (playd)
a joke on my friends cat. He
put a mouse in he's bed
The next morning the mouse
was torn up. Then we went
to go get the mour but it
was not there. The cat eat
it up. Then my friend was mad
at me. The next day she (callld) me
on the phone and said she
was srrie. My mouse and cat
(maid) friends been on they
(play) together and he nace (play)
    a joke

different spellings for the same /sh/ phoneme. Your knowledge of individual spellings is also far greater than what you learned through spelling instruction. At most, your elementary school spelling curriculum would have covered four to six thousand words; if you were required to learn spelling words formally in high school, that would have added at most another few thousand. How many words do adults know how to spell? *Webster's Ninth New Collegiate Dictionary* (1983) contains about 160,000 entries, and from a rough glance at it, I'd estimate that most literate adults could probably spell at least around half the words in it. (Take a look at a dictionary yourself and see if you agree with my approximation.) Even if 80,000 words is too high an estimate, I think we'd all agree that we can spell far more words than those we learned formally. We learn to spell words from seeing them in print and, often, from using them in our writing.

MINI-LESSON #4
Past tense words ending in -ed

Goal: To help students realize that most past tense endings are spelled *-ed*.

Appropriate audience: Students who are spelling past tense verbs phonetically, or omitting the ending, rather than abstracting out the *-ed* ending.

Teacher background knowledge: The past tense ending has three pronunciations, as heard in *walked, played,* and *wanted* but is usually spelled the same. Most exceptions are those where another part of the word changes, such as *sleep/slept* and *make/made*.

Major points to cover:
1. Take a group dictation of a story that took place in the past (e.g., a description of a field trip). Ideally, the dictation would grow out of your curriculum rather than being just a spelling exercise.

2. Ask the students to identify the words that show what people did (or the verbs, if they know that terminology). Ask what the spellings of all (or most, if there are irregular verbs) of the verbs have in common.

3. Point out that past tense verbs usually end in *-ed* and suggest that they look for this the next time they are editing. Suggest that if they are able to do a good job of finding them, they can add "Check for *-ed* endings" to their personal editing checklist.

Follow-up (optional): Have students report back on past tense verbs they found in their own writing.

This is true for children as well. On the average, children already know how to spell about 65 percent of the words in their spelling books before they've even studied them (Manolakes, 1975; Stetson & Boutin, 1980). This doesn't mean that learning individual words has no place in the curriculum, as I'll discuss later. But we do need to recognize that mere exposure to print through reading is an invaluable contributor to learning to spell many words. I'd like to share an example of what this might look like in practice. (See also Spelling Celebration #17.) Table 5–2 shows "before" and "after" spellings of the word *giraffe* by seven second- and third-grade children.

The children had been involved in a science unit on mammals for about a month and were given a list of mammal names to spell both before and after the unit. (Their teacher didn't do any instruction related to the spelling of mammal names.) Their invented spellings of *giraffe* show the kind of growth that takes place through incidental learning. Of the seven children, Darren spelled *giraffe* correctly both before and after the unit, two children, Erica and Mike, had learned to spell it by the end of the unit, and the other four had invented spellings both before and after. Of those four, Alison's "after" invented spelling

 Spelling Celebration

Incidental learning of words

Elaine, fourth grade: "We went to the CORVLFAROV (*carnival*)."

One week later: "I went to the *carnival*."

Elaine's first spelling of *carnival* occurred in a fictional personal narrative. Writing rapidly, she wrote the letters CORO, changed the second *o* to a *v*, and went on, looking back at her first spelling when she repeated the word two lines later. Many of her invented spellings of longer words were like this: jumbles of letters that, although bearing some slight resemblance to the word, worked mainly as placeholders. A surprise, however, came exactly a week later when Elaine, writing a rodeo story, paused briefly to think, wrote *carnival* correctly, and went on. Surprised at the dramatic improvement, I asked her how she had known how to spell it when a week earlier she hadn't. She replied casually, "Oh, I saw it on Susie's paper and I remembered it." My hunch is that when she saw the word on her friend's paper, something clicked as she realized (consciously or unconsciously), "Oh, *that's* how you spell *carnival*!" And don't most of us learn how to spell most words this way? We don't practice them five times, write them in sentences, unscramble them, and take tests on them. We just see them as we read and remember them. Even adults who are not strong natural spellers know many, many words that they learned not formally but incidentally, in the course of reading. Wide reading may be the single best avenue to good spelling.

---

is clearly an improvement over her earlier one since she spelled more phonemes correctly. I think you could also make a case for Jay's and Lacey's "after" spellings looking a little better than their earlier ones. It's important to recognize that invented spellings may get better before they become correct. More specifically, although all the children included *r*, which is predictable, in their earlier spellings of *giraffe*, there were improvements in the spelling of all the other phonemes of the word, all of which have more than one possible spelling. A straight phonetic spelling would produce something like Jay's JORAF. The improvement is likely to have come, therefore, from seeing the word in print and remembering something about how it looked, even if they didn't remember every letter at this point. (You may find that when you write a word you've only recently added to your writing vocabulary, you remember most of the spelling but get stuck on one or two letters. These are likely to be less predictable letters, such as those representing the schwa vowel.)

The point of all this isn't that children should never choose to actively memorize spellings of words but rather that much learning will take place without formal memorization, as a result of both maturation and increasing

TABLE 5–2
Before and After Spellings of Giraffe

	Phoneme						
	/j/	/ə/	/r/	/a/	/f/	spelling	# OK
Correct	g	i	r	a-e	ff	giraffe	5
	Before						
Alison	J	E	R	A	F	JERAF	1
Darren	G	I	R	A-E	FF	GIRAFFE	5
Erica	J	OO	R	A	F	JOORAF	1
Jay	J		R	A	R	JRAR	1
Lacey	D		R		VRF	DRVRF	1
Mike	J		R	A-E	FF	JRAFFE	3
Sally	G		R	A-E	F	GRAFE	3
TOTAL OK	2	1	7	3	2		
	After						
Alison	G	I	R	A	F	GIRAF	3
Darren	G	I	R	A-E	FF	GIRAFFE	5
Erica	G	I	R	A-E	FF	GIRAFFE	5
Jay	J	O	R	A	F	JORAF	1
Lacey	D		R	A	F	DRAF	1
Mike	G	I	R	A-E	FF	GIRAFFE	5
Sally	G		R	A-E	F	GRAFE	3
TOTAL OK	5	4	7	4	3		

exposure to print. This also doesn't mean that all children will naturally become excellent spellers of all words because, as we all know, even among adults there's a wide range of spelling proficiency. (Spelling strategies, discussed in Chapter 6, are the most important area of growth for older writers who want to spell better than they do already.)

Sometimes it's hard for teachers to let go of control and trust incidental, informal learning; we may feel it would be nice if we could just help kids learn all the words they might ever want to use in their writing. But a classic article by Hildreth (1948) shows how futile an undertaking that would be. Using data from a study (Rinsland, 1945) that tabulated the vocabulary used in over six million words of elementary children's writing (and this was precomputer!), she

 Spelling Celebration

High-frequency words

Elaine, fourth grade: "*one day i went* . . . *OT* (to) *ROED* (ride) *the* round-up."

Here is a list of all the words Elaine used more than ten times in her writing during fourth grade. Each word is followed by the number of times it was used and the number of times it was misspelled. Words from the list that Elaine used in the sentence above are italicized in the sentence and in uppercase on the list.

THE	85	0	was	24	0
TO	60	1	it	18	0
we	44	0	in	17	0
and	42	0	DAY	16	0
I	38	0	said	16	7
then	29	3	my	13	0
WENT	28	1	ONE	13	1
a	25	0	she	13	0

It is, of course, not surprising that children tend to be very successful in writing the words that they use most often. These words make up a high proportion of written text. In my study of six third- and fourth-grade children (Wilde, 1986/1987), I found that 37 different words accounted for about 50 percent of their running text (out of about 1,600 different words altogether). The 37 words were spelled correctly about 98 percent of the time. When one of these words is occasionally misspelled, the way that *to* was in this example from Elaine, it's usually just a slip of the pen, rather than an indication that the writer has forgotten how to spell the word.

found that most words were used only occasionally. Taking a sample of 612 different words, out of a total of 14,571 that were used three or more times by the children, she found that only 3 percent of them were used a thousand times or more in those six million words. Extrapolated to the entire word list, this would come to about five hundred words used a thousand times or more (e.g., about 2 percent of the 25,632 different words that were used at least once). Hildreth's graph of the 612 words, reproduced as Table 5–3, is fascinating; the curve hugs the edges of the graph so closely that it's almost invisible. The table can be interpreted very easily by saying that many words were used only rarely, while only a few words were used frequently.

There are two important implications of Hildreth's findings. The first is that knowing how to spell a small number of words will enable writers to spell correctly a large proportion of what they write, if you consider the running text as a whole. I found, for instance (Wilde, 1986/1987), that out of 13,793 words written by six third and fourth graders, only 37 different words (out of a total of

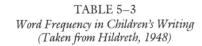

TABLE 5–3
Word Frequency in Children's Writing
(Taken from Hildreth, 1948)

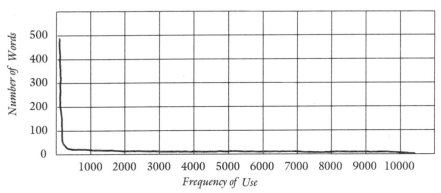

1,618) accounted for half of the total. These words were used anywhere from 61 to 1,013 times each. The great news for teachers is that the words children use a lot tend to be spelled correctly; the children I looked at spelled those 37 words correctly 97.6 percent of the time. When you look at the words themselves, it's obvious why this was so: The top ten words on the list were *the, and, to, I, was, a, he, we, went,* and *it*—all short, simple, common words. The children still did fairly well on what I called medium-frequency words, which were those used anywhere from two to sixty times: they were spelled 77.0 percent correctly. It's only on the low-frequency words, those used only once by any child in two years, that they dropped to a level of 56.4 percent correct spelling. Again, looking at these words makes the explanation obvious: Although many of the low-frequency words were also simple ones, invented spellings were often created for words like *unconscious, switchblade, planetarium,* and *especially.* (See Spelling Celebration #19.) This leads us into the second implication of Hildreth's study, which I'll let her describe:

> Those 23,000 seldom used but sometimes needed words [i.e., those appearing fewer than one hundred times in Rinsland's study] prevent even good spellers from making a perfect score. Beyond the first two or three thousand [most frequent] words each individual's vocabulary in functional writing becomes more and more diversified. One person needs "catastrophe"; another, "celery." One wants to write "Milwaukee"; another, "New Rochelle." In view of these circumstances, a person who does not have to stop to look up words every time he [or she] wants to write a letter or a report correctly that is intended for others to read is a genius comparable to the lightening calculator. . . . The teaching of spelling, instead of being largely mechanical drill to force the child to memorize as many words as possible before he [or she] leaves school, should give pupils more help in spelling for writing the material they need and wish to write everyday. (pp. 469–470)

She went on to suggest that spelling instruction beyond the learning of a basic vocabulary should focus primarily on strategies: proofreading, dictionary

Spelling Celebration

Low-frequency words

Anna, fourth grade: "We went to the *PLANA TEREUM* (*planetarium*). . . . We went on the *ESKLADER* (*escalator*) . . . We had CEREL (*cereal*) with BANNAS (*bananas*) and STRAW-BEERRS (*strawberries*)."

Anna used the three uppercase, italicized words above only once each during her fourth-grade writing. They are also long and fairly difficult words. It should come as no surprise that, just as children are very successful in spelling the words they use most often, they're likely to produce invented spellings for words they have never used before. This means that unless their vocabulary growth stagnates children are likely to continue to have a small proportion of invented spellings in their writing. This isn't a problem! As children continue to read widely, they'll become familiar with the written forms of more of the words that are already in their speaking vocabulary. As they develop strategies for finding out the spellings of words, they'll get better at correcting spellings for final drafts.

---

use, and the keeping of an individual dictionary. Elsewhere, Hildreth (1947) suggested that children are likely to learn the spellings of the several hundred most frequently used words through incidental learning by the end of third grade.

Thinking about what Hildreth has said, therefore, may make it easier for teachers to trust informal learning in spelling. Children will pick up many of the easier words on their own, and it's impossible to predict which of the more difficult words are worth learning, so we might as well let much of the learning of specific words be determined by the children themselves and focus instruction more on helping children to discover spelling patterns.

Instruction and the discovery of spelling patterns

I'd like to begin this discussion of discovery-based instruction with a mini-lesson for adults. Take a look at the following two lists of words:

-able	-ible
workable	visible
reliable	possible
laughable	edible
remarkable	legible
livable	incredible

Can you come up with a hypothesis as to why some words have the suffix *-able* and some *-ible*? You might even try to think of more than one possibility and see which rule works best. There are some words that don't fit the rule, but I haven't included any of those exceptions in my list. I've put the answer at the end of this chapter.

Although this isn't the same as a mini-lesson in a classroom since there is no chance for you to interact with me or other learners, I hope you got a sense of what it feels like to learn about spelling by looking at language data and trying to develop a theory for it. This, I think, is the major purpose that formal instruction in spelling can accomplish. (By the way, isn't it interesting that with all the formal spelling instruction most adults have had, most of us were never taught that fairly useful *-able/-ible* rule?) The first question to think about in planning such instruction is how much of it there should be and when it should occur. We can break spelling patterns for instruction into three groups: developmental patterns, variants, and orthographic patterns. The knowledge involved for each of them isn't really too extensive. The predictable developmental patterns in spelling that I'd focus instruction on are short vowel spellings, preconsonantal nasals, and possibly vowel omission before syllabic consonants.[4] The patterns in Appendix C that aren't marked *P*, including all the vowels, are variant spellings of phonemes, some arbitrary and some rule-governed, and Table 5–4 lists orthographic patterns comparable to what would be covered in textbooks for grades 1 through 6.

This is a reasonable amount of content to cover, so that, although spelling programs would allow six years to learn all of this, any teacher could easily cover most of it in the course of a year to the extent appropriate for his or her students. One mini-lesson on spelling patterns a week per child, conducted in small groups, would probably be sufficient. Obviously, first graders aren't ready to examine all the possible spellings of long *e* and sixth graders don't need to learn to include preconsonantal nasals, but how does one more specifically decide on developmentally appropriate instruction? The best way to do so is by looking at children's writing. If we look back at the writing samples from Chapter 3, we can see some examples. Carla, in writing about possible uses for a tin can (Figure 3–7), included a preconsonantal nasal in PANTE *(paint)* but omitted them in FEGER *(finger)* and STEREG *(string)*. She would probably be just at the right point for a lesson on preconsonantal nasals since her awareness of them was beginning to emerge. Interactions with children can also give you a sense of their knowledge base. Jay, a second grader, was writing about maps and wrote the

TABLE 5–4
Orthographic Patterns for Instruction

> Double consonants
> Within words
> Before suffixes
> Other changes before suffixes
> Change *y* to *i*
> Drop final *e*
> Silent letters (technically an
> arbitrary/historical pattern)

---

[4] If children don't pick up the predictable spellings for /sh/ and /y/ on their own, as Read (1975) suggests they might not, I'd include lessons on them as well.

word *longitude,* spelling it LONJETOOD. He then said, "I wonder how you spell *long;* I know it's at the beginning of the word." He sounded out *long* as *l-o-g,* then went back and erased the *n* in his spelling of *longitude.* After he was done writing, I asked him about the *n:* why he'd had it there originally when it didn't fit his later sense of what the spelling should be. He replied by saying, roughly, that he'd heard it but it's like when you're sounding something out and you hear it but it's not really there. Read (1975) gave a more formal description of the same phenomenon, "When children spell PUP . . . for *pump,* there is probably nothing wrong with their hearing; they simply have no special symbol for the nasalized vowel that is the largest difference between *pump* and *pup"* (p. 116).

Pulling together small groups of children who are clearly ready for mini-lessons on specific topics will be the most effective form of instruction, particularly for lessons on developmental features and rule-governed orthographic patterns. But lessons on arbitrary variant spellings like all the possible spellings of long *e* could be conducted very profitably with a whole class since a wide range of background knowledge could be accommodated. A checklist or general awareness of children's knowledge, as seen in their spellings, is probably the best way to maintain an ongoing matching of instruction to learners and to ensure that you don't waste their time by teaching them what they already know.

Instruction in developmental patterns

Let's take a look now at what this instruction would look like, beginning with preconsonantal nasals. Mini-lesson #5, both shows how to increase awareness of this particular spelling pattern and provides a model for these lessons in general. (In the case of this and other developmental spelling patterns, the role of instruction is to give a slight boost to growth that would no doubt occur on its own anyway.)

In the case of short vowel spellings, instruction would be most appropriate for children who have begun to use standard spellings of short vowels as well as or instead of early phonetic ones like BAD for *bed.* Activities similar to those used to familiarize children with consonant letters would work well. For short *a,* you could find poems with a lot of short *a* words to read, make a bulletin board or individual books of short *a* words (pictures with captions written by students), make lists of rhyming words to develop poems from, and so on. At some point you would probably want to do a mini-lesson that points out the relatively consistent spelling of the phoneme. ("Let's think of words that rhyme with *cat* . . . with *tab.* " After writing them on the board, ask the children to generalize about the sound/spelling relationship.) The same process would be used for the other short vowels. This instruction would be focused on the usual, single-letter spelling of each vowel. Alternative spellings like the short *u* in *month* would be covered later (and with older children) as variants. Instruction about vowels before the syllabic consonants *r, l, m,* and *n* would be similar to that for preconsonantal nasals, helping children to see that their spellings are different from what they might intuitively seem to be but still predictable. The children can be led to understand that words like *her, ball, him,* and *pen* are all written with vowels even though it's hard to hear them as separate sounds. (When syllabic

♦

MINI-LESSON #5
Preconsonantal nasals

Goal: To help children learn to include preconsonantal nasals consistently in their spellings.

Appropriate audience: Children who have begun to include preconsonantal nasals occasionally. (The lesson may also benefit children who haven't yet included them.)

Teacher background knowledge: Young writers tend to omit the nasal sounds /m/, /n/, and /ng/ before consonants in their spellings, not because they don't hear them but because they classify them as part of the vowel rather than as phonemes with their own spellings.

Major points to cover:
1. Say the words *cap* and *camp* and ask the students what the difference between them is. Encourage them to think out loud and express themselves in their own words, however convoluted. The point isn't to arrive at a right answer but for them to conceptualize their perceptions. Repeat with another pair of words, this time with an *n* (e.g., *pat* and *pant*); see if they are able to generalize from their understanding of the first pair.

2. If and when you feel the students have satisfactorily explained to themselves what they hear, write the two pairs of words on the board and ask what they notice and why they think the words are spelled the way they are. Again, let them express the relationships in their own way, with the goal of helping them to understand that this is how the sounds they hear are represented in writing.

3. (Optional) You might want to continue by drawing a comparison to words with a nasal but no following consonant, so that your blackboard list would look like this:

cam	camp	cap
pan	pant	pat

Follow-up (optional): Compose a group poem using preconsonantal nasals, by generating a list of rhyming words[5] and then building a poem (probably a silly or nonsense poem) around them.

♦

consonants occur in unaccented syllables, as in *mother, little, bottom,* and *button,* the vowel is both more difficult to hear and harder to predict a spelling for, so those patterns should be saved for a later lesson.)

---

[5] A rhyming dictionary is a useful classroom resource.

Mini-Lesson #6
Arbitrary spellings of long e

Goal: To make students aware of the variety of possible spellings of long *e*.

Appropriate audience: Students who have moved beyond the single letter *e* as a spelling for long *e* and have begun to explore other possibilities. (See Bennett's double *e*'s and the *y* in BENY, Figure 3–6).

Teacher background knowledge: Long *e* has a variety of spellings, as seen in b*e*, h*ea*p, pl*ea*se, n*ee*d, ch*ee*se, c*ei*ling, f*ie*ld, chlor*i*ne, alg*ae*, ph*oe*nix, p*eo*ple, happ*y*, hock*ey*, and qu*ay*.[8] The variation is basically arbitrary, having occurred largely for historical reasons, although *e* is common in two-syllable words and at the ends of words, while *ee* and *ea* are common in monosyllables.

Major points to cover:
1. Ask the children for as many words as they can think of that contain the vowel sound heard in *bee*. List them, preferably on chart paper, in columns according to spelling. Label the columns *e, ee,* and so on.

2. If possible, stop the lesson at this point and invite the children to add words to the chart as they think of them or read them during the next day.

3. When the lesson resumes, you may want to add columns for any spellings your students haven't yet thought of, particularly spellings that occur in familiar words. Continue by discussing which spellings are most common, and ask the class to formulate a good strategy for spelling a long *e* word they've never seen in print or can't remember the spelling of. (A good approximation might be, "Try *ee* or *ea* in the middle of one-syllable words and *e* elsewhere.")

Follow-up (optional): Suggest that students continue to add to the long *e* chart, which can be kept in the room as a spelling resource.

Instruction in variant spellings

Many of the sounds of English have more than one possible spelling; these occur for either arbitrary or rule-governed reasons.[6] A basic mini-lesson plan for each category can be adapted for any appropriate phoneme. Again, mini-lessons should be used with children who are ready for them and need them (e.g., for a child who always uses the right letter to spell /j/, a lesson on it would be a waste of time.) The phonemes whose variant spellings occur, on the whole, arbitrarily, are as follows:[7]

---

[6] In some cases the rules are too obscure or abstract to be worth exploring in elementary school, so I've labeled them as arbitrary patterns.

[7] The consonant /zh/, as in az*u*re, is an arbitrarily spelled one that is probably too rare to be worth teaching about in elementary school.

[8] *Webster's Ninth New Collegiate Dictionary* (1983, pp. 37–39) lists all common spellings of English phonemes, or teachers can generate their own lists.

> All long vowels except for a few rule-governed spellings
>> described in Appendix D.
> The vowels /ŏŏ/ and /ōō/
> Most spellings of /aw/
> Schwa (see Mini-lesson #10, Chapter 6)
> Vowels before /r/

I've chosen long *e* for a sample mini-lesson (#6).

This standard mini-lesson will work especially well with the long and rounded vowels, while the schwa vowel is best dealt with in a strategy lesson. Vowels before *r* can be confusing, but they can be dealt with in separate mini-lessons (e.g., the vowel in *stare* acts like long *a*). Vowels before *r* in unaccented syllables, as in answ*er*, can be incorporated into a lesson on the schwa.

Some variant spellings do follow rules and lend themselves to a different type of mini-lesson. The rules suitable for elementary school use are listed in Appendix D[9] and are most appropriate for children old enough (at least second or third grade) to understand the abstractions involved and whose spelling is a fair ways beyond being purely phonetic. (You could also make a case, documented through looking at children's writing, that the failure to follow these rules produces so few invented spellings by the age children could profit from lessons on them that such lessons wouldn't be worth the instructional time it would involve. Nevertheless, I've provided the ideas for those who would like to try them.)

In deciding which children to involve in mini-lessons on rule-governed variant spellings, you could either observe spellings in their writing or give a brief diagnostic test since some of these patterns may not turn up very frequently in natural writing. Let's consider variant spellings of /s/. A diagnostic test might consist of five words that follow the rule, perhaps *mess, ceiling, slip, cycle,* and *missing.* You could also ask children to explain orally or in writing how they know how to spell /s/ when they're writing a word they haven't seen. (If they just respond that they'd use the letter *s,* you might want to probe and ask if that's always true.) Carol's writing sample (Figure 5–2) shows that a lesson on /s/ would be appropriate for her.[10] Her spellings of /s/ break down as follows:

Used s correctly		Used c correctly	Failed to use c
planets	atmosphere	ice	EXEPT
sun	DESTANY		PERSENT
star	same		
Earth's	ABSULUT		

The spelling that's most revealing here is PERSENT for *percent.* In most cases, *s* was the right spelling and Carol used it. The one time she used *c* appropriately, in *ice,* doesn't tell us much because she could have just known the

---

9 The rule for double consonants is an orthographic one applying to all letters, so it's not included in the appendix. Also, most of the rules have exceptions, often many of them.

10 The corrected spellings were written by her teacher, who was helping her edit.

FIGURE 5–2   *Carol: Plute*

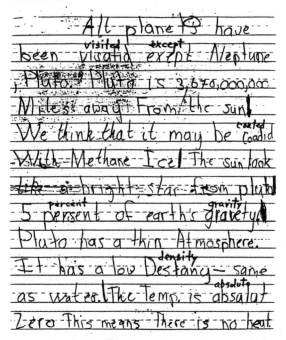

word. EXEPT for *except* is an interesting spelling; she correctly followed the rule for spelling /ks/ with *x;* it's only because the word is an exception that it should have had a *c* in it.[11] But in PERSENT we can see that she appears not to realize that /s/ tends to be spelled with a *c* before *e*. Although she could have written it by analogy to *sent,* the writing sample does seem to indicate that a lesson on spelling /s/, as seen in Mini-lesson #7 would be reasonable for Carol and a small group of similar children. By contrast, Daniel, (Figure 3–4), also tended to spell /s/ with *s* and /ks/ with *x,* but he was still spelling at such a beginning level that a lesson on variant spellings would almost certainly have been over his head. Mini-lessons for the other rules described in Appendix D would be very similar.

Instruction and orthographic rules

As we saw back in Table 5–4, there are only a few major orthographic rules that need to be covered in elementary school. Wheat (1932) discovered that only four spelling rules are consistent enough to be worth teaching as rules. Three of those are orthographic rules: consonant doubling, changing *y* to *i*, and dropping *e*, all before suffixes. (The fourth is the old rule about *i* before *e* except after *c*.) All three of these rules are very straightforward:

1. When a word ends in a single vowel and single consonant, double the consonant before adding *-ed* or *-ing* if the word is a monosyllable or has stress on the final syllable (see Spelling Celebration #20).
2. When a word ends in a consonant and *y*, change the *y* to *i* before adding most suffixes (except for those beginning with *i*).

---

[11] This is for historical reasons; it derives from two parts corresponding to *ex* and *cept*.

◆

MINI-LESSON *#7*
Variant spellings of /s/

Goal: To help children understand the rules governing the spelling of /s/.

Appropriate audience: Students whose invented spellings of /s/ indicate that in unknown words they tend to either spell it with *s* or spell it randomly.

Teacher background knowledge: See Appendix D.

Major points to cover:

    1. Write the word *miss* on the blackboard and ask the children if they can think of other words with *ss*. Write *city* and *mice* and ask for other words where *c* spells /s/.

    2. After mentioning that /s/ is usually spelled with *s*, ask if they can figure out a rule that tells them when to spell it with *ss* or *c* instead. Guide them toward discovering the rule as stated in Appendix D.

    3. Point out that the rule has *many* exceptions (e.g., *seat, science, this*) but that it can help them come up with a reasonable invented spelling for a word they haven't seen in print.

Follow-up: The children may want to have a section in a spelling notebook where they list spelling rules and exceptions to them.

◆

    3. When a word ends in a silent final *e,* drop the *e* before adding suffixes starting with a vowel. (Dropping the *e* before *-ed* is intuitive and probably doesn't need to be taught.)

The children who can benefit from lessons on these rules are obvious: those who write inflected forms as root word plus suffix. (See CLAPING and COMEING in Figures 3–8 and 3–9 respectively.) One possible way to conduct a mini-lesson would be to ask students to write their own spellings for several words related to whichever one of the rules applies, then to show them a written text including those words and finally to discuss with the group how their own spellings differ from the standard. They could then work at figuring out what the rule is. In addition to words with suffixes, some other words have double letters in order to indicate that the preceding vowel is short.[12] A mini-lesson could examine pairs of words like *diner/dinner* and *super/supper,* asking the students to hypothesize about the reason for the double consonants. In order to grasp the double consonant rule for spelling, children need to be good enough readers to see intuitively the difference a single versus a double consonant makes in a word,

---

12 The one exception is double *r.* It indicates a vowel change, a subtle one, only on some words and only in dialects that pronounce word pairs like *Mary* and *marry* differently. Double *r* is best treated as an arbitrary variant.

Spelling Celebration

Consonant doubling

Dana, third grade: MIST (*missed*)

Dana, fourth grade: "At the same night [they] HELLED (*held*) the meeting."

Look at the two columns of words here and see if you can tell why the words in Column A have double letters and those in column B don't (examples taken from P. Smith, 1980, and Venezky, 1979):

Column A	Column B
matting	mating
stiff	leaf
umbrella	cinema
brass	bras
inn	in
poll	pole
fibbed	fixed
bedding	heading

Double consonants occur in English for several reasons, not just when an ending is added to a word. Learning when to double consonants is tricky because we can never hear them in a word; children have to figure out how they're used from their experience with language. The rule for consonant doubling before suffixes works pretty well, but doesn't account for a lot of the other double consonants in our language. The two examples from Dana both involve past tense, but couldn't have been prevented by knowledge of the past tense doubling rule. *Missed* has a double letter in the root word because words don't usually end with a single *s* unless they're plurals. *Held*, of course, isn't the past tense of *hell* but of *hold*; it's an irregular past tense that doesn't use the *-ed* ending. Dana wrote two reasonable spellings that happened not to be the right ones because he didn't know those particular words, not because he didn't understand double letters!

(Answers to why the words in Column A are doubled: *matting/mating*, preserves short vowel; *stiff/leaf*, prevents single final *f* after single vowel; *umbrella/cinema*, shows that stress is on second syllable; *brass/bras*, avoids looking like a plural; *inn/in*, prevents two-letter content word; *poll/pole*, distinguishes homophones; *fibbed/fixed, x* doesn't double; *bedding/heading*, consonants don't double after vowel digraphs.)

---

rather than trying to formally apply a rule. If they can't tell from looking at the spelling *happy that it would be pronounced with a long *a*, it's unlikely that they'll remember to double consonants through a rule that requires identifying a short vowel. You could also have a mini-lesson on the four consonants that are usually doubled at the ends of words (as in sti*ff*, be*ll*, me*ss*, and bu*zz*).

Silent letters, which exist largely for historical reasons, can be treated like orthographic rules for instructional purposes. The silent letters that children are most likely to see and use are the *k* found before *n*, as in *knife*, the *w* found before *r*, as in *wr*ite, and the *gh* found in words like *night*. (Silent final *e* is better treated with variant vowel spellings and can be generalized across all the long vowels.) Since, by definition, there's no way to predict from hearing a word if it has a silent letter, the best way to learn about silent-letter words is by compiling a list. A mini-lesson could focus on eliciting words with silent *k*, *w*, and *gh* that children know and then creating a permanent chart for the classroom that students could continue to add to. The chart could have columns for *kn, wr, gh,* and "other," where students could list any words they found with silent *b* (debt, bomb), *h* (hour), *p* (pterodactyl), and so on.

Should word lists be a part of spelling curriculum?

I consider formal study of word lists to be an optional but reasonable part of spelling curriculum and instruction. As discussed earlier, the vast majority of the words we know how to spell are the product of incidental learning, which I think can profitably be supplemented by exploring the spelling patterns that bring some sense of order to our language. But memorizing the spellings of words is a traditional part of school curriculum that children, parents, teachers, and principals may be reluctant to give up. I think that spelling lists are acceptable in a whole-language curriculum if they follow three principles: individualization, limited quantity, and limited time. First of all, the words that children work on memorizing should be unique to each individual since children know and need to know very different words. They also certainly shouldn't have to study words they already know. Ideally, children should pick their own words, based on interest and on words they use a lot but don't yet spell consistently. The teacher can also provide a helpful nudge: "Don't you get tired of having to correct THAY every time you edit? Why don't you just learn how to spell *they*?" Teachers might also suggest that children choose words related to a week's mini-lesson, such as long *e* words. I've heard of teachers who are dissatisfied with spelling books creating lists based on their curriculum, but I think that this method can be misguided; children may be required to learn long lists of words that are developmentally too difficult for them. A better option would be to make a list of twenty words related to the curriculum and ask the children to pick five that they don't already know how to spell.

Five words a week, whether completely self-selected or partially chosen from a teacher list, is an appropriate number. What many people don't realize is that, as mentioned earlier, children already know how to spell about 65 percent of the words in spelling books before they even study them (Manolakes, 1975; Stetson & Boutin, 1980), so that they're learning at most only about five to seven new words a week anyway. Five words a week is about 180 in a school year, which is plenty since incidental learning is also going on. Five words a week also insures that an appropriately small amount of time each week will be spent on memorizing words. A good procedure is to have students pick their words on Monday and then practice them on their own time during the week, which would work well as homework. The best study method for memorizing words has been extensively researched, and is described at the beginning of most spelling books. Basically, it involves looking at the word, thinking about its spelling and/or saying the letters out loud, covering the word and writing it, checking the results, and repeating if necessary. You can suggest to students that they have their partners or parents test them periodically during the week to see if they've learned the words yet. On Fridays, partners can test each other for a final evaluation. Once words have been learned, they can be entered in an individual spelling dictionary or, if the classroom has a computer, in a text file for each child, which can be alphabetized and printed out regularly.

Sometimes teachers worry that with a method like this one, children may cheat by picking words they already know how to spell. The most important avenue for dealing with this problem is through helping children to take owner-ship of the process. When initiating the practice at the start of the school year, you can talk to students about how valuable it is to know how to spell words that they are using in their writing, and how rewarding it will be to have learned 180 new words during the school year. If grading can be downplayed, so that children don't avoid challenging words because they're worried about getting 100 percent on their Friday tests, so much the better.

What about spelling books?

What I've described so far is a way of developing knowledge about spelling that's completely independent of textbooks. But many teachers may be reluctant to give up the security of spelling books or are required to use them. I'd like to discuss what I think are the major problems with spelling books but then make some suggestions for using them in a more appropriate manner if one wants or needs to use them at all. A more extensive critique of spelling books, including a discussion of why they are so widely used, appears in Wilde (1990b.)

Reasons not to use spelling books

The major criticisms of spelling books can be summarized in four statements.

1. *Spelling books are boring.*

    When teachers speak openly, they're likely to admit that this is the main reason that they'd like to be free of spelling textbooks. The books' instructional methods are always didactic and never based on discovery, and the texts are full of low-level exercises that involve filling in blanks with little or no thinking. For example, "Write the list words that begin with consonants. Then write the words that begin with vowels"; "Fill in the blank: 'Do not [speed] when driving on busy streets.' "[13] These exercises are designed mainly to help children practice the spelling words, which can be done more efficiently by the procedure described earlier for memorizing spellings, and to build awareness of spelling patterns, which can be done more effectively through mini-lessons. Why have spelling books turned out to be so boring? Mainly because they're set up to provide a workbook-type, "teacher-proof" program, which

---

[13] All examples are taken from fourth-grade lessons on long *e* chosen from several recent popular spelling series.

requires no writing, discussion, or teacher input, and produces easy-to-correct right and wrong answers. Although this may be a convenience, particularly for teachers who aren't aware of other ways to teach spelling, is it really a good way for children to spend time?

2. *Spelling books take too much time for the results they produce.*
   The major intention of spelling books is for children to learn words. But, as mentioned earlier, children already know how to spell most of the words in the programs. One study (Stetson & Boutin, 1980) found that second graders learned an average of only 2.9 words a week, in 75 minutes of instructional time. In today's busy classrooms, can we really afford to spend over an hour a week for the purpose of learning to spell three words? If learning three or more words a week is important, it can be done far more efficiently through individual study.

3. *Spelling books repeat the same material, misleadingly labeled "skills", year after year.*
   Every spelling series has an extensive scope and sequence chart, with corresponding objectives for each lesson. A sample objective might be, "Each student will correctly spell words that have the long *e* sound spelled by the letters *ey, ee, ea,* or *y.* " This example is taken from fourth grade, and variations on most objectives usually appear every year from first through sixth grade. The scope and sequence charts imply that students are mastering skills; one would reasonably assume that such skills would help students to go beyond the memorization of words to the prediction of new spellings. But what the textbooks define as skills are primarily descriptions of sound/letter relationships, some of which are predictable and picked up early on by children who write with invented spelling and others of which describe variant spellings, like those for long *e.* (There are also discussions of compounds, homophones, etymology, and so on.) Since English spelling is too irregular for one to learn skills that would reliably predict unknown spellings accurately, all the textbooks are doing is supplementing word memorization by directing students' attention to spelling patterns over and over again every year, with just the individual words changing. In Chapter 6, where I discuss strategies, I'll describe how correct spellings are produced through an interaction of knowledge and strategy, rather than through skill mastery.

4. *Spelling books claim to integrate language arts but actually fragment it.*
   In order to fill the fifteen or more minutes a day usually allotted to spelling, textbooks usually include activities typically belonging to the broader language arts program, such as writing, grammar, handwriting, vocabulary, and dictionary use; teachers' manuals may even speak of "integrating the language arts." In a whole-language program, spelling is integrated into language arts largely through its role in writing done for meaningful, authentic purposes. Spelling books do it the other way around, using writing as a tool for practice of spelling words, often in the form of the most artificial, old-fashioned kinds of

story-starters that writing process teachers abandoned long ago. ("Your best friend is away for the summer. She missed your costume party. Write a letter to her. Describe the party. What were some of the costumes? What did you eat? What did you do? You may want to use some spelling words, such as *feast, sweet, need, peach, cream,* or *dream.*" This comes from a spelling series whose teachers' manual claims to provide "realistic writing situation[s].") A discussion of how grammar, handwriting, and vocabulary should be learned is beyond the scope of this book, but it certainly shouldn't be in the fragmented, decontextualized way that appears in spelling texts: isolated, fill-in-the-blanks exercises. (I'll discuss dictionary use as part of spelling strategies, in Chapter 6.) The proofreading exercises typically found in spelling books are, I believe, some of the worst activities found there since they ask students to correct artificial misspellings. The textbooks offer no evidence that this will transfer to student writing, and since visual knowledge is so powerful in learning to spell, there's a risk that students will tend to remember the misspellings they've seen in print in the exercises and confuse them with the correct spellings. (This would be a fascinating topic for a research study.) Proofreading should be developed as a strategy for use with one's own writing (See Chapter 6).

It may seem that I'm being extremely harsh on spelling books. In the interests of thinking through your own position, you might want to pick up a teachers' manual and take a good close look at both the introduction to the teacher and the actual lessons. Are claims borne out in practice? In what sense is the term "skills" used? Are the activities meaningful and intellectually challenging? To picture the books through student eyes, think about whether these kinds of activities would be useful to you if you were trying to learn how to spell some words that were already part of your oral language vocabulary.

How to use spelling books

For those teachers who aren't willing or able to abandon spelling books, there are still some ways to use them that are better than others. First of all, many of the criticisms I've raised can be circumvented by using just the lists but not the exercises. On Mondays, you could give a pretest, to be self-corrected[14], and have each student pick five words that he or she missed. Students can study these words during the week by following the same procedures I described earlier for self-selected word lists. Five words may seem like too few, but, as mentioned earlier, that's all that children are learning on the average anyway, and it seems fair to ask that everyone learn the same amount rather than putting an extra burden on the spellers who are less proficient to start with. Students who consistently miss fewer than five words on the pretest could be given a pretest from a harder book or choose words of their own to make a total of five. It's also important to establish

---

[14] This is a procedure for which there is very strong research support (Fitzsimmons & Loomer, 1978), and which should always be used if giving a spelling pretest. Having students trade papers with a partner for correction eliminates a valuable learning activity.

a grading policy that won't lead kids to intentionally misspell words on the pretest in order to have an easy week and still score 100 percent on the posttest.

Although you might feel that this way of using a spelling book wouldn't be acceptable to administrators, you could point out that by having students learn five words a week, you're accomplishing at least as much as textbooks do, but in far less time. Most of the exercises in the book exist mainly for the purpose of word practice, and you can point out how you're achieving other spelling book goals elsewhere in your curriculum (e.g., through the writing process). You might also choose to supplement the spelling lists through mini-lessons related to that week's spelling pattern, which would provide for more active learning than fill-in-the-blanks exercises. Mini-lessons, however, are generally more useful when geared to individual children's development as seen in invented spelling, rather than being used with a whole class.

If you feel it's necessary to use spelling exercises as well as the word lists, you may want to consider assigning them for homework rather than using class time but think carefully before doing so. I remember, a few years ago, trying to help a barely literate fourth grader do her spelling homework. The directions were incomprehensible to her, and even after I'd explained them, the exercises were too abstract to make much sense to her. She spent far too much time struggling through the homework, time that would have been much better spent in meaningful reading or writing. On the other hand, for many students the exercises are virtually as easy as they would be for an adult, and such children probably learn no more from doing them than adults would. Before assigning spelling exercises as homework, you might want to watch and interact with a few students as they do typical exercises in class, observing how they make sense of the activities and whether they appear to be learning anything from them. Spelling exercises chosen for homework should be both reasonably easy and benign in effect; I'd exclude all artificial proofreading exercises and story starters for writing because of the danger of negative effects on knowledge and enthusiasm respectively.

Answer to -able/-ible rule: Words ending with *-able* are usually those where the root can stand on its own as a word (*work, rely,* etc.).

· 6 ·

Developing Spelling Strategies

What do you do when you don't know how to spell a word? For me it depends on the word, on where I am, and on what I'm writing. If I'm talking to a friend who's giving me directions for getting to her house, and I don't know how to spell one of the street names, I'll just write something good enough to help me recognize the right street sign when I see it. If a friend is recommending a book or article by an unfamiliar author whose name doesn't have an obvious spelling, I'll usually ask, "How do you spell that?" so I can find the material in the library. If I'm writing an article, I'll use a variety of strategies: If I'm writing on the computer, I'll try my best guess and then use the spell-checker, either right after typing the word or later when I go through and spell check the whole article. Very occasionally, I'll look up a word in the dictionary, particularly if I'm also interested in refreshing my memory about the meaning or etymology of the word. If the word I'm stuck on is a proper name, I'll go back to an original source to confirm the spelling. Sometimes I'll try a few different versions of the word and see which looks right, maybe thinking about a rule or related word as I do so. Fortunately, most of the time, like most literate adults, I don't need to follow any of these procedures, because I already know how to spell the overwhelming majority of words I use as I write and don't need to give spelling any conscious attention. I'm sure that your own repertoire of spelling strategies is similar to mine.

We can think of spelling ability as being made up of three parts: knowledge of words and knowledge of spelling patterns, which were discussed in the last chapter, and spelling strategies, which are the way our knowledge is put into practice in the real world. Spelling strategies have been overlooked in traditional spelling programs that emphasize knowledge exclusively. Before the advent of writing process curriculum and the discovery of invented spelling, there were basically two spelling strategies suggested to children: ask the teacher or use the dictionary. It was simply assumed that correct spelling always had to be a part of writing, even in first grade, and that young writers had to rely on outside assistance, with a gradual change from using the teacher to a more independent reliance on the dictionary as they grew older. The biggest change since those

Spelling Celebration

Placeholder spellings

Elaine, fourth grade: "I was in the CHIEKCSEROS (circus)"

Elaine wrote many unusual spellings like this one that didn't seem to even be very good invented spellings. Is this a sign of a learning disability or a visual/perceptual problem? Educators are often too quick to jump to conclusions that there are medical reasons for problems that can be explained far more simply. In Elaine's case, she wrote unusual spellings when she was in a hurry and wanted to focus on what she was saying rather than how she was spelling the words. When she took the time to attempt a real invented spelling (i.e., an attempt at representing the word accurately), she did much better. The moral is: when in doubt, ask the writer where the spelling came from.

days has been the new understanding that invented spelling in first drafts is an appropriate strategy and that there are a variety of ways for children to refine their spellings in the editing process. This chapter provides a comprehensive, systematic approach to helping students answer for themselves the question, What do you do when you don't know how to spell a word? (Another discussion of spelling strategies appears in Wilde, 1989b, where I talk about how to look at strategies for evaluative purposes.)

Student ownership of the spelling process

The first area to consider in developing a spelling-strategy curriculum is students' attitudes toward the role of spelling in writing. This should be different at different age levels, and we'll have different goals for children at various points in their development. With children who are just beginning to write, the most important attitude is one of openness: a willingness to try out spellings in order to be able to write fluently and independently. Imagine how it would feel if our spelling system changed overnight, and we all had to learn new spellings for everything; as writers, we'd be best served by doing a lot of reading in the new spelling system and by using invented spellings as we wrote, focusing on fluency rather than on trying to spell everything right before putting it down on paper. Even beginning writers, however, should be introduced to the editing process (Calkins, 1986); the emphasis should be on initiation into the *process,* not on producing a perfect *product.* Editing for spelling might therefore involve correcting just a few spellings. Again, imagine yourself as a beginning writer grappling with a completely new spelling system for English; even if only your final drafts had to be perfectly spelled, you'd probably feel overwhelmed and choose to write as little as possible. Right from the start, children should be helped to discover the reason for correcting spellings: It is not to please the teacher or avoid red marks on one's paper (an inauthentic motivation) but as a courtesy to the reader. As children grow older, they need to realize that although invented spelling is still a legitimate strategy, they need to start aiming for 100 percent correct spelling in final drafts[1]. This can be approached through a mini-lesson where you discuss how students feel about spelling, whether and why they think it's important, and so on. Students generally do realize that at some point the outside world will expect that their invented spellings will give way to conventional ones (for instance, published authors don't use invented spelling), and you can explore ways for them to move in this direction.

By upper elementary school, you can discuss with students in more detail the role that spelling plays in the minds of prospective employers and the rest of the general public. Sometimes spelling is treated as almost a moral issue. I've seen a surprisingly large number of college professors turn livid about student papers with misspelled words, probably more than I've heard them complain about more important matters like a lack of authentic voice. But appropriate spelling is really more a matter of etiquette. Elementary students who have become real writers will realize that spelling is only a very small part of the process, but they also understand that a few misspelled words might cause a reader to discount or reject what they've written, particularly if it's a job application. Discussing the role of spelling as a matter of social conventions is more intellectually honest than telling students the main rationale for perfect spelling is communication; readers seeing a few misspelled words aren't upset because they can't understand what's intended but because they feel insulted that the writer didn't bother to proofread (or concerned that he or she didn't know how). There's a larger issue here, of course. Since incorrect spelling and punctuation are easier to spot in writing than, for instance, illogical thinking, the general public tends to seize on them as evidence of illiteracy and to periodically demand a back-to-basics focus on these fine points of language. In Chapter 9, I'll discuss some ways of addressing this issue with parents and administrators. I think that older elementary school students can both think about whether society puts disproportionate emphasis on the mechanics of written language and learn to function within that system.

Five strategies

In my work with young writers, I've seen five major spelling strategies at work, which I've called placeholder spelling; human resource use; textual resource use; generation, monitoring, and revision; and ownership (Wilde, 1989b). I see them as fitting into a rough hierarchy, in the sense that some are more sophisticated than others, but this doesn't mean that the simpler ones should be completely outgrown. Adults use all of these strategies. They're not a series of stages that one moves through but rather the elements of an expanding repertoire, although the proportion of each of them that one uses will change over time with one's development as a speller. The hierarchical nature of the strategies has to do with how sophisticated they are. Placeholder spelling is defined as writing something that one knows isn't correct, and probably isn't even close, in order to get

---

[1]This is true for final drafts that have a real audience or other authentic reasons for being finely polished. Teachers should not require that all or even most pieces of writing be taken to this point.

Spelling Celebration

Dictionaries and definitions

Gordon, fourth grade: "Little NIFE (knife) got SACRED (scared) when his FARTHER (father) said that he can CARY (carry) the deer with him."

At first glance, this appears to be just a permutation, a flipping of two of the letters in the word *scared*. But having watched Gordon write this, I know what *really* happened! On his first try at writing *scared*, he wrote SCERE, then erased it, commenting, "I used to know how to write it but I forgot how to spell it." He then got a dictionary, began skimming all the words starting with S, stopped when he got to *sacred*, and copied it onto his paper. When I asked him how he knew he'd chosen the right word, he began reading the definitions, which he hadn't looked at yet. His face lit up as he looked up and said, "See! It says right here that they play scary music in church."

---

something down on paper and move on. It's the least sophisticated strategy because it's an abandonment of any attempt to spell the word correctly. It's often, however, a valuable writing strategy. In using human resources, the writer asks someone else how to spell a word and is, therefore, choosing to at least aim for a correct spelling; writers use this strategy when they lack confidence in their own abilities or when they are in a hurry. Using textual resources, like dictionaries, is a more intellectually active process for the learner. Writers have developed even further still when they are able to generate, monitor, and revise their own spellings since they have come to realize the usefulness of their own knowledge base, without the use of outside resources at all. Finally, ownership is a strategy that doesn't even need to be consciously attended to; it's a matter of just knowing how to spell a word and writing it, as adults do with most words. I'll discuss each strategy in turn to give you some sense of how they work and how children can be helped to use them.

Placeholder spelling

In my description of my own spelling strategies, I described using placeholder spelling for writing a street name, without trying to spell it right, in taking down directions from a friend. Since I'm a good speller, what I write down is likely to be pretty close to the correct spelling, but I'm not taking the time to think about it, I'm just dashing it off. This is an appropriate strategy for the situation. I'd only be likely to ask my friend to spell the street name if it were so unusual that I couldn't come up with a spelling that made enough sense for me to feel I could recognize the street sign when I saw it. I also wouldn't get out a map in order to correct the spelling on my note to myself; I'd only look at the map if I wanted to confirm the directions visually or, perhaps, was curious about the spelling of the street, but even then I would be very unlikely to change what I'd written.

In Chapter 4, we saw a piece by Elaine that was full of unusual invented spellings (Figure 4–2). Elaine, who was in fourth grade at the time she wrote this, often produced some of the oddest spellings I've ever seen, such as COLD-ETOSC for *cartoons,* PALYEAN for *pumpkin,* and BEFXITST for *breakfast.* In writing these spellings, Elaine very consciously knew that they weren't correct and that she wasn't trying to produce a good invented spelling; when asked about one, she'd say, "I just wrote it any way." For writers who aren't strong spellers, or for any writers who are writing more difficult words than usual, this is a valuable writing strategy because it's the quickest way to get something down in writing without losing one's train of thought. (It would be even quicker, of course, to just leave a blank space, but children should be encouraged to at least put down a string of letters, which frequently will be like Elaine's. That is, the string of letters will often be about the right length and have some of the right letters.) These placeholder spellings are different from the letter strings that young children produce before they've begun doing real invented spelling; those earlier letter strings emulate the visual features of print before there is an understanding of the alphabetic principle in spelling, while placeholder spellings are created by children who could think out good invented spellings but have chosen not to. It might seem counterproductive to encourage children to spell badly, but in some cases it's very useful. Mini-lesson #8 shows how you might discuss placeholder spellings with children.

Human resources

Asking another person how to spell a word is a very natural, spontaneous spelling strategy. Most of us will do so if someone else is around and is likely to know how to spell the word. One version of this, asking the teacher, has long been common in North American classrooms, but this is the one human resource whose use I think should be discouraged. Remember, asking how to spell a word is a low-level spelling strategy because it involves turning to an outside authority rather than thinking for oneself. In my opinion, teachers, rather than spelling words for children, should ask them to come up with spellings on their own, or at most help them think through the invention process or help them use a textual resource. After all, we don't do kids' math problems for them. (The one exception I'd make is for very insecure children who are reluctant to write anything unless it's correct. You may need to offer, temporarily, to spell some words for them if they'll do the rest.) I think the same goes for editing. Children need to find and correct their own invented spellings; the teacher's role is to help them learn how to do this, not do it for them. The one exception is that I think it's legitimate for a writer who feels that a piece is ready for publication to ask the teacher, as final editor, to give it a last reading. (Even professional writers need copy editors.)

Children using *each other* as spelling resources is, however, much more productive because instead of an expert providing the right answer, equals are collaborating. Erica, a second grader, and Alison, a third grader, were working together one day on a story about a secret club. (Figure 6–1; this is just one section of a longer story.) They composed the story together, but Alison did the actual writing. It reads, "Then they said, 'Why don't you make a ladder out of rope,' and the other guys said, 'Good idea.' Then Erin said, 'Do you want to be

MINI-LESSON #8
Placeholder spelling

Goal: To add placeholder spelling to children's repertoire of spelling strategies.

Appropriate audience: This mini-lesson would be most valuable with children whose ideas far outstrip their spelling ability and whose writing fluency is often impaired by the amount of time it takes them to invent spellings. Placeholder spelling should be encouraged mainly after children already know how to spell many common, high-frequency words since a text with too many placeholder spellings won't be readable even to the author. (For less developed writers, inventing spellings more slowly is worth the time involved.)

Teacher background knowledge: None.

Major points to cover:

1. Ask students if they ever want to use hard words when they're writing, and how they go about getting them down on paper. (This lesson would fit in especially well when you're doing a content-area unit, such as dinosaurs, that involves a more extensive and difficult vocabulary than usual.)

2. Talk about the trade-off between fluency and accuracy; taking the time to think through an invented spelling can cause you to lose your train of thought. On the other hand, of course, the better your original spelling is, the less editing you'll have to do and the less likely it is that you'll forget what the word was.

3. Ask the students to try an experiment with you. Think of a fairly hard but familiar word, like *stegosaurus,* and ask them to write as quickly as they can a spelling just good enough for them to recognize the word later. (Of course, these spellings are always easier to identify later when written in the context of a larger text.) Next, have them write their best invented spelling for the same word. Finally, discuss the pros and cons of the two approaches and the occasions when it would be useful to use a placeholder spelling. (Remember, it's not a matter of one strategy being better than the other but of choosing the most appropriate one.)

4. (Optional) You could also talk about abbreviations, standard or invented ones, as placeholder spellings in first drafts. For instance, in my first, hand-written draft of this mini-lesson, rather than spelling out *placeholder* every time, I wrote "p/h."

Follow-up (optional): Have the group meet again in a few days to discuss their experiences with placeholder spelling.

FIGURE 6–1   *Erica and Alison: The Rope Ladder*

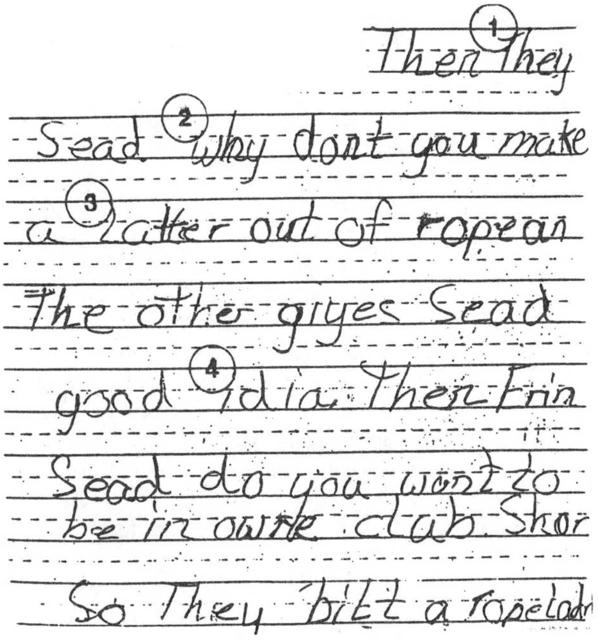

in our club?' 'Sure.' So they built a rope ladder." I observed the following interactions related to spelling. The numbers on Figure 6–1 are keyed to the following events:

1. Alison told Erica how to spell *they*.
2. Alison told Erica how to spell *why*.
3. After Erica had spelled *ladder* as LATER, Alison said, "I think *ladder* has two *t*'s," so Erica went back and added one.
4. After Erica wrote IDIYA for *idea*, Alison said, "You had everything right except there's no *y*," and Erica erased the *y*.

Although at first glance it may appear that these interactions weren't that helpful, that Alison was being bossy without always being very accurate, I saw it as a very positive episode. The feeling was very much one of two equal collaborators, with perhaps Alison, as the older one, providing a bit of extra input. Although Alison provided a few spellings, Erica invented many of her own. (Note the spelling of *ladder* in the last line; also, when I asked Erica about her spelling of OWRE for *our*, she articulated it as a two-syllable word to explain her spelling of it.) I believe that the process was valuable for both girls; Erica learned from Alison's greater knowledge, and Alison had the chance to think about spellings and to articulate her knowledge. Although Alison's suggested spellings weren't always correct, they were at least an improvement on Erica's original ones.

A story of Gordon's (Figure 6–2) also involved collaboration on spelling. Again, points in the text where the episodes occurred are marked with numbers.

23 Spelling Celebration

What if your friend doesn't know how to spell it either?

Elaine, fourth grade: "The big snak EAT (*ate*) all the PEPOLE (*people*)."

When Elaine was ready to write the *word* people in this story, she went and got a dictionary to look it up. Before she found it, however, her friend Addie wrote PEPOLE on a scrap of paper for her. Elaine ended up with an invented spelling, but not her own! When children collaborate as spellers, what really matters is process, not product. They learn that peers can be valuable resources, that teachers and books are not the only source of knowledge. It is, of course, important for teachers to realize the many sources of spellings when they look at children's writing. Not all invented spellings are a direct reflection of children's knowledge about words: some reflect *classmates'* knowledge of words, or imperfect copying from the dictionary, or slips of the pen, and so on. The more teachers observe all the strategies that children use as they spell, the more they will realize that there are a variety of possible causes for particular spellings.

1. Gordon originally spelled *treat* as TEAT, then asked me if it was spelled correctly and tried to sound it out. Garry, sitting nearby, suggested writing *tree* first, while Kate told Gordon to just add an *r* to what he had.

FIGURE 6–2 *Gordon: One Halloween Night*

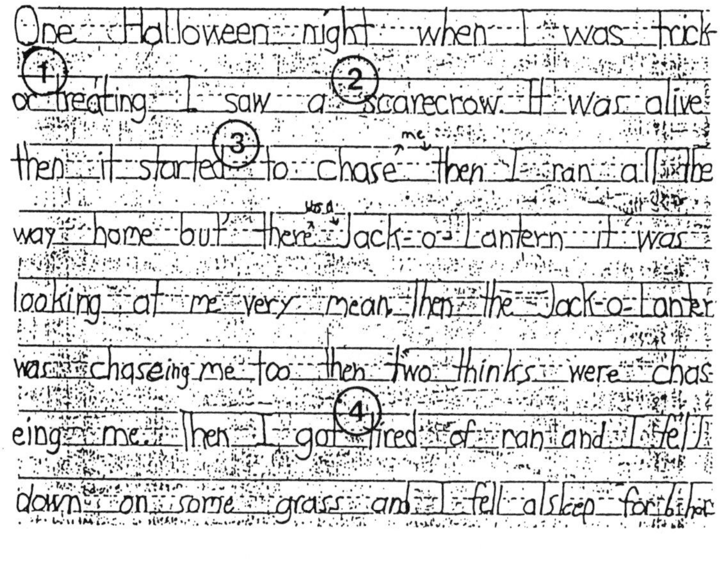
One Halloween night when I was trick-
or treating I saw a scarecrow. It was alive
then it started to chase me then I ran all the
way home but there was Jack-o-Lantern it was
looking at me very mean Then the Jack-o-Lanter
was chaseing me too then two thinks were chaseing me. Then I got tired of ran and I fell
down on some grass and I fell alsleep for [illegible]

2. In preparing to write *scarecrow,* Gordon looked in a Dr. Seuss dictionary but couldn't find it. Then he went to get a bigger dictionary. In the meantime, Annie brought back the Dr. Seuss dictionary, saying "Just spell *scare* and here's *crow.* " As he worked his way up to *sca-* words in the bigger dictionary, Alice had found *scare* in hers and told him the page number.

3. After writing *started,* Gordon offered to help Casey spell a word in her piece.

4. Looking for *tired* in the dictionary, Gordon got distracted by a picture of the solar system and read all the planet names aloud, with Casey joining him.

A few other similar episodes also occurred.

We see here some collaborations that go beyond the simple imparting of knowledge that Alison did for Erica. In spelling *treat,* the children were inventing together; although the choice of spelling was ultimately Gordon's, there was a collaborative effort where everyone was involved in thinking. Gordon started with a pretty good sense of the word, which others added to by focusing on a missing phoneme ("just add *r*") or analogy to another word ("write *tree* first"). Although the spelling ended up being correct in this case, the process was even more important.

In the case of collaborative dictionary use, the children were helping each other become proficient at a fairly complex task. Even though their use of dictionaries had a visible effect only on Gordon's writing, all of the children were getting more experience in dictionary use. In the case of reading the solar system words, one could say that Gordon and Casey weren't on task, since they had gotten away from Gordon's original intention of spelling *tired,* but I can only applaud the active intellectual curiosity that the children showed. Classrooms should be places where there's room to discover new knowledge serendipitously. Gordon's helping Casey also shows that children's collaborating in spelling needn't be a one-way street, where the same students who know more always help those who know less; instead, it can be truly interactive, with children sometimes imparting knowledge, sometimes helping each other figure things out but always relating as equals.

The teacher's role in encouraging students to use each other as spelling resources is one of describing and perhaps modeling the process. As a mini-lesson, you could have a few students come up to the blackboard and think out loud together about how to spell difficult words, followed by a discussion of the process and a suggestion that students might find it helpful to discuss spelling during writing time as they write and particularly as they edit. The classroom environment is also a crucial factor. Students obviously need to be allowed to talk if they are to be collaborators in spelling. It can also be very helpful to designate an area of the classroom as an editing center, where students can not only use dictionaries and other reference materials but also help each other edit their writing.

Using textual resources

When you don't know how to spell a word, and no one else around does either, you always have the option of going to a written text for the answer, including

24 Spelling Celebration

Living off the land

Darren, fourth grade: "We would have to CELL (call) *off* Christmas."

Gordon, third grade: "Once THEIR was a *parrot* named DRAW TOW (*two*)."

Donald Graves talks about children "living off the land" as writers. When children write in a print-rich environment, they'll use the resources of that environment to help them spell. Aside from the usual sources like dictionaries and word charts, children also find spellings wherever there is written language. Darren, while writing one day, jumped up and ran over to look at the light switch by the classroom door, came back, and wrote *off*. (Though we often wondered if he had done it merely to impress the researchers who were watching him write!) Gordon asked the researcher sitting next to him how to spell *parrot*. Although she didn't tell him, she had written his question in her field notes and he copied *parrot* from there. His parrot's unusual name came from the "Draw Two" card for the *Sorry* board game, which he miscopied. The more we fill our classrooms with written text, the more spellings children will be exposed to and the more resourceful they will be able to be.

---

but not limited to dictionaries. I see three components to helping children learn to use written language as a spelling resource: creating a print-rich environment, using dictionaries and other reference tools, and, for those settings where they're available, learning how to use computers and other electronic media to support spelling.

Creating a print-rich environment.　Often when I visit classrooms I'll see a class set of thirty copies of the same dictionary sitting on a shelf, and think how the same amount of money could have been better spent on thirty different reference books for supporting growth in spelling and vocabulary. Expanding one's vocabulary is an important developmental goal for the elementary school years, a goal which has the additional benefits of supporting spelling growth, through both incidental learning and the use of vocabulary reference materials for finding and checking spellings. We therefore need to see classrooms filled with print, both on the walls for quick reference and in other easily visible spots throughout the room, and in the form of books and other accessible reference material.

A print-rich environment might include the following, with the specifics varying according to grade level. (Some of the suggested types of books are described more extensively in the annotated bibliography in Appendix F.)

1. A wall chart of words commonly used in writing, perhaps the 220 Dolch words (Dolch, 1941, and available wideiy elsewhere).

2. Charts of vocabulary words related to content-area units, which are compiled by the class throughout the course of the units.

3. One or more copies each of dictionaries ranging from simple picture dictionaries to standard elementary school dictionaries, dictionaries for adults, and possibly even unabridged ones. *Webster's Collegiate Dictionary* is an especially good resource because it contains many tables and other valuable reference sections.

4. Picture glossaries, which contain many small, labeled pictures, usually grouped thematically. Many of these have been designed for children, but there are also some very useful ones intended for adults learning English as a second language.

5. A thesaurus or two, a rhyming dictionary, and other books about language.

6. Profusely illustrated adult reference books on content-area topics. These are especially useful if they have charts, tables, and so on, as well as good indexes. (I'll discuss content-area spelling at greater length in Chapter 8.)

7. A globe, one or more atlases, and a map collection.

8. Commercial charts and posters related to content-area study, such as anatomy charts, posters showing comparative sizes of mammals, and so on. These can be materials intended for adults as well as those designed for children's use. Students can also use reference books to make their own informational posters.

9. Personal dictionaries where students list both words they've learned recently and words they're likely to use in their writing but can't yet spell consistently.

In general, resources for a print-rich environment should vary widely in difficulty level since both children and the resources they need also vary. Although a simple picture dictionary may not be used much beyond fourth grade and an unabridged adult dictionary may be of little use before then, a rhyming dictionary or a detailed chart of the solar system would be a valuable addition to any level of elementary school classroom.

Children can be helped to use these resources both informally and through mini-lessons. When beginning a unit you might start with a brainstorming exercise, such as listing all the words students can think of that relate to outer space. This will provoke thinking about the topic, and it can also be the beginning of a vocabulary chart that will remain on the wall during the unit. When hanging up a new informational poster, you can talk about the kinds of information it includes, encouraging students to spend some time examining it on their own and reminding them that it can be a spelling resource. In doing a mini-lesson on how to use the index of an adult nonfiction book to find information for a research project, you can mention in passing that the index can also be a spelling resource. These examples make it clear that in many cases spelling is only one small part of the benefit of a print-rich environment; a variety of resources also supports growth in vocabulary and in knowledge in general.

Dictionary use.   Dictionaries are an important textual resource that are well worth spending some instructional time on. Both spelling books and language

TABLE 6–1
Learning to Use the Dictionary

Finding words
Choosing the best dictionary
Alphabetical order
Guide words
Choosing the right word
When you're stuck

Learning about words
Spellings
Pronunciation and syllables
Definitions
Etymology

arts textbooks tend to devote a fair amount of time to dictionary use, but since the textbooks are intended to be self-contained, they often use worksheets and other exercises rather than having students actually use dictionaries. Teachers conducting mini-lessons followed up with actual application in the writing process can, I believe, do a better job. Using a dictionary, for purposes including but not limited to finding spellings, involves integrating several component abilities listed in Table 6–1. (These are comparable to what a textbook would cover during the six grades of elementary school.)

In planning mini-lessons on dictionary use, what knowledge your students seem to need and how much they can handle at one time are the most important elements to think about. These are more important than covering a set list of "skills" during the course of the year. A good general goal is to help students develop their own well-integrated dictionary strategies, which will serve as one part of their overall spelling strategies. A sample mini-lesson (#9) describes how to help children who are able to get to the right beginning letter in the dictionary but then skim through all the words beginning with that letter rather than using a more precise search strategy. I'm sure that all teachers have seen children do this!

Rather than trying to provide detailed examples of how to conduct mini-lessons in every area of dictionary use, I'll just make a few suggestions about each of them. Language arts textbooks can also be a useful resource for topics to cover, which you can then develop in an interactive lesson of your own design, followed by practice in actual dictionaries. Be sure to look at textbooks critically to see that the ideas make sense; for instance, many texts will follow a dictionary lesson on alphabetical order with a list of words to alphabetize rather than the more relevant activity of using alphabetical order to actually look for a word in the dictionary. The reason for this is practical rather than pedagogical—the textbooks don't assume that children have access to a dictionary.

1. Choosing the best dictionary. If you have a range of dictionaries in the classroom, students can be helped to discover that they can use a picture dictionary to find words like *chair* quickly, but they will need a bigger one to find *surrounded*. There's a tradeoff between ease of use and comprehensiveness.

MINI-LESSON #9
Dictionary search strategies

Goal: To help children move beyond locating the initial letter in finding words in a dictionary.

Appropriate audience: Children who when looking for a word like *scarecrow* will efficiently find the beginning of the *s* section in the dictionary but then skim through all the *s* words in order.

Teacher background knowledge: None.

Major points to cover:
1. Each student or pair of students should have a dictionary. Ask each student to think of a word he or she doesn't know how to spell but might want to use in writing and to write down what the first three letters of the word might be. Have the students find the right section for the initial letter of their word in the dictionary. Ask them what they would usually do next at this point.

2. Tell the students that you're going to show them a way to find words more quickly. Point out the guide words on each page of the dictionary and have them work with a partner to hypothesize about what they are and how they work. You should help them discover that guide words show what the first and last words on each page are and that they are in alphabetical order. Ask the students how this might help them find a word, and help them discover that they can match the first three letters they've thought of with the first three letters of the guide words. To help them use alphabetical order more efficiently, talk about where an *sta-* word would be in relation to an *sho-* or *stu-* word, and how they can use guide words to skim quickly to the right page. Have the students try to find their words; you might also want to repeat the process with a few more words.

3. (Optional) Discuss the idea of generating an alternative first three letters if the first ones don't work. (Students also need a separate mini-lesson on a variety of strategies to use when you can't find a word, but this aspect of it would be appropriate here.)

Follow-up: Have the students use the strategy in their writing and/or editing over the next few days and report back about how it worked.

2. Alphabetical order. For beginning writers, finding the correct first letter in a simple picture dictionary is enough. They should always have an alphabet chart in easy view either on the wall or taped to their desks so that they don't need to recite the whole alphabet aloud to narrow down their search. By sixth grade, students should be able to use alphabetical order to find the right word quickly, choosing the right

25 Spelling Celebration

Scanning the dictionary

Elaine, fourth grade: "I am going to kill the witch. Because she kill my *sister*."

Elaine began her attempt to write the word *sister* by writing STERIS on the back of her paper. Recognizing that that spelling didn't look right, she opened the dictionary and began reading at the beginning of the s words. Scanning words for 10 pages or so, pausing on possible choices like *scissors* and *series*, she finally found *sister* and copied it onto her paper. Dictionaries aren't particularly easy for children to use. To find a word efficiently in the dictionary, it's helpful to have a sense of how it might be spelled, knowledge of how dictionaries are laid out (e.g., alphabetical order, guide words), and some way of recognizing when you've found the word you're looking for. Children who don't have this sophistication are likely to do as Elaine did: identify the probable initial letter of the word, then skim all words beginning with that letter until they think they've found it. I've even seen Elaine miss the right word when she came to it because she was scanning so many words! Do children need to "master dictionary skills"? I'd sooner talk about helping them to develop dictionary strategies, based on teacher assessment of what would be helpful. For instance, Elaine became much more efficient when her teacher suggested that she generate the likely first three letters of a spelling. A student who kept picking the wrong word from the dictionary could be helped to use definitions judiciously as a confirming strategy.

page and moving directly to the right spot rather than browsing or using trial and error. (Even a surprising number of adults have trouble with this.)

3. Guide words. See Mini-lesson #9.

4. Choosing the right word. Children need to understand about entries' being organized under a root word (e.g., when looking for a past tense verb) and about glancing at the definition to confirm that you've found the word you had in mind.

5. When you're stuck. An adult student of mine, a woman in her thirties who considered herself a poor speller, described how she tried to find *upholstery* in the dictionary, didn't find it under *ap-* and had no idea where else to look. She ended up writing a synonym instead. As the old truism goes, it's hard to find a word in the dictionary if you don't know how to spell it! Younger children can be encouraged to think of possible alternative spellings in a general way, and older students can discuss more specific spelling features, such as the schwa sound that *upholstery*

starts with, which can be spelled with any vowel letter. These mini-lessons can be paired with those on the spelling patterns described in Chapter 5, as well as fitting into a more general discussion of spelling strategies. (If a writer is *really* stuck, the dictionary may not be the best alternative.)

6. Spellings. This is usually straightforward, but some words may have alternative spellings or unusual plural forms.

7. Pronunciation and syllables. Even adults have trouble making sense of pronunciation guides, but you could do a mini-lesson on how to use the dictionary to help you with the *part* of a pronunciation you're unsure about (e.g., is the vowel long or short? which syllable has the accent?). This should probably be saved for middle to upper elementary grades since pronunciation symbols are fairly abstract. Learning about syllables isn't nearly as useful as all the instructional time usually spent on it would suggest, but in talking about hyphens (see Chapter 7), you can discuss using the dictionary as a guide for dividing words.

8. Definitions. Definitions, of course, go beyond using the dictionary for spelling and fit into a broader study of vocabulary; students should learn how to use dictionary definitions as a tool both to confirm that the right word has been found for spelling purposes and to clarify meanings when reading.

9. Etymology. I'll discuss the role of dictionary etymologies in Chapter 8 when talking about spelling and punctuation across the curriculum.

Computers and other electronic media.   Virtually every time I speak to a group of teachers about spelling, someone will ask, "Haven't computers with spell-checkers made spelling instruction obsolete?" People used to ask the same question about calculators and arithmetic instruction, and the answer is basically the same one: electronics have provided us with some useful tools, but you have to know enough to use them intelligently. Spell-checkers that are part of word processing programs usually work by flagging words that aren't in the program's wordlist and suggesting possible alternatives. For instance, when I typed in **flsg* (a possible typo for *flag),* the computer thought I might have intended to write *fig, flag, fling, flip, flit,* or *flog,* while for **accomodate* (a common adult mis-spelling), it offered *accommodate* as the only choice. For COMEING, a possible child's invented spelling, it suggested *combing, coming, chiming,* and *chumming.* The writer then has the choice of selecting one of the alternatives, editing the spelling directly, leaving the spelling alone, or adding the word to the computer's dictionary if it's a real but unlisted word. A hand held spell checker like the Franklin Spellmaster works similarly; you type in your own spelling or a pho-netic spelling, and it generates alternatives, often even more of them than a computer program does, putting more of a burden on the writer to choose the correct one. I find a spell-checker useful mainly for catching typographical errors although it doesn't flag the cases where I've correctly spelled the wrong word. For finding true misspellings rather than typos or homophones, spell-checkers are most useful for writers (adults or children) whose misspellings don't have much wrong with them: failing to double a consonant, for instance, or using the wrong letter to spell a schwa. For children whose spelling is still developing, I find them far less useful because children's invented spellings might be so far off that the computer would be unlikely to know what word was intended, or the child might not be a strong enough reader to pick out the correct choice. In addition, there are problems of access to electronic media; most people don't usually write on a computer (except in business settings), and few classrooms are well-enough supplied with computers for children to do much of their writing on them. Also, I'd sooner see parents with limited resources spend fifty dollars on interesting children's books about language than on a gadget like the Spell-master[2]. As in so many other areas, computers and related tools are helpful instruments rather than a panacea. They can be of some use to those elementary school writers who are already spelling most words correctly and whose invented spellings are good enough for the computer to match, but even then they are only a single part of one's collection of spelling strategies. For students who do have access to computers, however, whether in school or at home, it would certainly be useful to conduct a few mini-lessons about how to use a spell-checker.

Generation, monitoring, and revision

Since coming up with a spelling is to some extent a matter of judging between several plausible alternatives, we often write out two or three possible spellings to see which one looks right. As children acquire the greater knowledge base about spelling that allows them to do this productively, they discover that it's a much more efficient and self-reliant method than asking someone or going to the dictionary. As mature spellers produce a piece of writing, they *generate* spellings of words they don't already know, *monitor* whether or not those spellings look right, and then *revise* them if necessary. Children who are beginning to use invented spelling concentrate their efforts mainly on generating spellings, particularly in first drafts, but for them to grow as spellers it's crucial that they develop more of a visual sense of words and learn to proofread their own work.

In generating spellings, students can be encouraged to actively use all of their existing and growing knowledge base. Younger writers are best encouraged to think mainly about how a word sounds when they're first starting to invent spellings, but every time they have a mini-lesson that expands their knowledge, they can be shown how to apply this new knowledge as part of their strategy for generating spellings of new words. For instance, as part of a lesson on spelling /j/, you could ask students to try writing several words with /j/ that they don't already know and talk about how they applied their knowledge of how /j/ is likely to be spelled in different parts of a word. In discussing these strategies, you can examine how some spelling patterns are very regular and others aren't, so that /j/ is virtually always spelled with *j* before *a, o,* and *u* (*jag, jog, jug*) and with *dge* (*hedge*) at the ends of words but varies more before *e* and *i* (*gem, jet; gin, jig*). Students can even develop strategies for schwa, which varies widely and with little predictability, as seen in Mini-lesson #10.

---

[2] A promising new technology, however, is handheld spellcheckers with voice capacity; they seem particularly useful for readers, who can type in an unfamiliar word to hear it pronounced.

MINI-LESSON #10
Strategies for spelling schwa

Goal: To help students develop a strategy for generating a reasonable spelling of the schwa vowel.

Appropriate audience: Students whose spelling is good enough that they usually come up with reasonable spellings of vowel phonemes like the long and short vowels, and who use a fair number of words containing schwa in their writing.

Teacher background knowledge: The schwa vowel phoneme, / /, which occurs in unaccented syllables, doesn't have any consistent spelling pattern based on phonetics or orthographic rules, but its spelling can sometimes be predicted on the basis of a related word.

Major points to cover:
1. Write on the blackboard some words in which schwa in spelled with different letters, with those letters underlined (e.g., *a*bout, want*e*d, rap*i*d, c*o*nnect, and circ*u*s). Ask the students how they would describe the sound that the underlined letters represent. Ask if these words would be hard to spell if they hadn't seen them in print before. How would they know how to spell the unaccented vowel? (The answer, of course, is that they wouldn't. If they had seen *circus* in print, they could remember the spelling by thinking of the second syllable as being pronounced with a short *u,* but that's not the way it's usually said.)

2. Ask the students to write the following words, inventing the spellings if they need to (I've highlighted the schwas in each of them): phot*o*graph, thermom*e*ter, *e*xpect, and nat*i*ve. Ask them what strategies they used to spell the schwa vowels. Help them develop two strategies: think of a related word[3] where you can hear the vowel (phot*o*graphy, m*e*ter) and think of common prefixes and suffixes like the *ex-* and *-ive* found in many words.

3. Mention that for many schwa words, these strategies won't work, but they could try several possible spellings to see which one looks right or as an aid to finding the word in a dictionary. For instance, they could try writing **circas, *circos,* and *circus.* Students should also realize that schwa may be spelled with more than one letter (e.g., oc*ea*n, nat*io*n).

Follow-up (optional): You might want to create a chart with columns for words with different spellings of schwa that students could add to over time.

---

[3] Thinking of a related word is a good general spelling strategy that can also be dealt with in a separate mini-lesson.

 Spelling Celebration

Sounding out

Gordon, fourth grade: "[A jack-o'-lantern] was looking at me very *mean.* "

Gordon asked a friend how to spell *mean*, then decided to attempt it himself. He tried three spellings out loud: "M-e-n-e, m-e-n, m-e-a-n," and wrote down the third, correct one. Beginning spellers typically sound out words on the basis of attempting to find a single letter for each phoneme, and would be likely to produce MEN as a spelling for *mean*. Gordon, however, was operating on a more sophisticated level. He realized that long vowels can be spelled in a variety of ways and tried out alternative spellings for the long e vowel phoneme. Interestingly, he didn't need to write the spellings down to see which one looked right, although he had done so on other occasions.

Proofreading, the monitoring and revision of one's invented spellings, is an area of spelling curriculum that's been strangely neglected, considering the heavy emphasis that's usually put on correct spelling. Students are *expected* to proofread their writing for spelling, but not *taught* how to do so. Papers are handed in with misspellings, and the teacher (at all levels from elementary school to graduate school) chooses to act as a copy editor, marking spellings in that dreaded red ink. Proofreading for spelling isn't always easy to do. When you know how to spell a word but have made a typo or slip of the pen, you tend to read for meaning and overlook unexpected spellings (particularly if they're real words, like homophones), which is why a typo can persist through several readings of a manuscript by different people. It gets even harder when you think you're spelling a word right but aren't; you won't think there's anything to correct (and you can't take the time to look up *every* word you've written, just in case). Even if you know you don't know how to spell a word, it's not always easy to figure out or find the right spelling. Since proofreading is, therefore, fairly difficult, students need a lot of practice in doing it.

Through mini-lessons, you can help students develop a two-part proofreading strategy. As writers become more proficient spellers, they can move from editing a few of their spellings to aiming for 100 percent correctness. To proofread their writing for spelling, students need to do the following:

1. Flag possible invented spellings. Students can make two passes through a piece of writing, first marking the spellings they know are wrong, then looking for questionable ones, those that could be correct but may not be. This process will come more naturally to some students than others. Good spellers often spot instinctively when a word doesn't look right, while a poor speller may have to go through a piece much more painstakingly. If the piece was written on a computer, a spell-checker is a very valuable tool for this stage of proofreading, particularly for weaker spellers.

2. Determine possible spellings and narrow them down to the correct one. At this point, writers can draw on their entire repertoire of strategies: writing a few alternatives to see if one looks right, using a dictionary or other reference material, or asking someone (which shouldn't be overused by students since they need to develop independence as proofreaders).

For a final draft that's going to be published or otherwise disseminated, it's appropriate for the teacher to serve as a final copy editor after students have done their best, but even then, rather than circling and correcting spellings, it's more useful to help students find and correct any remaining errors themselves. Some teachers have students edit each others' work, and although this is useful at a late stage of the editing process, students should first do as good a job as they can on their own, with a classmate serving only to catch errors that may have been inadvertently overlooked. Even then, I think it's best done informally, with one student saying to another, "Could you look this over and see if I missed anything?" (much as adults do), rather than having a basket where pieces are left for a student editing team to red-pencil corrections in the way that a traditional teacher would.

Piaget talked about autonomy as the aim of education (Kamii, 1984), and building a good strong proofreading component into spelling curriculum is one of the most important ways to develop writers who can autonomously produce writing that's spelled well enough to meet society's often extremely high standards. Some people are naturally better spellers than others and can produce correctly spelled texts with little effort, but everybody can learn to proofread. Building the kind of knowledge base in spelling described in Chapter 5 will bring writers to the point where they know a large number of words and are aware of spelling patterns, but proofreading ability is necessary to bring some older spellers from the 93.5 percent or better level of correctness that they'll produce in first drafts[4] to the near 100 percent level that's expected by many employers, professors, and other readers.

Ownership

The final spelling strategy is a simple one: ownership of a spelling means that you know how to spell a word and can write it without consciously thinking about the spelling. Observe yourself sometime when you're writing rapidly using words that you know. You'll probably find that words come out without your needing to think about the individual letters in them; you think only of the word, and it emerges through an integrated movement sequence (Lashley, 1951), whether by pen or by keyboard, if you're a touch typist. The individual letters are all there, but were produced automatically rather than needing to be consciously thought of as a sequence of letters. We also write words that we have to attend to more closely, thinking about each letter, but we still know these

---

[4] The most recent National Assessment of Educational Progress (NAEP) studies (Applebee, et al., 1987) cited a level of 6.5 percent spelling errors for 17 year olds at the bottom tenth percentile.

FIGURE 6–3   *Hannah: My New Shampoo*

words and can spell them correctly the first time through. Fortunately, writers very quickly attain ownership of most words that they write. The National Assessment of Educational Progress (NAEP) studies (Applebee, et al., 1987) found that even at the 10th percentile (those students who spelled worse than 90 percent of all students surveyed), nine year olds spelled 80 percent of words in an open-ended writing task correctly, while those at the 75th percentile produced spellings that were 98.1 percent correct. The kinds of curriculum described in Chapter 5 will contribute to children's growing store of known words, but a good deal of this growth will occur on its own through incidental learning. Teachers can support it mainly by encouraging students to reflect on how many words they do know how to spell and reminding them that the more words they know, the less they'll need to use their other spelling strategies.

Strategies for less proficient spellers

You may have noticed that in Chapter 5, I didn't devote any attention to special spelling curriculum for special education, at-risk, or learning disabled students. Acquisition of spelling knowledge is a developmental process, and children defined as learning disabled produce invented spellings very much like those of other children, with the major differences being that less sophisticated spellings persist until a later age (Moats, 1983). Curriculum related to spelling knowledge for these children should, like that for all children, grow out of the invented spelling that they produce in their writing. The major difference is that they may need more individualized attention and more time to pick up spellings and spelling patterns. Some of these children may also need a slightly different kind of support in developing spelling strategies, largely because of a lack of self-confidence. This can be seen with Hannah, an eight year old whose mother asked me for an opinion on her invented spelling. When I sat down to work with Hannah, she was extremely reluctant to write anything at all because she didn't know how to spell many

FIGURE 6–4   *Gordon: One Halloween Night*

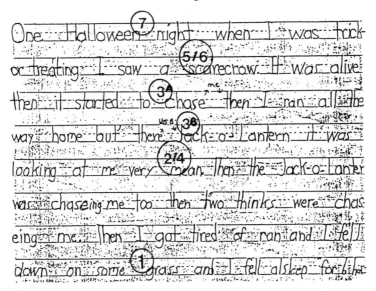

words. She copied a picture from a book we'd read and, with great reluctance, wrote, "This is my new shampoo" (Figure 6–3).

When I suggested to Hannah that it might be fun to get a shampoo bottle and compare her spelling, which I thought might provide some reinforcing visual sense of the word, she was crushed to discover that she'd left out a letter rather than pleased that she'd come so close, even though we'd discussed the concept of invented spelling. Unfortunately, children who have a developmental lag in spelling often get more discouraged as they grow older since they see an increasing gap between their spellings and other children's. What they need most is encouragement to use the strategies that promote the greatest fluency—place-holder spelling and generating invented spellings—with a corresponding de-emphasis on getting a correct spelling the first time out. Even proofreading should focus primarily on learning how to proofread and correcting only a few spellings per piece, rather than on creating a perfect product. Also, the more you can create a classroom climate that honors invented spelling and recognizes its developmental nature, the better these children (and of course all children) will be served. What less proficient spellers need most while their spelling is still somewhat immature (e.g., with correct spellings less than 80 percent or so of the total) is a lot of reading and writing that will give them the space to explore the spelling system at their own pace. Fortunately, Hannah did write fluently when she didn't feel under pressure. In Chapter 9 we'll look at and evaluate another sample of her writing.

Integrating spelling strategies

I began this chapter by describing my own use of spelling strategies and would like to conclude it by showing how one child used all the spelling strategies we've looked at. I've reproduced one of Gordon's pieces again as Figure 6–4, with numbers again representing points where he did or said something.

1. Placeholder spelling. By the time Gordon came to the end of his story he was tired and wrote GREES as a quick, not very accurate, spelling for *grass*. It didn't look right to him, and he said, "Is that how you spell *grass*? Oh, I'm just going to leave it." He later went back and corrected it while rereading his piece.

2. Human resources. Gordon asked Casey how to spell *mean* (but didn't get a response).

3A./3B. Textual resources. Gordon went to the dictionary to find *chase* but spotted a picture of a Jack-o-lantern and decided to leave the dictionary open to that page to use later in his story.

4. Generation. Gordon tried three possible spellings of *mean* out loud (*m-e-n-e, m-e-n,* and *m-e-a-n*) and wrote the correct one. Since spelling is part of written language, students should usually be encouraged to try possible spellings in writing, but here Gordon spontaneously chose to do so orally.

5. Monitoring. After writing *scarecrow,* with the help from Annie described earlier, Gordon covered up *scare* and said, "Look: here's *crow,* and here's *scare,*" thus monitoring his spelling and confirming it was correct.

6. Revision. In writing *scarecrow,* Gordon initially wrote *sco,* then erased the *o,* saying, "I forgot there's no *o* in it." Revision is, of course, always preceded, as it was here, by generation and monitoring.

7. Ownership. After writing *Halloween,* Gordon remarked, "I know how to spell *Halloween* now!"

   Although it's unlikely that you'll see all these spelling strategies at work during a single piece of writing like this, all children can be helped to develop this full range of strategies and to learn which are most appropriate for different situations. Spelling strategies have for too long been the missing component in spelling curriculum and instruction; they have a tremendous role to play in helping children to become even more autonomous as their spelling competence increases.

· 7 ·

Learning to Punctuate

Punctuation, including capitalization, has to do with how we use written language to represent information other than the words themselves: grammatical divisions like sentences and clauses, meaning like exclamations and proper names, instructions to the reader, and so on. Punctuation can provide unambiguous, discrete information, as when quotation marks indicate dialogue, or subtler shades of meaning, as in the choice of a semicolon rather than a period to separate two clauses. Like learning to spell, learning to punctuate is developmental; children's hypotheses about punctuation grow out of their experience with written language and evolve over time. Their writing is influenced by punctuation rules but not fully defined by them since the rules lack precision. Even adults don't always use punctuation successfully and probably do best when they have an intuitive understanding based on experience with written language rather than trying to follow rules. Although we usually think of punctuation in terms of special characters, the first type of punctuation that children become aware of is the spaces that divide one word from another because they stand out visually in the written texts that emergent readers see. (See Spelling Celebration #27.) As children become aware of punctuation marks, they'll begin to use them in their writing, a process which can be strongly supported by instruction. Just as with spelling, curriculum and instruction in punctuation will be most useful when grounded in extensive reading and writing; when children are encouraged to write independently right from the beginning, even if errors occur; and when instruction builds on children's existing knowledge base, rather than assuming a blank slate. Although a fair amount of space is devoted to punctuation in language arts textbooks, they tend to focus on extensive rules for a few punctuation marks (one textbook series listed twelve separate comma "skills") rather than exploring a wide variety of punctuation. I'd like to suggest a three-part curriculum in punctuation (Table 7–1), with roughly equal attention devoted to the three parts over the entire seven years of elementary school. Most of the discussion is about the first group of punctuation marks because they're the ones that lend themselves most to focused instruction.

119

27 Spelling Celebration

Word boundaries and compound words

Anna, fourth grade: "We went to the *PLANA TEREUM* (*planetarium*)."

Rachel, fourth grade: "His name *YOUSTBE* (*used to be*) JHON (*John*)."

Gordon, fourth grade: (November) "I was COMEING home from a *FOOT BALL* game"; (December) "I gave Santa some *CUP-CAKES*."

One of the tasks of young writers is to discover where one word ends and the next begins: where to leave spaces between letters. Oral language is a continuous stream that contains pauses but not between each word. Beginning writers often follow a common progression: first, they're likely to write letters with no spaces between them; second, they then leave spaces more or less at random because they've noticed them in written texts; and third, they use spaces based on some sense of a concept of word. The spellings of *planetarium* and *used to be* shown here illustrate that fine tuning of the concept of word boundaries continues over time. (In some cases it persists into adulthood; many adults write *a lot* as one word.) Compound words are a special case of word boundaries. Writers need to learn when two words that go together are written as one (e.g., *football* is one word while *golf ball* is two). As Gordon went to write *football*, he asked if it was one word or two, then decided to write it as two words, but with a smaller space than usual between them because "they go together," thereby inventing a new feature for English spelling: the half-space. A few weeks later, he invented the spelling *cup-cakes*, and when asked about it said that either a hyphen or a small space can be used when two words go together. Interestingly, many compound words are written with hyphens, and in Great Britain *cup-cakes* is one of them!

The first section, the basics, concerns those punctuation marks that it's reasonable to expect that children will be able to use by the time they finish elementary school. Since most of them can be at least somewhat unpredictable in how they're used and do not have clear-cut rules that can be applied mechanically, children's use of them will be refined over time; instruction in the early grades should focus on a general sense of what they are and how to use them, while older children can learn about more subtle uses. The punctuation marks that I've referred to as enriched are not often dealt with much in elementary school textbooks but can greatly enhance children's writing. Calkins (1980) cited many of these in her description of how third graders in a writing classroom had a much more elaborated knowledge of punctuation than those in a skills classroom who did little writing. Learning about these more advanced

TABLE 7–1
A Curriculum in Punctuation

The basics
1. Sentence boundary punctuation (period, question mark, exclamation point) 2. Commas 3. Capital letters 4. Quotation marks 5. Apostrophes
Enriched punctuation
1. Writer's tools (asterisk, caret, hyphen, paragraph mark, parentheses) 2. Advanced punctuation marks (colon, dash, ellipsis, italics/underlining, semicolon)
Fun with punctuation
1. Playing with visual features 2. Inventing punctuation marks

punctuation marks is best done in the context of the writing process and in a spirit of "here's an interesting new punctuation mark that you might want to try." Finally, children can be encouraged to have fun with punctuation and other visual features of written language, exploring the ways that we can express meaning in text other than through the words themselves and inventing new punctuation marks when there seems to be a need for them. In planning curriculum in punctuation for an entire year, teachers can make a list of what they might like to cover and then either plan a schedule of mini-lessons or wait for appropriate times for instruction to emerge during the year. Some mini-lessons would work well with an entire class, such as introducing periods to first graders, while others will grow spontaneously out of what you see as the next step in particular children's development. (I'll provide suggestions for both types of instruction.) As always, teaching will be most effective if it's part of a broader reading and writing curriculum. For instance, if children read and write a wide variety of text formats, they'll be exposed to and learn about a broad range of punctuation types and uses. If children write letters, they'll learn a few specialized uses of the comma; if they read a lot of fiction, they'll be exposed to various uses of quotation marks. If they write simple research reports, they can begin learning about the uses of punctuation in bibliographic citation.

When you teach about punctuation yourself rather than from a textbook, you may need to refresh your own knowledge. Do you still remember what an appositive is? This is important both for organizing instruction and for answering questions when they come up. I'd like to recommend three sources. *Webster's Ninth New Collegiate Dictionary* (1983) has an excellent reference section on punctuation and capitalization, which gives a concise summary, with examples, of the major uses of 16 punctuation marks, as well as a complete list of capitaliza-

FIGURE 7–1   *Elaine: One Day I Went to a Christmas Party*

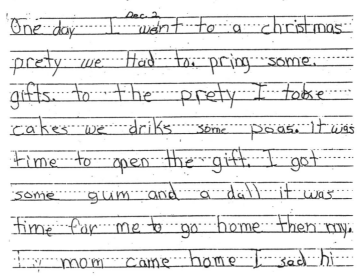

tion rules. The best book-length punctuation handbook I've seen is *Punctuate It Right!* (Shaw, 1963), which includes even more punctuation marks and gives detailed descriptions of their use. Finally, *The Well-Tempered Sentence* (Gordon, 1983) has straightforward content couched in an amusing form; the standard punctuation rules are illustrated with sentences that sound as if they were taken from a very weird Gothic romance. For instance, she used this sentence to illustrate comma use: "Georgia, after lifting her petticoats, turned the corner in her clattering heels."

Learning basic punctuation marks

I'd like to share a story by Elaine (Figure 7–1) to illustrate how children's hypotheses about punctuation can be distorted by inappropriate instruction. The story reads, "One day I went to a Christmas party. We had to bring some gifts to the party. I took cakes. We drank some punch. It was time to open the gifts. I got some gum and a doll. It was time for me to go home. Then my mom came home. I said 'hi.' " Although some of Elaine's periods were used appropriately (those in the fourth and fifth lines), most of them seem randomly placed, which was typical of her writing at the time this piece was written in the middle of fourth grade. When asked about how she decided where to use periods, Elaine typically stated one or more of a series of vague and half-baked ideas: they go at the end of a sentence, which she couldn't define any further; they go at the end of a line (see the second and seventh lines of this story); you need them to break up the story, and it matters where they go but she wasn't sure where they went; and my favorite, "periods and capitals go together," which sometimes led her to put periods before proper names and the pronoun *I*. Elaine was generally confused about periods, not using any of her rules consistently, although I think sometimes her instincts led her to use them appropriately. Her two rules about the ends of sentences and about periods and capitals make sense to adults because we already know how to punctuate, but to a child who was just given the rules but not shown how to apply them in her own writing, they just made things worse. Shortly after this piece was written, Elaine's teacher (not the one who had taught her those rules) sat down with her and read one of her stories out loud, asking her where she thought the sentences ended. Elaine was able to respond correctly, based on her general knowledge of language. Rather than giving her a rule for using periods, her teacher asked her just to listen in the future to where she thought the sentences ended, and from that point on, Elaine's use of periods was close to perfect, with her mistakes never again being odd like the ones in this piece. I think that this is an excellent model for teaching children about punctuation: helping them to tap into and operationalize their existing instinctive knowledge about written language.

Sentence-boundary punctuation

Although periods are much smaller than letters, children do begin to notice them in their reading at a fairly young age and start using them in their writing; they're likely to use them first at the end of a piece of writing and often at the ends of lines, particularly if they use a basal reader where each sentence starts on a separate line. A mini-lesson (#11) can help beginning writers start to give periods, and their accompanying capitals, more conscious attention as they write.

Older students will probably continue to need some instruction dealing with dividing sentences, instruction that will work best if based on their particular perceived needs. Run-on sentences and sentence fragments are the most likely structures that will need to be dealt with, most effectively by helping students edit their own writing. If students have a reasonable sense of what a sentence is, run-on ones are usually due to rapid writing focused on ideas rather than mechanics; if such students check sentence boundaries as they edit, they'll usually catch them easily. A related issue is when students create long sentences where independent clauses are linked with coordinating conjunctions such as "and"; they can be helped in the revision process to craft shorter, more discrete sentences. Sentence fragments are a little trickier because they tend to reflect natural speech patterns and sometimes fall within the realm of stylistic variation. Teachers need to realize that many old chestnuts about punctuation and grammar don't reflect normal good writing practice; it's acceptable in many cases to start sentences with "and" or "but," and a sentence fragment can be used to create an effect, as in, "Give. Till it hurts," in an advertisement for a charity. You might want to look for acceptable and effective sentence fragments in literature and periodicals, both to develop your own ear for them and to share with your students. However, students *do* need to learn that it's not acceptable to write, "One night. I was coming home. . . . " and similar fragments. The best way to do so is in an editing conference, where you compare the student's version of a sentence with a correctly punctuated one and ask them to describe the difference and whether they can tell why their version is wrong.[1] Rather than trying to

---

[1] This is a good general strategy for dealing with punctuation errors; rather than giving a *rule* to apply, you can help students develop *instincts* about punctuation, with a rule serving in some cases to describe those instincts more coherently.

MINI-LESSON #11
Learning to divide sentences

Goal: To help beginning writers learn to use periods and capital letters more consciously to separate sentences.

Appropriate audience: Beginning writers who are writing fairly fluently but who are using periods randomly, occasionally, or not at all. This lesson is appropriate for use with a whole class, although there's greater opportunity for discussion if small groups are used.

Teacher background knowledge: Although sentences can be described as consisting of a complete thought or as being composed of a subject and predicate, these aren't definitions that will clearly determine where one sentence ends and the next begins to someone who doesn't already have an intuitive sentence sense. Students, especially beginners, are best served by developing a feel for sentence boundaries rather than trying to use an abstract rule.

Major points to cover:

1. Each student should bring a book that he or she is familiar with and can read. Ask students to open their books and look for the little dots that come after some words. Ask them if they've noticed these marks before, if they know what they're called, and why they think they're used. Allow an open-ended discussion that will both give you a sense of the children's background knowledge and give them an opportunity to explore and share ideas.

2. Build on the children's discussion to bring out the idea that these marks are called periods and are used to divide up a piece of writing into sentences. At this point, you should have available a brief written text, about five sentences long, from a children's book, either made into a transparency or written on chart paper. A Big Book would also work, as long as children can see the periods easily. First, read the passage aloud, without showing the text to the students, running the sentences together without the usual intonation. Ask how it sounds. Then reread it with normal intonation at sentence breaks, asking the students to describe the difference. Then show them the written text and read it aloud again with appropriate intonation, asking them to notice the punctuation as you read. Point out how the text is divided into units called sentences, each beginning with a capital and ending with a period. Next, have them read aloud to a partner from their book, using the punctuation to provide appropriate intonation.

3. Ask the students to discuss how they would know where to use capitals and periods in their own writing, guiding them to a good workable explanation expressed in their own words. You should guide them towards a statement something like, "You just listen for what sounds like a new sentence." It's *not* accurate to say you put a period whenever you pause since other pauses occur in speech. You can talk about how they can choose to punctuate sentences while writing their first drafts and/or when editing.

Follow-up: Meet again in a few days; ask students to bring a piece they've just written and talk about how they used periods and capitals. They might also want to add "Checking sentences" to their editing checklist for writing. At this point in children's development, you shouldn't expect that sentences will always be punctuated correctly; the point is that they have begun developing an intuitive concept of what a sentence is.

♦

teach a rule that can then be stated consistently, it's more realistic to help students be aware of fragments as they produce them and learn to monitor for them in their own writing. Once the concept is developed, the appropriate vocabulary can follow; if students can describe in their own words what's wrong with their punctuation (e.g., "It's like I broke the sentence into two pieces"), you can mention to them that a piece of a sentence that can't stand on its own is called a fragment, which will provide a vocabulary for future discussion.

Question marks and exclamation points are the other two sentence boundary punctuation marks, and both are easy and enjoyable to learn. They can best be introduced through literature; given a book with many question marks (e.g., *Brown Bear, Brown Bear, What Do You See?* by Bill Martin, Jr., 1983) or exclamation points, children can very easily define for themselves how they're used. They might also find it fun to learn that you can use both at once for an excited question (e.g., "You paid $500 for *that*?!") and that someone has even invented a combined question/exclamation mark called the interrobang (‽).

Commas

Commas are used in two major ways: in several special, clearly defined cases such as dates and to divide grammatical units within sentences. Since the first ones are easy to define in rules while the second ones aren't, you might want to treat them separately for instructional purposes. The most important special uses of commas are dates, geographical names, salutations and closings of letters, before quotations, and in numbers of four or more digits. These can easily be introduced in context; the first three, in fact, are all part of letter-writing, so that the first time students write letters it would be very easy to show the usual layout of a letter, with comma use as one part of it. For the other, more subtle uses of commas, you should begin by refreshing your own knowledge of how and where they're used, using one of the punctuation reference books mentioned earlier, and then ask students to go on a comma hunt, asking them to keep an eye out for commas within sentences in their reading for a few days, and then bring an example or two when you meet with them for a mini-lesson. Since younger children aren't usually writing sentences complex enough to need commas and since understanding their use requires a fair amount of experience with written language, instruction on commas within sentences isn't really necessary or useful until at least third or fourth grade.

In the mini-lesson, you should focus on helping the students describe in their own words when and why they think commas are used, using your own background knowledge to help them see patterns. For instance, different students may have found examples of commas used for clauses separated by *and* or for adjectives in a series. You may or may not choose to use words like "clause" and "adjective" in your discussion, but if you do, they should be used only to label concepts that students have already worked through rather than preceding discussion.

Capital letters

Capital letters are quite easy to use; most of the time straightforward rules apply. The most important cases to cover in elementary school are the first word of a sentence (including quotations), and proper names (including places, organizations, people, holidays, titles of books and other media, and the pronoun I). In some cases, the distinction between proper and common nouns is subtle (e.g., the state of Washington vs. Washington State), so you might want to have a reference book on hand to settle any questions that come up. A capital letter hunt would be an excellent way to help students discover the variety of proper names that are capitalized; you could make a class chart of categories of capitalized names, and also discuss why some names (e.g., those of animals) aren't capitalized. A more advanced discussion could focus on why the same word is sometimes capitalized and sometimes not. For instance, *Mary* is always a proper name, but a common noun like *tyrannosaurus* can sometimes be used as a proper one—"The other dinosaurs feared Tyrannosaurus." Dictionary entries also indicate when a word is usually capitalized and can therefore be used as a reference source for capitalization. Children have few problems with capitalization once they understand the basic idea, and, of course, once they've moved from all uppercase to primarily lowercase writing, so that their capitalization errors will occur mainly with ambiguous cases.

Quotation marks

If children write fiction, they're likely to need to use quotation marks to represent dialogue. Working with play scripts is one way to move into using quotation marks. In a script, dialogue is represented as following the speaker's name and a colon:

Hamlet: To be or not to be. . . .

If students would like to turn a script into a narrative (or the reverse), it's very easy to show how quotation marks are another way of marking off who's speaking, with a comma used to separate the quotation from a dialogue carrier:

Hamlet said, "To be or not to be. . . . "

The delightful series of books starting with "The Day Jimmy's Boa Ate the Wash" (Noble, 1984, with illustrations by Steven Kellogg) are also an excellent tool to use in exploring quotation marks. These books are written entirely in dialogue, bouncing back and forth between mother and child with no dialogue carriers, so that the entire text of the book is enclosed in pairs of quotation marks. It might be fun for children to write and illustrate their own all-dialogue stories.

FIGURE 7–2 *Gordon: The Day the Indian Got Power from God*

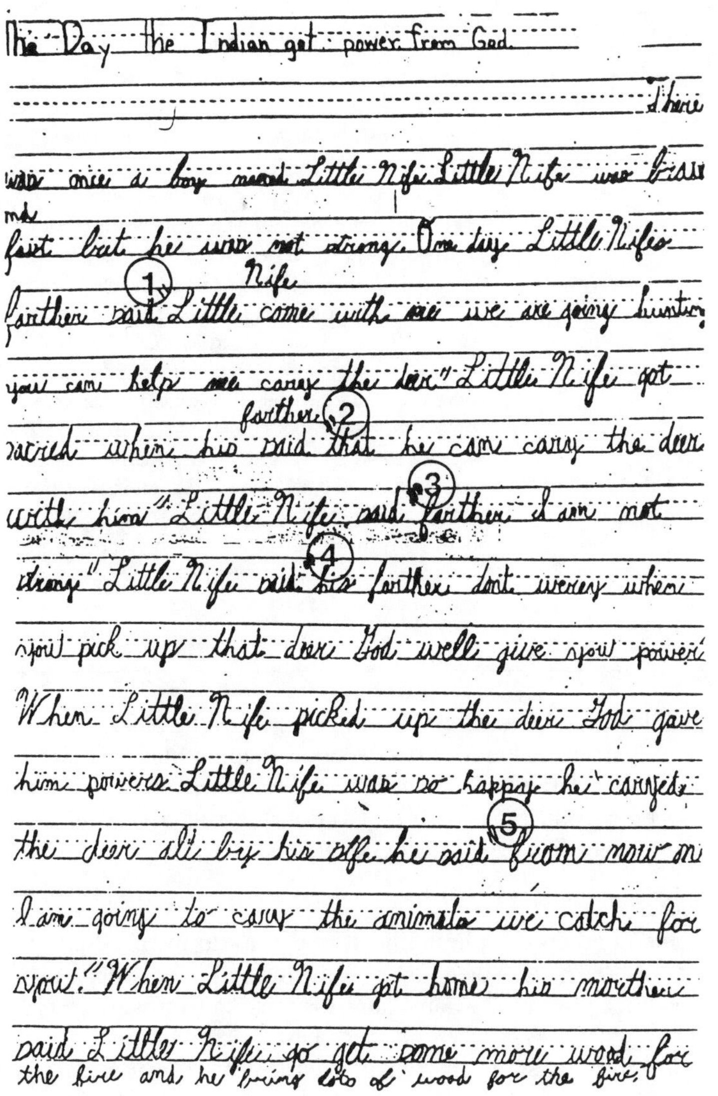
The Day the Indian got power from God.
There was once a boy named Little Nife Little Nife was fast but he was not strong. One day Little Nifes farther said Little Nife come with me we are going hunting you can help me carry the deer" Little Nife got scared when his farther said that he can carry the deer with him" Little Nife said farther I am not strong" Little Nife said his farther dont worry when you pick up that deer God well give you power When Little Nife picked up the deer God gave him power Little Nife was so happy he carryed the deer all by his selfe he said from now on I am going to carry the animals we catch for you." When Little Nife got home his mother said Little Nife go get some more wood for the fire and he bring lots of wood for the fire.

Once children have a good sense that quotation marks are used to enclose dialogue, they may be ready for a more advanced lesson. As mentioned in Chapter 1, Gordon, when he was in fourth grade, worked from a hypothesis that the first quotation mark goes after *said* and the second one after the speaker has finished talking. This worked most of the time, but Figure 7–2 shows two cases where it didn't.

The quotation marks labeled **1, 3,** and **5** are appropriate, but **2** marks an indirect quotation and **4** a divided quotation ("Little Knife," said his father, "don't worry. . . . "), where the rule doesn't work. This piece provides an excellent opportunity for one-to-one instruction during an editing session. One way

28 Spelling Celebration

Apostrophes

Danny, second grade: "the heart PUMP'S blood. when YOU'R born you have cartalage on YOU'R head. when YOU'R EYE'S see something it GO'S to YOU'R brain. . . *there's* cartelage to separate [your bones]."

Apostrophes are a tricky element of our spelling system. You can't tell from listening to a word whether it has an apostrophe in it. Rather, you have to understand the two special kinds of words where one is used: contractions, where two words are combined and possessives (not including possessive pronouns like *his* and *its*). Children typically become aware of apostrophes and experiment with them before using them appropriately. This experimentation is often based on a hypothesis about how apostrophes work. When Danny was asked when he knew to use them, he said it was when you have a word and then add a letter. This hypothesis isn't totally incorrect; it's just overgeneralized. He uses apostrophes here mainly for words ending with s (correctly in the case of *there's*), but he also spells the homophones *your* and *you're* both as YOU'R.

---

to approach it would be to have Gordon go through the piece and underline all the words that are actually spoken as dialogue, helping him see that the indirect quotation isn't the father's actual words since *he* rather than *you* was used. This would also be a good time to show Gordon the rule for using a comma to separate quotations from their dialogue carriers.

Apostrophes

Children often find apostrophes difficult to use, as do many adults, judging by how often they're omitted or inserted in menus and other public print. (Years ago, I saw a huge poster for a Canadian Broadcasting Company special with the CBC's slogan written as "Television at it's best." I couldn't resist writing on it, "Punctuation at its worst.") Children often either leave out apostrophes or, once they're aware of them, overgeneralize them, particularly to plurals, perhaps explaining this use of apostrophes by saying they're used on words ending in *s*. (See also Spelling Celebration #28.) Apostrophes are actually fairly uncomplicated; their two main uses are for contractions and possessives. (A less common use is for some special case plurals, such as *p's and q's* and *Levi's*.) There are very few contractions in common use, and after a mini-lesson, it would be easy to make a chart of them for reference purposes, which children could add to as they think of more. Possessives are probably problematic mainly because they get confused with plurals but perhaps also because possessive pronouns don't have apostrophes. For a mini-lesson, you could make a list like the following:

Ann's car
Jim's house

Spelling Celebration

Explanations and non sequiturs

Gordon, fourth grade: "*..BUT'* there was a Jack-o-Lantern"

Children's hypotheses about how the spelling system works may not always be conscious ones, and their attempts to put these hypotheses into words may not always make a lot of sense. When Gordon was asked why he had an apostrophe at the end of *but* (which he also sometimes wrote BU'T), he replied, "It's like *don't*, sort of bad news." My hunch is that on some level he had made a connection between *but* and *don't*, probably based on their both having a negative meaning and being short words ending in *t*, and as a result he placed them into the same mental category, leading to overgeneralization of the apostrophe. Was this a conscious process? Not very likely! Like much of the schematic system by which we make sense of the world around us, our understanding of the spelling system remains largely tacit and beneath our awareness, although if asked, we can try to put it into words, as Gordon did here.

the spider's web
a child's toy

Ask the students what they see and if they can suggest a rule for apostrophes. I'd suggest *not* contrasting possessives with plurals, which have an *s* with no apostrophe. You risk creating a confusion between them, although you could contrast *her* car, *his* house, *its* web, and so on. You might also want to wait until children are writing singular possessives comfortably before introducing plural ones (the spiders' webs, etc.) Although punctuation often seems to take up a large amount of time in elementary school, conducting small amounts of instruction in the five areas of punctuation I've just described would pretty well cover what appears in most scope and sequence charts for punctuation. Such instruction should be repeated at different levels of sophistication for different grade levels; children will be capable of understanding more subtle uses of each punctuation mark as they grow older.

Enriched punctuation

There are several punctuation marks that are rarely dealt with in standard text-book treatments but that children are capable of using, either as tools for the composition and revision process or to express subtle shades of meaning.

Writers' tools

When writers write in longhand, what they have to say doesn't always fit neatly on the page. They may run out of room at the end of a line, decide to add a word or a sentence, or change where a paragraph begins. Although we can all impro-vise ways to do this, special punctuation marks for these purposes already exist, and young writers might enjoy learning them. Also, as writers become more sophisticated, they may also want to set off part of their message from the main body of the text, making it parenthetical or putting it in a footnote. There are at least five punctuation and editing marks that deal in some way with text layout, which I've called writers' tools: the asterisk, caret, hyphen, paragraph mark (¶), and parentheses. Since none of them is obligatory, they can be introduced very informally, with an attitude of, "By the way, here's a new punctuation mark that you might want to try out."

When students first begin doing revision of their writing, you can show them the asterisk, caret, and paragraph mark as tools for inserting and rearranging text. Because these are primarily conveniences for the writer rather than conventionalized signals to the reader, they can be used very casually, and children find them both easy and pleasant to use. As older children begin reading material that includes footnotes (using either asterisks or numerals) and parentheses, you can bring these marks into their awareness and encourage them to use them in their own writing. The hyphen has two uses: dividing words at the end of lines (see the discussion of Figure 1–2 in Chapter 1), which can be explored with a mini-lesson, and in compound words.

Advanced punctuation marks

Children who are fairly proficient writers may be ready to learn even in elementary school about some punctuation marks that not even adults use very often. The colon, dash, and semicolon can be useful when children have begun to write longer, more complex sentences, and when they start writing research projects that involve quoting from other writers, they can learn about ellipses (three dots used to show omission in a quotation) and underlining the titles of books (the handwritten equivalent of italics), as well as learning new uses for familiar punctuation marks like quotation marks and parentheses. These advanced punctuation marks are never necessary to teach in elementary school, but may very well be useful for some students in their writing. Teachers of upper grades may want to keep an ongoing punctuation chart or notebook in the room that students can turn to as a reminder of all the punctuation marks they know and how they're used. You might also want to issue an ongoing invitation to students to keep an eye out as they read for punctuation marks that they haven't seen before to be discussed and added to the class list.

Fun with punctuation

If we think of punctuation as all the features of written language other than the letters themselves, it's clear that in addition to learning the usual punctuation marks, children can play around with the system as a whole. They can do this in two ways: experimenting with visual features and inventing their own punctuation marks. Children will often spontaneously write words bigger, use multiple underlinings, make words bolder by pressing down hard on their pencils, and create letters that are shapes rather than just lines. One of my favorite examples comes from Spencer, Figure 7–3, who saved himself some time by using the same *S* to start both his name and the heading of his spelling paper but then immediately squandered it by taking the time to draw outline letters.

To some extent, the printing press has impoverished the visual possibilities of handwritten text; printed text is linear and standardized, and handwritten text

FIGURE 7–3   *Spencer: Spelling*

follows the same pattern, as if we assumed that all writing would eventually find its way into print. But children need not be bound by these constraints, at least not in all of their writing, and can be encouraged to use visual means to express some of their ideas. It's hard to define what form this experimentation might take, but for a start you can suggest to children that size, boldness, shape, directionality, and color can vary in written language; as students begin to explore these features, they'll be inspired by seeing each other's work.

Children might also want to try inventing their own punctuation marks, to fill a real need or just for fun. Yetta Goodman (1979) shared the story of a child who invented a "sadlamation mark," to use for sentences like "My dog died," and Gordon (see Figure 6–1) created little arrows to use when inserting a word. (Since he hadn't yet learned about the caret, he invented his own equivalent.) Frumkes (1983), a humorist, invented some tongue-in-cheek punctuation marks that seem surprisingly handy:

> The Delta-Sarc: Indicates spoken sarcasm. "I'll just bet you do△"
> The Sigh: Used to emphasize resignation. "Oh well, I guess so⌐ "
> The Answer Mark: Opposite of a question mark. "How much is
> that?" "Twenty-five dollars∠"

Looking at other people's invented punctuation marks and coming up with their own can lead students into discussions on the whole nature of punctuation. Older students might want to research the history of punctuation or explore the etymology of the names of punctuation marks.

If punctuation is dealt with in classrooms as a courtesy to readers, a tool for the writing process, and an avenue of exploration, it need not be dull and dry. Although it's not as intrinsically exciting as many other areas of study, students are likely to find it reasonably interesting if it's dealt with in small doses, focusing on students' own purposes for using it in the context of real writing.

· 8 ·

Spelling Across the Curriculum

I n this chapter, I'd like to examine two areas of curriculum that support spelling and punctuation growth indirectly: thematic units in the content areas and treating language itself as a content area through the study of topics like etymology. As mentioned earlier, growth in spelling and punctuation will often occur incidentally, as a side effect of some other kind of learning that is being pursued for its own sake. In showing how this might take place, I'll explore two kinds of examples: writing samples and descriptions from a single content-area unit conducted by one teacher and an assortment of suggestions for turning language itself into a content area.

Learning about mammals:
An experience with content-area spelling[1]
Claudia Rossi, who teaches a diverse group of students in a combined first, second, and third grade classroom, builds much of her curriculum around thematic units that involve reading, writing, and small group research projects. During these units, Claudia's room fills up with resources and visuals, including many books of widely varying reading levels. Claudia believes in building her units around a solid core of shared knowledge, accompanied by freedom for children to explore and expand their knowledge in a variety of directions. The writing that they do in each unit usually takes two forms: an individual booklet or project, which may consist of writing either a daily log or a more polished report, and a group project, most typically written on chart paper by a group scribe and then shared orally with the class as a whole. During all of this writing, students are encouraged to use invented spelling, although they sometimes edit spelling for final drafts. Although spelling is rarely if ever a focus in these units, I believe the kind of wide learning through literacy that takes place here, and that

---

[1]My work in Claudia Rossi's classroom was supported by a grant from the Research Foundation of the National Council of Teachers of English.

FIGURE 8–1 *Alison: Mammals*

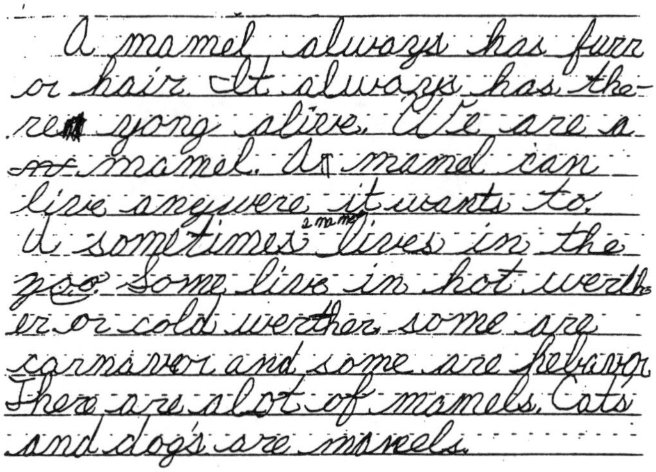
A mamel alwazs has furr
or hair. It alwazs has there yong alive. We are a
mamel. A mamd can
live anywere it wants to.
a sometimes lives in the
zoo. Some live in hot werther or cold werther. some are
carnavor and some are hebavor.
Ther are a lot of mamels. Cats
and dogs are mamels.

can take place in all content-area learning, makes a powerful indirect contribution to growth in spelling.

New vocabulary

First of all, children learn new vocabulary in the content areas: they see it in print and then have the opportunity to use it in their writing. Claudia believes that curriculum should be expansionary: rather than focusing on mastery of the small amount of material that would normally be included in a primary-grade textbook on a topic like mammals, she conducted discussions that included both basic concepts and adult scientific terminology like *herbivore* and *carnivore*. Although she didn't expect all of her students (particularly the first graders) to remember all of the material, she realized that at least they were being exposed to knowledge they would encounter more formally later on. They were likely to remember some of it and, at the very least, gain a sense of being respectfully treated as young intellectuals. Alison, early in the unit on mammals, wrote a summary of the knowledge she'd been acquiring in Claudia's lessons. Figure 8–1 reads: "A mammal always has fur or hair. It always has their young alive. We are a mammal. A mammal can live anywhere it wants to. Sometimes a mammal lives in the zoo. Some live in hot weather or cold weather. Some are carnivore and some are herbivore. There are a lot of mammals. Cats and dogs are mammals."

Although most of the piece is written in everyday language, Alison did include the technical terms *carnivore* (CARNAVOR) and *herbivore* (HEBAVOR). Topics like science and social studies are, therefore, content areas where children's vocabulary will be expanded, where they can hear new words during instruction, use them in their own oral language, recognize them in their reading, and use them in their writing. When teachers expose learners to the sophisticated vocabulary of content area subjects, children's spelling knowledge can actively expand. One note of caution is necessary: *herbivore* and *carnivore*

30 Spelling Celebration

Dinosaur spelling

Three second graders' spellings of *Tyrannosaurus Rex*:

Tami: TRRESAERU RAX (before), TYRNNSURUS REX (after)

Jamie: TUNTSUOSREX (before), TYRANNOSURUS REX (after)

Helen: TYAWINASOURES REX (before), TYRANRO-SURUS REX (after)

These three children were members of a second-grade class that spent three weeks reading and writing about dinosaurs. At the beginning and end of the unit, they were asked to write all the dinosaur names they could think of. Several of the children included *Tyrannosaurus Rex* both times, including these three, whose spellings are typical of the class as a whole. These examples suggest two important points. The first is that a good deal of spelling can be learned incidentally. During the dinosaur unit, no formal attention was given to spelling. The children had a different dinosaur book read to them each day and wrote their own booklets. A master list of dinosaur names was compiled, and the children added to it as they thought of new ones. The children were encouraged to look at the chart and at any of the books, if they wished to, as they wrote. (Their writing contained a mixture of correct and invented spellings.) Their spellings at the end of the unit showed an obviously greater visual awareness of these long and difficult words. This leads to my second observation: spellings don't have to be correct to be good. On traditional spelling tests, you're either right or you're wrong; only a few of these children had progressed to the point where more dinosaur names were spelled correctly, but in almost all cases the spellings were more logical and a closer approximation to the correct spelling. This should be acknowledged as a valuable sign of growth. Let's expose kids to big words and encourage them to use such words as they write, realizing that language growth may often be gradual and incremental rather than discrete.

wouldn't be appropriate words to *require* primary-grade children to learn as spelling words. As mentioned in Chapter 5, some teachers have changed their spelling programs by eliminating the textbook and instead choose up to 15 words from content-area subjects for their students to learn each week. This could be an extremely difficult task for many children. (Would you want to have to learn to spell 15 new scientific terms every week?) Experience and encouragement, rather than mastery, is an appropriate focus.

Although the longer and more difficult a word is, the more invented its spelling is likely to be, it's plausible that repeated exposure to a word will lead to

31 Spelling Celebration

Avoiding hard words

Gordon, fourth grade: "The mountains USE to be volcanoes."

Gordon had been reading about Hawaii and decided to write about the intriguing fact that many of the mountains there were once volcanoes. He was temporarily stumped when he couldn't figure out how to spell *used to be* and considered writing, "The mountains were volcanoes a long time ago but they aren't now." He finally, with the help of the dictionary, came up with a spelling that made sense to him.

Gordon was a confident speller who recognized how silly it would be to write a much longer and more convoluted sentence just because he didn't know how to spell a word. Yet consider all the children in classrooms where they are expected to use only correct spellings when they write. Children will consult resources like the dictionary and other people comfortably when it's a matter of choice, but if they feel they need to do so for every word they don't know, they are likely to begin limiting their expression to words they do know how to spell. Wouldn't you?

---

better invented spellings of it before the writer internalizes the correct one. There is evidence that meanings of words are learned incrementally (Nagy, Herman, & Anderson, 1985) from repeated exposure to vocabulary in context, and I think the same may be true of learning to spell. If you take a look again at the before and after spellings of *giraffe* shown earlier, in Table 5–2, you'll see that of the four children who began the word with a *j* before the mammal unit, three of them afterwards used spellings that began with *g*. The spelling/sound correspondences of English would allow for either letter at the beginning of *giraffe*. (*G* is used because the word comes from Italian, which has no *j*.) Read's preschool subjects (1975) spelled this sound with *g* by itself or in combination with another letter nearly 60 percent of the time, presumably because it's the more common letter. But they also spelled it with *j* about 40 percent of the time, a spelling that's also common and perhaps more consistent. In the case of any individual word, unless /j/ precedes *a, o,* or *u,* even a sophisticated speller who hasn't seen the word before can only guess whether to use *g* or *j*. Once the word has been seen, however, there's a fair chance of remembering it, although the process is incremental since we're attending to so much else other than spelling patterns as we read. Even adults often aren't completely sure of all the letters in longer words they've seen in print, particularly the more unpredictable letters like those for schwa vowel spellings.

As we saw earlier with Mike, a member of Claudia's class writing about the bones of the human body (Figure 1–1), invented spelling enables children to write at the outer boundaries of their knowledge and vocabulary, regardless of their level of sophistication as spellers. Jay's writing about koalas (Figure 8–2)

FIGURE 8–2   *Jay: Koala Bears*

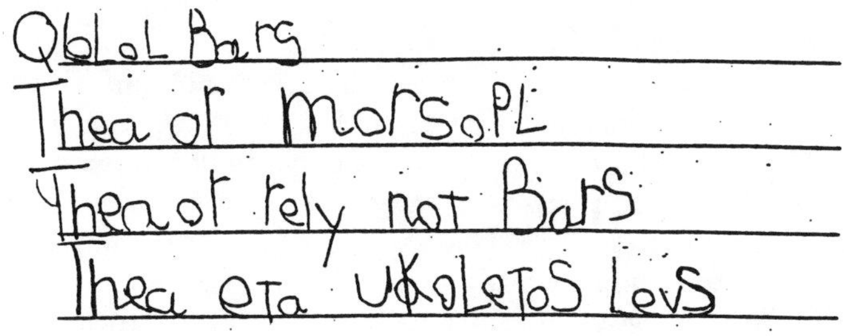

is a good example of this. His piece reads: "Koala bears. They are marsupials. They are really not bears. They eat eucalyptus leaves."

Jay was a child, in the middle of second grade at the time this piece was written, who had been categorized by the school as both gifted and learning disabled. He had a wide variety of intellectual interests, particularly in the area of nature, which he learned about largely from the public television programs that he watched avidly. Writing, however, was often slow and difficult for him, and his spelling tended to be largely phonetic at best. Claudia's classroom was a wonderful place for Jay to grow intellectually, not only because of the wide range of resources and activities available to him there but because of the freedom to use resources widely and to express himself despite his limitations. Invented spelling in the content areas is perhaps particularly important for the less sophisticated spellers in a class; they need to be free to write at length using the vocabulary of what they are learning without feeling that spellings need to be correct in a first or even perhaps in a final draft. For Jay, who had only one correct spelling in 14 words in this short piece, editing every invented spelling for a final draft would be too great a burden. By contrast, Darren, whose piece appears in Figure 8–3, knew about as much as Jay did about koalas but could spell far better and could be encouraged to aim for a perfect final draft.

Claudia supplies a variety of written language resources for every content-area unit. The reading ability of her students encompassed the usual range that one would expect in a class containing grades one through three (including mainstreamed special education students), and the content-area materials she made available were even broader in scope. For the mammal unit she had, both as part of her classroom collection and on loan from the school district library, a wide variety of informational books on mammals in general and on specific

FIGURE 8–3   *Darren: Koala Bears*

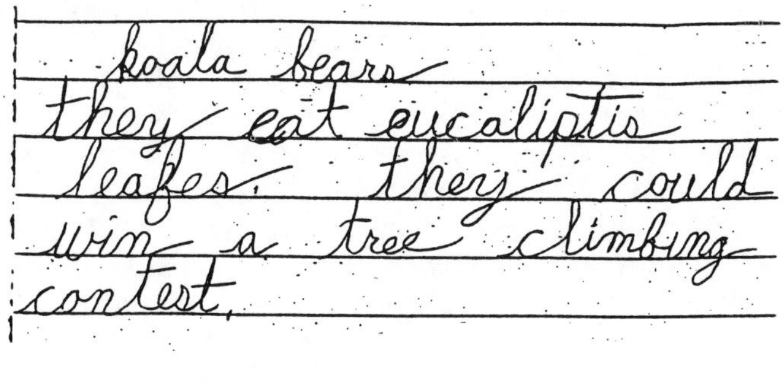

mammals, including the Knopf *Eyewitness* books on mammals (Parker, 1989), series such as The National Geographic books intended for both primary and older readers, *Zoobooks* published by the San Diego Zoo, and many others. She also had an assortment of the kind of adult reference and nonfiction books that are filled with pictures, like field guides and books that are intended both to inform and entertain a lay audience, such as a book about mammals from the *Life Nature Library* series. The classroom was one that provided plenty of time for children to interact with books, both during "mammals" time and at other points in the day, and the children made extensive use of all these materials, both reading and looking at them individually and exploring them with friends, sometimes for fun and sometimes to find specific information. Their exposure to written language about mammals wasn't limited to books; as the unit progressed, the walls of the classroom filled up with murals, charts, bulletin boards, and student reports, so that their visual field was filled with written and pictorial reminders of what they were studying. The children were also all given a list of 107 mammals to keep in their desks for reference. (See Table 8–1.)

Two vignettes illustrate typical ways that the children used these materials. First, multiage groups of about five students each had a particular mammal to research and report on. They began by generating some questions and then moved into using books, a few for each group, to discover whatever they could. Claudia and other adults in the room moved among the groups, helping them to use tables of contents and indexes to find information about their mammals, as well as helping with the reading of text passages. For instance, when I looked at the Eyewitness *Mammal* book (Parker, 1989) with the hippopotamus group, I helped a second grader find *hippopotamus* in the index and explored with her a description and picture of the hippo's yawn. In each group, the older and more proficient readers read more of the text and found more specific information, but all of the students actively participated in examining pictures and discussing their mammal. The younger students often spotted a provocative picture of their mammal and asked an older one to read the accompanying caption or other text. As information was uncovered, children would clamor for the group scribe to record it on a large piece of chart paper, which was shared with the class a few days later. The atmosphere was one of excitement about knowledge and joyous discovery. Claudia's goal for this activity was not to have the children produce a rigorously researched and organized report but to give them a general sense of what collaborative text-based research is like: posing questions about a topic and using printed and visual resources to both look for answers and discover new information, and then recording one's findings in one's own words.

What role does spelling play in all of this? An appropriately incidental and peripheral one. The focus of the activity was on knowledge exploration, but as part of that exploration, children were being exposed to print in a different way than by sitting down and reading a book straight through. In scanning indexes, reading picture captions, and working through text that was more difficult than what they usually saw in story books, they were being actively exposed to a wide range of the written version of content-area vocabulary, all of it a contribution to their evolving knowledge base about spelling.

Lacey's experience with *Simon & Schuster's Guide to Mammals* (Boitani & Bartoli, 1983) is another example of how the content-area materials in Claudia's

TABLE 8–1
107 Mammals

aardvark	giraffe	orangutan
alpaca	gnu	otter
anteater	goat	panda
antelope	gopher	peccary
ape	gorilla	platypus
armadillo	hartebeest	porcupine
baboon	hedgehog	porpoise
badger	hippopotamus	prairie dog
bandicoot	hog	rabbit
bat	horse	raccoon
bear	ibex	rat
beaver	impala	reindeer
bison	jackal	rhinoceros
boar	jaguar	seal
bongo	kangaroo	sheep
camel	kinkajou	shrew
caribou	koala	skunk
cat	lemming	sloth
chamois	lemur	springbok
cheetah	leopard	squirrel
chimpanzee	lion	tapir
chinchilla	llama	Tasmanian devil
chipmunk	lynx	tiger
civet	manatee	vicuna
coatimundi	mandrill	wallaby
cougar	marmoset	walrus
coyote	mink	wapiti
deer	mole	warthog
dik-dik	mongoose	whale
dingo	monkey	wolf
dog	moose	wolverine
dolphin	mouse	wombat
eland	muskrat	woodchuck
elephant	ocelot	yak
fox	okapi	zebra
gibbon	opossum	

room provided opportunities to explore knowledge in one's own way. This book, a guide to 426 species of mammals, displays photographs and descriptions of two mammals on each two-page spread, arranged categorically throughout the book as a whole; it's an excellent source for either reference or browsing. I came in one day and saw this book on the desk of Lacey, a second grader who was often moody and reluctant to do schoolwork, perhaps at least partly because she wasn't a very strong reader or writer. I noticed she had a bookmark about a third of the way through the book and said, "Oh, I see you've been looking at the mammal book." "No," she proudly corrected me, "I'm *reading* it," and she informed me that she was planning to read the entire book. Since most of the text in this adult book was well beyond her ability to read, I knew that for her reading it meant looking at each picture and often reading the English (but presumably not the Latin!) name of the animal. But this process should not be

FIGURE 8–4   *Sally: Animal List*

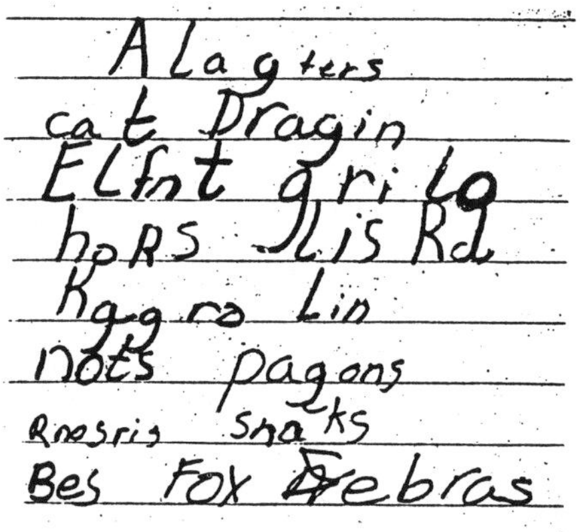

viewed condescendingly. In her reading of the *Guide to Mammals,* Lacey was exploring the topic in far greater breadth than would a second-grade science textbook (where she might be exposed to perhaps 20 different mammals), as well as getting a strong sense of accomplishment from finishing an adult book. The book occupied pride of place on Lacey's desk for weeks. Again, spelling is a small and incidental part of this. Lacey's focus was primarily on the pictures and to some extent on being able to read the names of animals she recognized. But in reading those names, she was being exposed to hundreds of discrete and largely new pieces of data about spelling that would at least partially become part of her increasing knowledge base about written language. I'm not in any way trying to suggest that children will remember the spelling of any word they see in print; to the contrary, it's likely to require multiple exposures (cf. Nagy, Herman, & Anderson, 1985). But the kind of wide ranging exploratory curriculum that Claudia builds with her students offers, along with exposure to a variety of knowledge, exposure to many, many new written words.

Spelling strategies

It's interesting to see how children do and don't make use of written text as a spelling resource for their own expository writing. Sally decided to write a list of animals and used the book *Animalia* (Base, 1986) for ideas. The book is arranged alphabetically, largely reflected in Sally's text, seen in Figure 8–4, which reads: "Alligators, cat, dragon, elephant, gorilla, horse, lizard, kangaroo, lion, newts, penguins, rhinoceros, snakes, bees, fox, zebras." She did not, however, copy any spellings from the book, preferring to invent them. Lacey, by contrast, was usually not very comfortable writing her own spellings, and in her list of mammals (Figure 8–5) tried as much as possible to find words in written text around the room, copying *monkey* from a list of activities ("Make [a] paper monkey"), *lions* from a worksheet, and *zebras* from an animal facts bulletin board, as well as inventing spellings. Her text reads: "Monkey, birds, wild dogs, wild cats, lizards, lions, pigs, frog, zebras."

Strategies for spelling in the content areas can be integrated into one's general discussion of spelling strategies with students (see Chapter 6), perhaps focusing particularly on the use of specialized reference books such as encyclope-

FIGURE 8–5   *Lacey: Animal List*

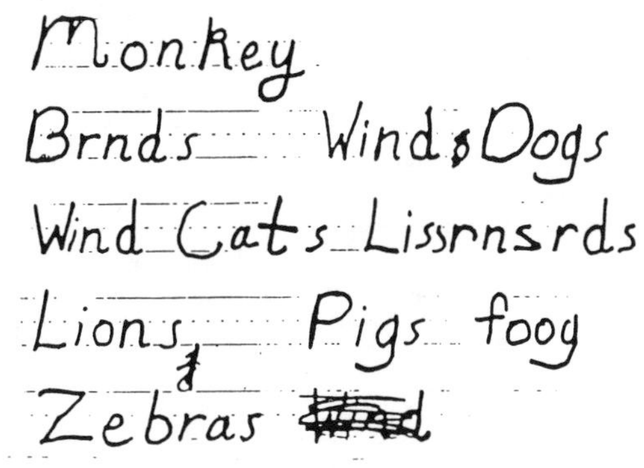

Monkey
Brnds   Wind Dogs
Wind Cats Lissrnsrds
Lions,   Pigs fooy
Zebras ~~Wind~~

dias, field guides, and topical dictionaries, as well as the use of special text features (like indexes, glossaries, and tables) for spelling reference. Of course, any special reference materials that the teacher can either provide or generate with students, such as a photocopied alphabetical listing of mammals to keep in one's desk, is a way of providing support that will uniquely suit the needs of a particular classroom and teaching unit. The discussion with students of this use of reference materials also needs to recognize the appropriateness of when to use them: usually in final draft editing.

Evaluating content-area spelling

Teachers may want to ask children to learn the spelling of several words from each content-area unit. These words, no more than a few a week, are best chosen by the children themselves to allow for differences in interest and ability. But as a broader form of evaluation, teachers may also find it interesting to conduct pre- and posttests of content-area vocabulary words, not for grading purposes but to track spelling growth generally. This will be particularly valuable for students who are mature enough as spellers to be spelling many common words correctly but are still inventing spellings for new vocabulary words. As part of the research I was doing in Claudia's classroom, I gave her students a focused and an open-ended test both before and after the mammal unit. The focused test was a list of twelve mammal names, ranging from easy (*cat*) to difficult (*rhinoceros*). The children weren't asked to study or otherwise concentrate on the words during the unit. Table 8–2 summarizes before and after spellings for eight second and third graders. From this table, one can get a good sense of the spelling development of these children as a group; their spellings of the first four words (of three to five letters each) were for the most part either correct or logical. As the words got longer, spellings often became more anomalous, although in many cases, logical spellings of longer words look unusual just because there are more letters to get wrong and the correct spelling isn't very predictable: HIPAPADAMISS looks odd but isn't really a bad spelling. One also notices that there wasn't a great shift to a larger number of correct spellings in the posttest; 23 words out of 96 were spelled correctly on the pretest and 29 on the posttest, and not always the same ones. (See Table 8–3.) Also, there was quite a bit of variation between children; Lacey and Jay produced a lot of the nonlogical invented spellings,

TABLE 8–2
Before and After Mammal Spellings

| | CAT | | LION | | MOOSE | |
	BEFORE	AFTER	BEFORE	AFTER	BEFORE	AFTER
ERICA	cat	cat	liyiane	liyn	moos	moose
LACEY	cat	cat	lorn	lion	mos	moos
JAY	cat	cat	lien	line	mos	mos
MIKE	cat	cat	lian	lion	mousse	mouse
SALLY	cat	cat	line	line	loes	mose
DARREN	cat	cat	lion	lion	moose	moose
ALISON	cat	cat	lion	loin	moose	moose
JAMES	cat	cat	lion	lion	mouse	moose

| | ZEBRA | | GIRAFFE | | JAGUAR | |
	BEFORE	AFTER	BEFORE	AFTER	BEFORE	AFTER
ERICA	zibra	zibru	jooraf	giraffe	jagwor	agwiyr
LACEY	zoebo	zedras	drvrf	draf	jagwoyr	jagyr
JAY	zibe	zopo	jrar	joraf	jagor	jagur
MIKE	zebra	zebra	jraffe	giraffe	jaguar	jagur
SALLY	zebra	zeber	grafe	grafe	jagwire	jagwir
DARREN	zebra	zebrah	giraffe	giraffes	jagware	jaguar
ALISON	zebra	zebra	girrafe	giraf	jagure	gagware
JAMES	zeybra	zebra	jeraf	giraffe	jagwarg	jaguar

| | CHEETAH | | KANGAROO | | SQUIRREL | |
	BEFORE	AFTER	BEFORE	AFTER	BEFORE	AFTER
ERICA	chida	chitgh	kangaroe	kengrroow	skrowle	sqrels
LACEY	ceet	ceta	kacroo	kagrroo	scals	srol
JAY	chte	ceto	kagero	kagro	swrl	sor
MIKE	cheetah	chetah	kangero	kangaro	squerl	squrels
SALLY	ceat	ceeta	kakaroe	kekaro	skrlqs	skrlos
DARREN	cheetah	cheeta	kangaroo	kangaroo	squirl	squirril
ALISON	cheeta	chetha	kangaroo	kangarure	squirell	squrel
JAMES	cheta	cheeta	kagarar	kangaroo	sqorwerl	squirrel

| | AARDVARK | | HIPPOPOTAMUS | | RHINOCEROS | |
	BEFORE	AFTER	BEFORE	AFTER	BEFORE	AFTER
ERICA	ordforke	ardvork	hipopotumis	hippopodumis	rinuoruse	rinorsoris
LACEY	andbark	ondbc	hipopomis	hioopotumis	wanosris	rinrrrs
JAY	ovork	ordvnk	hpoeptoms	hopota	rinors	rorse
MIKE	ardvark	aardvark	hipapotamas	hipopato-patamus	rinonosurus	rhinosaros
SALLY	abverk	edvrk	hpoppomes	hpoptomis	ronosores	ronsris
DARREN	ardevarke	ardvarke	hipopotomus	hippopotomus	rhinosaurus	rhinosoraus
ALISON	ardvark	ardfark	hippopatamus	hippopamis	rhinosurrus	rinoasis
JAMES	ardfark	ardvark	hipapadamiss	hippopotums	rinasaris	rhinoseres

while Darren and James produced many of the correct ones. Although a more detailed analysis could be conducted, for the classroom teacher a before and after list of words like this would probably be most useful as a general indicator of a class's spelling knowledge of content-area words. Incidentally, the developmen-

TABLE 8–3
Summary of Before and After Mammal Spellings

	Correct Before	Misspelled Before	Total After
Correct After	16	13	29
Misspelled After	7	60	67
Total Before	23	73	96

tal level of this group as indicated by their invented spellings suggests that for most of them, the simpler mammal names would be the more appropriate choice for self-selected spelling words.

The students' spellings of as many mammal names as they could generate on their own after a whole-class oral brainstorming session appears as Appendix E. These are taken from fourteen second and third graders, with before and after spellings collapsed. It's interesting mainly for seeing the variety of spellings children are likely to produce, again with short, simple words being spelled better. The classroom teacher doesn't, of course, have the time to compile a whole class's responses in this way, but can certainly benefit from eyeballing individual children's papers. This kind of open-ended pretest and posttest also serves an even more important function of providing a sense of each child's knowledge base about the topic.

Language as a content area

There are probably few areas of study that seem less appropriate for elementary school children at first glance than linguistics, the scientific and historical study of human language. Probably most teachers have never taken a linguistics course, would be hard pressed to justify finding room for it in a busy elementary school curriculum, and are likely to find it rather forbidding as a field of study anyway. But children are already being exposed to a fairly extensive linguistics curriculum in many classrooms, but rather than being called linguistics, it's called phonics, spelling, punctuation, grammar, usage, vocabulary, and so on. If we were to add up the amount of time spent on all these areas in a typical classroom, we would find that a very large part indeed of the school day is often being spent studying linguistics (defined as any study of language as an object in its own right). Linguistics is learning *about* language, rather than directly learning to become better at *using* it—although the two are often confused. A full critique of phonics, grammar, usage, and vocabulary instructional practices, as found in and influenced by textbooks, is beyond the scope of this book, but many of the criticisms I made of spelling books in Chapter 5 are relevant here: linguistics is generally taught in a dull, decontextualized, and spuriously systematic way.

The usual rationale for this extensive teaching of linguistics in elementary schools is one of helping children acquire the skills needed to be effective users of oral and particularly written language, rather than as knowledge interesting in its own right. Many whole-language teachers have rejected this model of literacy acquisition and have eliminated linguistic study (in the form of skill and drill exercises) from their classrooms. But a question that very much deserves to be raised is whether linguistics in some other form has a place in the elementary curriculum. I'd like to propose that we consider exploring language with children the way we would explore any other subject of interest (like mammals, or communities, or folktales), through exploration and discovery. Linguistics would make an excellent subject for a theme study or thematic unit once a year, as well as being suited to less extensive activities, some of them one-shot, some ongoing. One way to conceptualize what these activities might consist of is by thinking in terms of traditional subject matter divisions within linguistics: phonetics and by extension graphics (the study of sounds and of spelling); syntax (the study of grammar, i.e., how sentences are put together); semantics (the study of meaning); and applied areas such as sociolinguistics (the study of language in social context), as well as the related topics of language history and geography. Since phonetics and graphics are most closely tied to spelling, I'll discuss them at greater length than the other topics.

Exploring the sounds and spellings of language

Geller (1985) has written about how children's spontaneous language play is not just pleasurable but also entails a significant amount of language learning and exploration. Starting in preschool, teachers can help children explore the way that the sounds of our language add another level to speech beyond that of communicating ideas. When language includes rhythm, rhyme, and alliteration, homonyms (as in puns), onomatopoeia, and repetition of pattern like that found in predictable books, there's a layer of language involved that can't be summed up by a paraphrase. Geller's book explores the roots of language play and suggests a variety of ways that children can explore it in the classroom. For instance, children can try out and practice tongue twisters (a short but fiendish one that Geller mentions is "unique New York") and then examine what defines a tongue twister as a prelude to creating their own, a surprisingly difficult task. A teacher wanting to introduce children to playful exploration of our phonetic system can best do it with a light hand, introducing a variety of literature with patterned language and letting children discover the phonetic relationships themselves. With only a little encouragement, children will move from enjoying rhyme, tongue twisters, homophone puns (e.g., Gwynne, 1970, 1975), and so on, to discussing the principles involved and creating their own. Golick (1987) also has an excellent collection of language games to introduce to students; the sections on rhyming games, alliteration and other poetic devices, and secret languages all use sound as the basis for word games. For instance, an old favorite is the riddle game where a clue is given for a pair of rhyming words: thus a seafood platter is a "fish dish," and an ominous member of the clergy a "sinister minister." Games and activities can also focus directly on spelling; some classics are Ghost and Geography, also found in Golick's book under "Alphabet Games", as well as Hangman, familiar in a new guise from the television program "Wheel of Fortune."

For a more academic look at language, but one that, unlike most grammar textbooks, focuses on knowledge rather than skills, *Answering Students' Questions About Words* (Tompkins & Yaden, 1986) is an excellent resource. After a 20-

32 Spelling Celebration

Looking for homophones

Gordon, fourth grade (orally): "I wonder which *there*?"

Gordon on three occasions showed an active awareness of homophones. First, one day after he had helped a friend to find *marry* in the dictionary, he said, "Now I have to find *Mary*" (for his own story), then said, "I think it's M-A-R-Y." These two words were homophones for him; when asked, he showed awareness that words can be pronounced the same and spelled differently. Another time, when planning to write *there*, he stopped after writing the first four letters and said, "I wonder which *there* (*their*)?" and successfully found the right spelling in the dictionary. When asked how he knew it was the right one, he answered, "'Cause I seen it," suggesting he had some intuitive visual sense of which was which. Two weeks later, as his class was studying homophones, while looking for *hospital* in the dictionary, he spotted *homophone* as a guide word at the top of a page. He exclaimed, "Homophones! That's what we're doing!" and wrote down the page number so he could show his teacher later. These three examples illustrate the active, varied role that children can play in learning about language systems. For Gordon, learning about homophones wasn't a matter of learning to spell lists of pairs of words but rather an exploration of a language phenomenon.

page introduction providing the teacher with background knowledge about the history of the English language, the remaining 50 pages of this source book develop a series of activities out of questions that students frequently ask about language at the level of individual words. Each section gives background information and suggests a few activities for students to carry out. The level of sophistication of the activities is primarily upper elementary and middle school, but many of them could be adapted downward. In the area of spelling specifically, the book shows how students can be helped to think about the complexity of sound/symbol relationships in English (which could be extended to a study of the first language of bilingual students), as well as to learn about the history of silent letters. Students who have explored homophones for fun might find it interesting to learn about the etymology of many of them. Tompkins and Yaden suggest specific examples to research.

Other aspects of language

The linguistic study of grammar, also known as syntax, is very different from the layperson's (including most classroom teachers') understanding of the term "grammar." To a linguist, the grammar of a language is a set of rules that, if precisely enough specified, could be programmed into a computer that could then generate any sentence in the language. Syntacticians try to define patterns such as how statements are turned into questions and why a sentence like "flying planes can be dangerous" can have two very different meanings while "the dog chased the cat" and "the cat was chased by the dog" have the same meaning. Elementary school grammar books contain only the palest reflection of this work, in the often exhaustive treatment given to identifying parts of speech and parts of sentences under the rubric of being skills that one needs for writing. If syntax is treated instead as an area of linguistic knowledge that might be of interest in its own right, it soon becomes obvious that it's an area beyond the expertise of most elementary teachers and not really very interesting to children anyway. Children need the opportunity to *use* the grammar of their language as they speak and write, but this develops through practice, not formal study.

Usage, however, which often involves syntax, can be explored as part of sociolinguistics. The term "grammar" is often used to refer to prescriptions for so-called correct use of language, such as avoiding *ain't* and double negatives. In most cases, this is an issue of class and cultural differences in language being differentially valued. Many whole-language teachers have merely dropped any attempt to change children's language, but it's also possible to study dialects as part of a unit on language. *Students' Right to Their Own Language* (National Council of Teachers of English, 1974) and *The Story of English* (McCrum, Cran, & MacNeil, 1986) are good starting points for teachers to develop their own knowledge in this area. A study of how dialect is represented in literature could focus on how spelling is used to represent speech more directly than usual, as can be seen in texts ranging from the multiple Mississippi River dialects of *Huckleberry Finn* (Twain, 1884/1959; see his introductory explanatory note about dialect) to the use of Black dialect by modern African-American writers like Lucille Clifton (e.g., *All Us Come Cross the Water*, 1973).

Moving on to the semantic system of language, Tompkins and Yaden are again an excellent resource. The bulk of the activities in their book deal with etymology, providing an overview of language geography and history, as well as the history of people and places that have given rise to so many of our words. For children who are old enough to understand the etymological entries in the dictionary, exploring the origins of individual words not only is interesting in its own right but provides extra practice in dictionary use. There are also an increasing number of informational books for children that deal with the history and origin of words; many of these are listed in Appendix F, "Books About Language for Teachers and Young Readers."

Another way in which learning about spelling can be tied into a broader social context is by looking at how spelling changes over time, with advertising and brand names perhaps serving as the cutting edge in today's society. Students might enjoy conducting an invented spelling hunt in the supermarket and the yellow pages, looking for creative spellings and speculating on the reason for them. A copy shop named "Kwik Kopy" may be using one spelling (instead of three) for the same sound to bring out the alliteration, while "Froot Loops" may be spelled the way they are because there isn't any real *f-r-u-i-t* in them!

In planning linguistics as a content area for instruction, teachers might want to work it into other curriculum areas or set aside separate times for it. One simple procedure is to put a "Word of the Day" on the chalkboard each morning, inviting students to discover its meaning, research its etymology, or explore

TABLE 8–4
Some Questions About Words

1. What do ZIP code, Jeep, and scuba have in common? (They are all acronyms.)

2. What's a 9-letter word with only one vowel? (strengths)

3. What's the opposite of antepenultimate? (third)

4. What consonant never doubles before a suffix? (x)

5. How are helicopter & pterodactyl related? (They both include the root *pter*, meaning *wing*.)

6. Can you come up with an example of a palindrome and a pangram? ("Madam, I'm Adam," which reads the same backwards and forwards, and "The quick brown fox jumps over the lazy dog," which contains all the letters of the alphabet.)

7. What 2 consonant letters are unnecessary because their sounds can always be spelled by another letter? (c and q)

8. Where do the words denim and jeans come from? (*De Nimes* means "from [the town of] Nimes," while *jeans* derives from Genoa, Italy.)

what's special about it. Some of my favorites (with answers) are listed in Table 8–4; teachers can use Tompkins and Yaden as well as some of the books listed in Appendix F to help them generate their own lists of interesting words.

Many areas of study across the curriculum lend themselves to inquiry into language; a unit on Asia could include learning a little about Asian writing systems, as well as examining English words derived from Asian languages, while a study of mammals could include a map showing the worldwide etymology of mammal names. It would also be valuable every year to have a unit of study focused just on language. Tompkins and Yaden include a sample plan for such a unit (1986, pp. 24–5) growing out of their list of some 25 questions that students often ask; better yet, teachers can ask students what their own questions about language are so that the curriculum can grow directly out of their interests.

Although many of these teaching ideas are particularly suited to older children, even beginning readers and writers can start thinking about how language works and how interesting it can be. Hodges (1981) discovered that spelling bee champions (surely the epitome of what we want our spelling curricula to accomplish!) are characterized by their broad general interest in words: not just their spellings but their meanings, their histories, and their relationships to other words. These are the kinds of students who, as adults, will watch public broadcasting programs like "The Story of English" and will have the knowledge base to enjoy and appreciate an extra layer of meaning in what they read. If teachers can generate, for themselves and for their students, an attitude of interest in and curiosity about language and how it works, not every student will be a spelling bee champion, but all students can have positive feelings about exploring a fascinating human creation.

· 9 ·

Evaluation, Grading, Parents, and Administrators

S ome of the knottiest questions about spelling are those that deal with matters at least somewhat apart from the day-to-day process of working with children. Teachers wonder how they can know if their programs are working and whether some learners need extra attention or a different approach of some kind. In addition to concerns about evaluation in this broader sense, teachers also wonder how to assign a report card grade for spelling if they're no longer using spelling books and wonder if their students will do all right on the spelling sections of standardized tests. This gives rise to thoughts about what people outside of the classroom will think about spelling curriculum; many teachers never attempt to innovate in the area of spelling (or quickly abandon any changes) because of actual or potential criticism from parents, colleagues, and principals. I must admit a certain bias in dealing with these issues. I feel that in our democratic society, the drive for public schools to be appropriately responsive to community needs through accountability has distorted many of our purposes. Elaborate evaluation systems are now a large part of many published curricula; evaluative activities are often mistaken for instruction (Durkin, 1978–9), and, worst of all, educational goals are determined (in policy and/or in practice) in response to the scope and sequence of standardized tests. Doesn't it sometimes seem like the tail is wagging the dog?

Despite this concern over distorted priorities, it's a necessary and even welcome fact of life that teachers are responsible for monitoring children's learning, communicating the results of that monitoring to parents and others, and conveying our purposes to the broader community, in and out of school. In the case of spelling, as in other areas, appropriate evaluation grows out of curriculum rather than either controlling it or being tacked on as an afterthought. Communication with parents and administrators will often, at least initially, focus on evaluation since the question they are most likely to ask about a nontraditional curriculum is Does it work?

When I speak to teachers or parents about spelling and punctuation, the questions I hear most often and with the highest level of anxiety are related to evaluation; because of this, I've organized this chapter around responses to questions.

How do I know if my students are growing as spellers?

The first part of the answer to this question is an easy one: for most students, it'll be obvious that they're growing. Given a good spelling curriculum, with plenty of opportunities to read and write, chances to explore spelling patterns, and an appropriate focus on editing, children's spelling will follow predictable maturational patterns. A portfolio of each child's writing collected throughout the school year gives us data to remember where he or she started from; often growth is obvious from just the briefest look at how a child's spellings have changed over time. For instance, in January of third grade, Gordon wrote a piece about hiking in the Grand Canyon (Figure 9–1), and nine months (but only about six months of school) later, in October of fourth grade, wrote about PacMan (Figure 9–2). The first piece, excerpted from a longer story, reads, "When we got down the canyon we climbed some hills. When we were climbing the hills a volcano exploded and we almost fell down into the water." The second piece, also an excerpt, is correctly spelled except for GOST/ghost and BRUNING/burning. It's evident that Gordon's spelling improved both quantitatively (proportion of correct spellings) and qualitatively (maturity of invented spellings) during this time period. (These two pieces are representative of his writing as a whole at each point in time.)

    With younger children, growth will be more rapid and dramatic, while in older students who are already spelling well, change may be more subtle but is of less concern because so little more growth is necessary to reach adult stan-

FIGURE 9–1   *Gordon: Grand Canyon*

> When we got donw the Canyon we
> Clameyd Some hellS. Nhon We Wher
> Clmeing the hellS A Voninyon ElxeBed
> And We AWas fell donw intothe
> werter!

FIGURE 9–2   *Gordon: PacMan*

> Pac Man is eating the gost biby.
>
> Mrs. Pac Man is looking for baby Pac Man.
> the Sun is bruning the tree the tree is
> Saying ouch.

33 Spelling Celebration

"Regression" in spelling

Gordon, fourth grade: "Me and Michael went to the *UNVSTE* (*university*) . . . We went to VIST (*visit*) Dian and Sandy and *UATA* (*Yetta*)."

Gordon's two spellings highlighted here are less sophisticated than his usual invented spellings. In UNVSTE he represented only consonants and those vowels that "said their name" in the word. In writing *Yetta* (Yes, that's Yetta Goodman!), he began with the letter u, whose name (/yu/) begins with the phoneme /y/. These are patterns typical of much younger or less proficient spellers. What's going on? Why did he regress? The content of his two sentences here provides a clue. He had just returned from an exciting overnight field trip to the city involving visits to the university and a mall, as well as a picnic dinner and a swim. His piece was written after returning to school early the following morning, after a night with very little sleep. He was just tired! Children's *competence* in spelling grows consistently and gradually, given appropriate experience. Their *performance* may vary for any number of reasons.

---

dards. Gordon, by early in fourth grade, was spelling at about 85 percent accuracy and needed mainly to keep expanding his stock of known words and work on proofreading ability. For most older children like this, you could help them provide their own answers about ongoing learning by having them reflect periodically, perhaps in writing, perhaps in small group discussions, on the question, How am I growing as a speller? Each child can define for himself or herself whether growth is occurring through knowing more new words, easily getting more words right in first drafts, coming up with better spellings of hard words, proofreading and using resources more effectively, and so on. The children themselves are the best judge of where they've been, where they are, and where they need to go.

This may seem vague to some teachers who would like benchmarks to measure children against rather than observing growth on its own terms, but I'm not sure that learning can be predicted or quantified much more precisely, although apparent precision of scope and sequence charts and standardized tests may have fooled us into thinking it can be. In other areas of writing (or speech for that matter), we don't try to quantify; for instance, classroom teachers don't attempt to track sentence length or sophistication of story grammar in children's writing, or to measure the number of new words children use in their speech. It seems that for the majority of students who are actively involved in learning about spelling as part of a larger writing curriculum, any attempt to define a correct amount of growth isn't really appropriate. The reason for wanting this knowledge would be to adjust the curriculum to achieve more growth. But I'd sooner rely on a teacher's general instinct that a class or some individuals in it need to work on getting more spellings right automatically in first drafts or push themselves to use more big words even though they're hard to proofread, and so on, rather than trying to generate curriculum changes by comparing students to some external standard, with all the extra time and energy that this would take away from other matters. I think, therefore, that a good rule of thumb for tracking spelling growth for most students is to glance through their writing portfolios every couple of months, focusing on spelling growth; you'll discover that most children are doing fine, and you can flag those few who aren't.[1] This leads to the next question.

How can I identify and work with students having problems in spelling?

Every classroom will have children who are either far less adept in spelling than the rest of the class, or aren't showing progress, or both. Often these children are so self-conscious and unhappy about their spelling that it inhibits them from writing at all. Often they need to learn to focus *less* on spelling to feel relaxed enough to write more and build the fluency that will pave the way for a later refocus on conventions.

Before looking at some writing samples from children who were struggling with spelling, we need to consider again the issue of learning disabilities. Is it true that some children produce unusual spellings because they have some type of visual/perceptual problem that makes it difficult for them to see or transcribe words properly? Although many articles have been published with that suggestion, Moats (1983) conducted a study comparing the spellings of normal second graders and a group of older students who had been classified as dyslexic. She found there were no real differences between them in either phonetic accuracy or letter order errors. If anything, the dyslexics were slightly *better* at phonemic segmentation and more knowledgeable about spelling rules although they made more copying errors and had more problems with letter formation. In her discussion of other studies, she suggested that researchers who thought of "underlying process dysfunctions" as the cause of dyslexics' seemingly unusual invented spellings may have been assuming qualitative differences where none existed, perhaps because of a lack of knowledge about what normal invented spelling looks like.

Another issue is whether evidence of a presumed spelling disability would make any difference in how to work with children. In my experience, in most cases, what children with problems in spelling need first is to work on building confidence. Second, such children can participate in the same kinds of curriculum that are helpful for all children, supplemented by additional one-on-one work with the teacher. Reverting to isolated skill-and-drill exercises can end up making things worse. It makes spelling boring and isolates it from writing, and also reinforces a sense of stigma in the child. Let's look now at some writing samples from students with various kinds of spelling problems.

---

[1] If most children aren't doing well, then it may be time to reassess your spelling curriculum as a whole.

FIGURE 9–3   *Bill: First Alphabet*

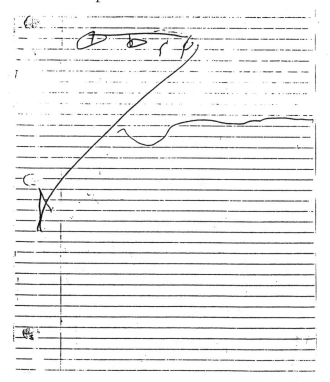

Bill: A non-writer

Bill was eight years old when a tutor started working with him on his reading and writing. In their first session, the tutor, Tom, asked him to write the alphabet (Figure 9–3). Bill produced shapes that looked somewhat like the first four letters and then, in disgust and frustration, scrawled his pencil across the paper and refused to write any more. Tom worked hard at building rapport with Bill and encouraged him to try again. At their second session, he was able to write the entire alphabet successfully (Figure 9–4). (Tom wisely chose not to focus on handwriting at all, realizing that fluency and confidence were the most important goals at this point.) By their fourth session (Figure 9–5), Bill was able to write a message using letter strings, and at their sixth session produced his first text using real invented spellings (Figure 9–6) His piece reads, "The old phone number is [555]-1347. My new phone number is [555]-2749. Mom is cleaning the oven."

FIGURE 9–4   *Bill: Second Alphabet*

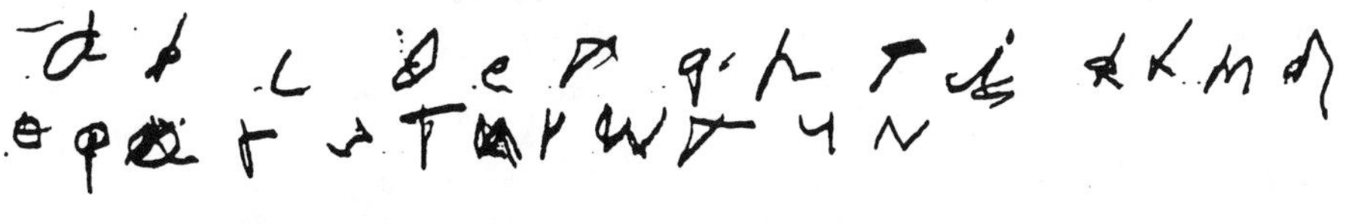

FIGURE 9–5   *Bill: Letter Strings*

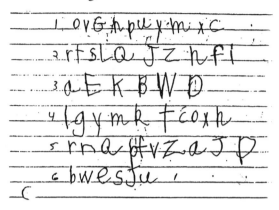

FIGURE 9–6   *Bill: The Old Phone Number*

Tom's work with Bill demonstrates the power that a small amount of individual attention can have. Bill was basically a nonwriter who, because of his feeling that he couldn't write, was in danger of never being willing to take the risks that would help him become a writer. Tom's major achievement was to help Bill discover that he could use writing to express his thoughts and feelings;[2] in doing so, Bill also applied the knowledge he'd already been absorbing about written language and very quickly advanced to the point where he was producing good, logical invented spellings as well as some correctly spelled words. Not all nonwriters will progress this rapidly, but all will benefit from the same kinds

---

[2] For example, a later piece read: "I like my mom. She loves me very, very much and I love her very, very much. I have a picnic lunch with my dad and my mom."

FIGURE 9–7   *Jay: Your Rib Cage*

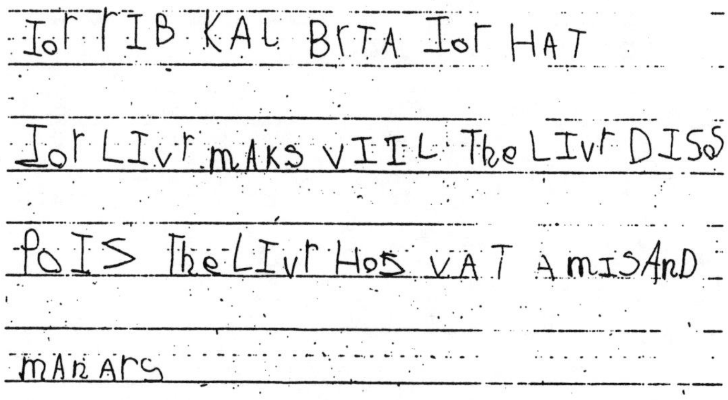

IoF FIB KAL BITA IoF HAT

IoF LIVF mAKS VIIL Tḣe LIVF DISS

PoIS Tḣe LIVF HoS VAT A mISAnD

mA n Ars

of encouragement that are used with younger beginning writers, where they're given opportunities to express themselves through coming up with spellings that make sense to them.

Jay: Ideas outstripping spelling

In the last chapter, we saw a piece about koalas from Jay (Figure 8–2), who had been classified by his school as both learning disabled and gifted. Another piece by Jay again shows how the ideas he wanted to express were often fairly well developed, even though writing them down wasn't always easy for him. Figure 9–7 was written at the end of first grade; it reads, "Your rib cage protects your heart. Your liver makes bile. The liver dissolves poison. The liver has vitamins and minerals." Writing for Jay was usually fairly slow and laborious, with each word sounded out slowly and written letter by letter. When he had the chance, he would often choose to write with his friend Darren, both of them composing out loud but Darren doing most of the actual writing. Although this piece about the liver has some invented spellings that seem unusual, they *are* logical and are perhaps due to the slowness of Jay's sounding-out process. For instance, the word *your,* when said slowly, can sound like a short *i* followed by the word *or,* and the two *i*'s in VIIL (bile) may be Jay's way of indicating the long vowel. (The *v* is close in sound to *b* and may represent a misperception of this uncommon word.) Although some final consonants are missing, this is typical in younger children writing words of two or more syllables. The main thing to be concerned about with Jay's spelling is its slowness and the consequent inhibiting of his ability to express himself. Jay could benefit from two kinds of help: practice in speeding up and using a less painstaking, less precise strategy for creating spellings, and at least occasional opportunities to express his many varied ideas in ways that wouldn't be impeded by his spelling, such as orally, in art, or with someone to collaborate with or transcribe for him.

Elaine: Unusual spellings

Many of Elaine's spellings, as seen in Figure 9–8, are the kind that might strike a layperson as indicating a learning disability. (This piece reads, "I [went] to the fun house. I got scared. Then I started to cry. I was a ghost. My friend was a

FIGURE 9–8   *Elaine: I Went to the Fun House*

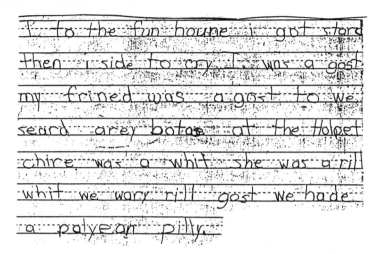

ghost. My friend was a ghost too. We scared everybody at the hospital. Cheri was a witch. She was a really [*sic*] witch. We were really ghosts. We had a pumpkin pie.") However, these spellings are best seen not as a sign of pathology but as a good way for Elaine to get her thoughts down on paper quickly. Unlike Jay, she wrote rapidly, and although her spellings may not look any worse than his to an untrained eye, they're often far less logical; AREY BOTAE isn't much like *everybody,* nor are HOLPET and PILLY very good spellings for *hospital* and *pie.* SIDE (*started*) and PALYEAN (*pumpkin*) seem particularly unusual, like Elaine wasn't even thinking about how the words might be spelled. At the time she wrote this piece, however (early in fourth grade), she had realized that it was really all right to invent spellings and had decided that her priority during writing time was usually to get as many of her ideas down on paper as possible. For a stronger speller, this goal wouldn't have been incompatible with logical spellings, but for Elaine to produce reasonable spellings, she needed more time than she was willing to take in her first drafts, so she cheerfully proceeded to write "any way" the words she didn't know, realizing that they were close enough for her to read back in context. Although a writer like Elaine needs to realize (as she did) that more precise spelling is helpful for a reader, she didn't really need any remedial help. By continuing to write (as well as reading to increase her visual knowledge of words), she was teaching herself how to spell.

Hannah: A fearful writer

Hannah, whose writing we saw in Figure 6–3, was nine when she wrote her piece about a monkey (Figure 9–9). She had some of the same inhibitions as Bill and many unusual spellings like Elaine. The piece, excerpted from a longer story, reads, "There once was a monkey named Anthony and he did not like people or animals or yellow ripe bananas. One day he went out to look for yellow brown mushy bananas. All of the animals followed him but he did not know that they were following him." Hannah was reluctant to write around anyone who she thought might judge her and felt very self-conscious because she was so far

[34] Spelling Celebration

Recopying

Elaine, third grade: "I went to my ENTESC (*auntie's*) house." (next page): "My ANETSC (*auntie*) came after me."

Sometimes teachers worry that if their students are allowed to use invented spelling, these spellings will somehow imprint themselves on the brain through frequent repetition so that the correct spellings will never be learned. Elaine's two spellings of *auntie*('s) are an interesting piece of countervailing evidence. On the first page of her story, Elaine wrote ENTESC (*auntie's*), then went back and looked at that first spelling when she was ready to write another form of the same word (*auntie*). Not only had the first spelling not, we might say, "stuck in her brain," she had so little intuitive sense of the word that she didn't even copy her own spelling of it correctly! My hunch is that children realize that their invented spellings are different from standard spellings and don't put any energy (conscious or unconscious) into remembering them. It is only when they have some familiarity with the real spelling that something clicks in their head when they produce the right version—the spelling only then becomes consistent. (Many of the persistent invented spellings that we see in children's writing are the right spelling of the wrong word, often a homophone. This is a very different issue.)

---

behind her peers in spelling, but she felt comfortable writing personal or imaginative stories if the audience was only herself and her family. The biggest difference between her and Elaine was one of attitude and confidence. Teachers working with students like Hannah need to resist the temptation to focus first on improving their spelling, as problematic as it may seem. The most valuable approach to take with Hannah would be one of encouraging her to write as much as possible and to read widely, publishing and displaying her work without making her do any proofreading, and praising her for writing hard words

FIGURE 9–9   *Hannah: A Monkey Named Anthony*

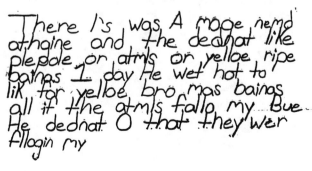

and coming up with good invented spellings. Only when her fear was greatly reduced would I begin talking to her about final form.

Diane: An older writer

Diane, a fifth grader, is typical of many older children who aren't spelling as well as their teachers would like. Her piece about division seems at first glance to be very badly spelled. Figure 9–10, reads, "What is hard in division. Composition. Division is hard for me in many ways but usually because I do not know all my multiplication. And I think it is harder when the number does not go into the base number. And I just do not like division [,] period. Problem solving." However, a closer look reveals that her invented spellings reflect just a few types of problems. Three words (*composition, division, multiplication*) show that she hadn't yet generalized *-tion/-sion* endings (as well as having left out a few other letters), while seven other words (*because, number, does, and, period, problem*, and *solving*) are only off by one letter and three others appear as reasonable phonetic spellings (*usually, when,* and *just*).

    Diane would probably benefit most not from a focus on learning more words but from help in proofreading, as well as drawing her attention to some patterns like common word endings. Diane's handwriting (including the use of *m* for *n* in two words) suggests that she's a quick writer who is not highly concerned with surface form. For many older writers like Diane who are still misspelling many words, examining their invented spellings is likely to reveal a few customary error patterns that account for many of the individual spellings. Perhaps with older children, the most important task for the teacher is to help writers develop a sense of ownership about their spelling. If Diane could come to realize that it's in her own best interest (for her life both in and outside of school) to be able to produce appropriately spelled final drafts, she and her teacher could work as partners toward this common goal.

FIGURE 9–10   *Diane: Division*

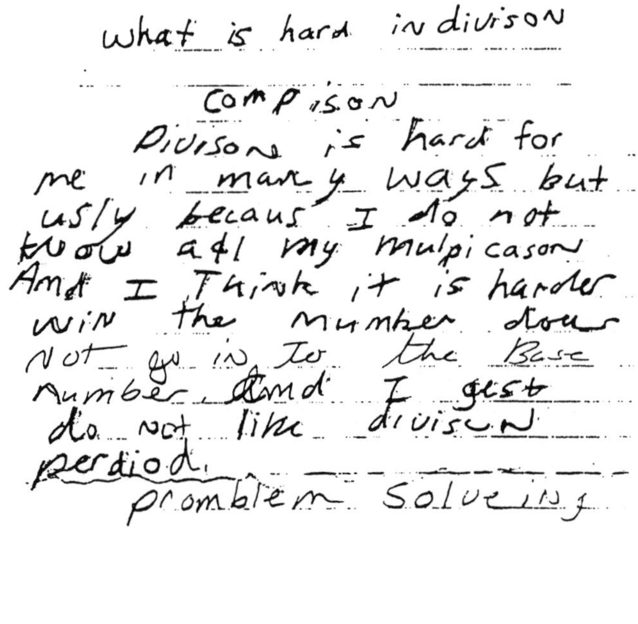

Older students probably aren't helped in the long run by a carrot-and-stick attitude (e.g., "Your grade will be lowered for every misspelled word") or by being given long lists of words to memorize, but they may appreciate being helped to discover what kinds of invented spellings they tend to produce a lot of. They might even enjoy collecting and coding their invented spellings as part of a self-remediation plan. I (Wilde, 1989a) describe such a coding system that may also be of use to teachers who wish to analyze their students' invented spelling in more detail. The idea of self-analysis has been used for miscues and the reading process under the name of retrospective miscue analysis (Miller & Woodley, 1983; Marek, 1989).

By the upper elementary grades, some students will be naturally good spellers, while others have to work harder at it; this is true for many adults as well, who are often critical of themselves for being such poor spellers and avoid writing when possible. A teacher working on spelling with older learners can probably help them most by focusing on strategies. There may be some inborn natural spelling ability that can't be learned, the kind of visual awareness that makes misspelled words leap out at you from a menu, but anyone can learn to flag possible misspellings in one's own writing and use appropriate resources to correct them. Remember the former student of mine, mentioned in Chapter 5, who wanted to write the word *upholstery,* looked for it in the dictionary under *ap-,* and then gave up and used another word instead. It would have been tremendously helpful if a teacher at some point in her educational career had helped her to develop a range of strategies to use in situations like this. Two obvious ones are to look in the dictionary under *ep-, ip-,* and so on or, even simpler, to look up the definition for *sofa,* which is bound to include some variant of *upholstery.*

Roberto: ESL and spelling

Although teachers may be concerned that ESL students will have particular difficulties with spelling, they usually won't need any special help; their spelling in English will benefit most from activities that will help to develop their English proficiency generally. The teacher's role is primarily (if she or he has the neces-sary knowledge) to notice invented spellings that reflect the pronunciation and/ or spelling system of the child's first language and keep an eye out to see if there are any persistent problems. The following invented spellings occurred in one piece by Roberto, a Hispanic fifth grader: CAINE for *kind*; CHURT for *shot,* and BATROOM for *bathroom* (Figure 9–11).

Each of the spellings is at least potentially influenced by Spanish. CAINE is orthographic (the long *i* vowel in Spanish is typically spelled *ai,* as in *bailar,* meaning *dance*), while the consonant errors in CHURT and BATROOM are likely to be related to pronunciation: /sh/ and /th/ don't exist in Spanish, and in each case Roberto spelled appropriately a closely related sound that does occur in Spanish. Although such spelling patterns are likely to occur often in the writing of younger children since all young children spell phonetically, they become less consistent over time. Roberto's piece also contained appropriate spellings of all three of the problematic sounds (e.g., *white, pushed,* and *with* were spelled correctly). The task of the ESL student in learning to spell in English is not essentially different from that of native speakers of English; phonetic

FIGURE 9–11   *Roberto: ESL Spelling*

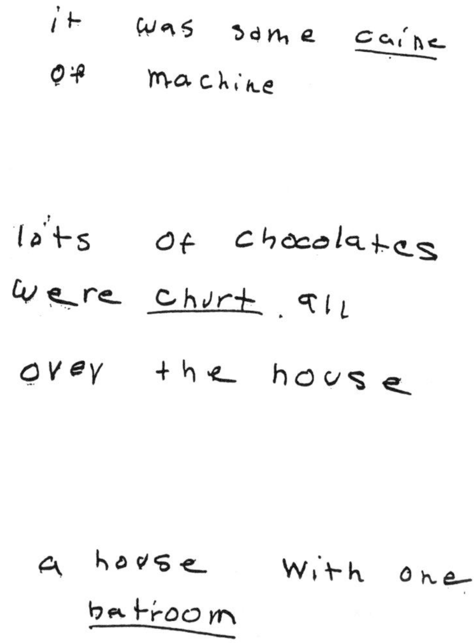

it   was   some   caine
of   machine

lots   of   chocolates
were   churt . all

over   the   house

a   house   with   one
batroom

spellings and predictions based on orthographic rules must be supplemented by an awareness of how arbitrary spelling can be and by knowledge of how to spell many individual words. The major difference is that the child is working to integrate the phonetic and spelling systems of more than one language. Although they will mutually influence each other for a time, the end result is a highly positive one: someone who is literate in two languages.[3]

Some general advice

In working with children needing extra help in spelling, it's important to remember that their developmental profile is likely to be different from that of other children their age, and that instruction should be geared to development rather than age or grade level. As discussed in Chapter 5, what beginning spellers need most is opportunities to explore the writing system, a base that is later supplemented by more instructionally focused examination of spelling patterns and later still by strategy refinement with a focus on proofreading. A sixth grader who's inhibited as a writer because of insecurity about spelling isn't ready to think about perfect final drafts yet. Spellers who aren't doing well need to follow at least generally the same developmental process as other children, even if it comes at a later age. In many cases, the emotions associated with years of what the child may see as failure make developmental appropriateness even more necessary; a child who freezes up and refuses to write if it seems that people

---

[3] Recent evidence (Jimenez, forthcoming) suggests that bilingual students indeed develop an awareness that they are learning two different writing systems, in which some features are alike and others are not.

Spelling Celebration

The complexity of invented spellings

Three different children: "EAT (*ate*)"

Gordon, fourth grade: "Don't WEREY (*worry*). God will give you power."

These two spellings reveal how complex any single invented spelling can be and how many levels can be operating at once. Although EAT may not seem like a very reasonable spelling for *ate*. since it is not obviously phonetically logical the way that AIT would be, it is understandable on several levels. First of all, *ea* is used in a few other words (such as *great*) to represent long a before *t*. Second, the spelling contains all of the right letters; only their order is wrong. Finally, *eat* and *ate* are of course two forms of the same verb. The spelling therefore has three possible explanations. In the case of WEREY, both the *o* and the double *r* in *worry* are not obvious spellings. Vowel spellings after *w* tend to be a little different than elsewhere, and double *r*'s signal very subtle vowel shifts that don't occur in all dialects. This explains why the word is hard to spell, but why this particular spelling? My hunch is that Gordon wrote the word *were*, then added the ending. Because so much is going on at once, rather than trying to put any single invented spelling into a particular category, we may be better off trying to discover how many *different* possible explanations we can think of!

might criticize her spelling may not even be amenable to a mini-lesson on spelling patterns, and it might be enough for the time being just to get her writing more freely.

It isn't, therefore, appropriate to focus instruction on how children *should* be spelling at whatever age they are, and it also doesn't seem valuable to put a lot of energy into diagnosing a so-called spelling stage (Henderson, 1981) to base instruction on. Although developmental changes in types of spelling definitely exist so that a child's spelling of *beat* may change over time from B to BT to BET to BETE, a representative sample of any one child's writing at one point in time is likely to show a variety of patterns. For instance, although Gordon's Grand Canyon story (Figure 9–1) includes some relatively immature spellings (e.g., HELLS/hills, ELXEBED/exploded), he also shows higher level awareness in features like the WH of WHETH (with) and a silent final *e* in CLMEING (climbing), as well as many correctly spelled words. One-to-one work focusing on self-confidence, strategies, and exploration growing out of the patterns actually seen in children's writing rather than a structured program based on assigning children to a spelling stage is likely to be the most valuable type of instruction for those having trouble with spelling.

How can I document children's knowledge about spelling?

Teachers may very well feel that their professional sense of children's spelling knowledge and growth should be supplemented with written documentation,

36 Spelling Celebration

Permutations

Elaine, fourth grade: "We AET (*ate*) some POPCONR (*popcorn*)."

Sometimes writers will produce a spelling that seems more visual than phonetic: one which has all the right letters but in the wrong order. I call these permutations. In my study of six elementary school children (Wilde, 1986/1987), 8 percent of *all* their invented spellings were permutations. Producing a permutation is likely to involve a fair amount of knowledge about a word's spelling; for instance, a child who spells *clothes* as COLTHES is probably more familiar with the word than a child who spells it phonetically as KLOZ. An interesting historical comparison: Masters (1927) listed 221 invented spellings of *pneumonia* written by students from eighth grade through college age. Eighteen of the spellings (8 percent) were permutations. Many of the typographical errors that touch typists make are permutations; some permutations of handwritten words may even be "typos of the pencil" of words that the writer knows how to spell.

especially if they no longer have a weekly record of spelling test scores. There are a variety of materials one can collect that preserve various types of evidence about spelling. Teachers won't want to save all of these for all children; one's choices will depend on how much concern one has about spelling (for a class as a whole and for individual children), expectations of parents and administrators, and the amount of time available. Some of the options include

1. *Writing samples and related data*
   a. Samples of first drafts (to indicate children's "natural" level of proficiency)
   b. Samples of final drafts (before any final editing is done by the teacher, to indicate children's proficiency at proofreading)
   c. A record of percentages of correctly spelled words in first- and/or final-draft pieces (to show general growth trends, although the percentage of correct spelling can vary widely from one piece to the next: Y. Goodman,1984)
   d. Redictation to a child of a piece written months earlier, with "before" and "after" spellings compared
   e. Coding of children's invented spellings over time to determine their general level of sophistication as spellers (Wilde, 1989a, is a detailed exploration of such a coding system. Since it's not amenable to a quick summary, readers who are interested in using it should refer to the original article.)

37 Spelling Celebration

The importance of spelling

Elaine, fourth grade: It's important to be a good speller because "they're going to ask you to spell something when you go to high school . . . and you're not going to know what it is and they're going to get mad."

Gordon, fourth grade: It's important to be a good speller because if you are "police ladies or men you have to write nice so they can understand."

If you were to ask a cross section of adults why spelling is important, their answers would probably fall into two categories exemplified by Elaine's and Gordon's reactions. Some would see spelling as primarily a matter of etiquette in the low-level sense of minding your p's and q's; correct spelling is something you do to make a good impression, to stay out of trouble, so that people won't think you're ignorant. (Elaine also said that even adults need to be good spellers because otherwise "everybody's going to think that you don't go to school . . . and your mother doesn't care.") By contrast, other people, like Gordon, think of correct spelling as primarily a communication tool, a courtesy to others, etiquette in the higher-level Golden Rule sense. Which attitude would we rather have our students hold? Through interviewing children, we can discover what beliefs they hold about the importance of spelling. Through communicating our own attitudes, we can influence those beliefs.

---

2. *Word lists* (to be compiled as running lists by the children themselves)
   a. Words students already know how to spell
   b. New words learned each week
   c. Words students would like to learn in the future
3. *Written self-evaluation*

   Children can write periodically on topics like, "What I know about spelling," "What I learned in today's spelling mini-lesson," "What I do when I don't know how to spell a word." These can be repeated periodically and compared over time.

Many of these kinds of data can be collected easily as part of the regular curriculum and analyzed only if necessary. As mentioned earlier, for most children, when parents ask, Is my child improving in spelling? showing them writing samples a few months apart will be adequate documentation. A cumulative list of words the child knows how to spell can also be impressive. For children whose growth is less obvious, it might be necessary to go back over writing samples and count up percentages of correct spelling, as well as coding invented spellings, in order to find out if there is growth, either quantitative or qualitative, that is occurring but is too subtle to see directly.

TABLE 9–1
Spelling Interview

	Spelling Concepts and Attitudes
1	Is spelling important? Why?
2	How do you feel about spelling? Do you like trying to figure out how to spell words?
3	When is it important to spell correctly?
4	Who's a good speller that you know? What makes him/her a good speller? Does he/she ever make a spelling mistake?
5	How do people learn how to spell? How did you learn how to spell? Are you still learning?
6	Why do you think words are spelled the way they are?
	Spelling Strategies
7	What do you do when you don't know how to spell a word?
8	What else could you do?
9	Where in the classroom would you look if you wanted to find how to spell a word?
10	If you were at home, where would you look?
11	How do you know when you've spelled something right?
12	What do you do when you haven't spelled something right?
	Questions about Specific Spellings
13	How did you figure out how to spell this word?
14	Why did you change this spelling?
15	Pick out some words that you think are spelled wrong. Tell/show me how you could change them to the right spelling.

Can talking with children help one evaluate their spelling?

Talking with children about spelling can provide some interesting insights. I've developed an interview format (Table 9–1) that can be used to get children discussing their thoughts about how spelling works and how they spell, as well as their feelings about spelling. These questions can be used in a variety of ways. The class could be asked to write responses to one of the questions, perhaps preceded by a group discussion to stimulate thinking. The teacher could choose a question to discuss individually with each child during one week's writing conferences. For children who are struggling with spelling, the teacher might want to make the time for a more in-depth one-on-one interview, using the questions as the basis for an extended discussion about spelling concepts and strategies. When the questions are used orally with individual children, the

TABLE 9–2
Lacey's Interview

1	R	What do you do when you're writing and you don't know how to spell a word?
2	L	Sound it out.
3	R	Okay. What else, what else could you do?
4	L	I don't know.
5	R	Could you ask somebody to help you?
6	L	Yeah, I have some people.
7	R	If you were in your classroom and you wanted to figure out how to spell a word, where could you look?
8	L	On something
9	R	Okay, for instance?
10	L	I even sound it out.
11	R	Where's something you could look on?
12	L	In the piece of paper.
13	R	Okay, and what kind of piece of paper might you find a word on that you wanted to spell?
14	L	Typed.
15	R	A typed paper? Okay.
16	L	A wrote paper, a piece of paper that someone wrote already.
17	R	Oh, a piece of paper that somebody's [written] already?
18	L	Um hm, and typewriter.
19	R	Okay, and maybe they wrote it on a typewriter?
20	L	Yeah.
21	R	Okay, where else in your classroom could you look?
22	L	I don't know.
23	R	You don't know huh? If you were at home and wanted to know how to spell a word, where would you look?
24	L	I don't know.

discussion itself is of value instructionally and the teacher may also want to take notes and perhaps even make an audio or video recording in order to use the child's answers evaluatively.

Interviews can be very revealing of both differences between children and differences across time. Tables 9–2 and 9–3 show two children, Lacey and Mike

TABLE 9–3
Mike's Interview

1	R	What do you do when you're writing and you don't know how to spell a word?
2	M	Sound it out.
3	R	What else could you do?
4	M	Write it down the way you first had thought? What I usually do is write it down the way it came off the top of my head, then look it over and I correct it if it's spelled incorrectly.
5	R	Anything else you could do?
6	M	Well you could, you could always just think of the word. If you've already written it once, you could then go back and think of it since you memorized it and just write it down that way.
7	R	If you were in your classroom and you were doing some writing, where could you look if you wanted to find out how to spell a word?
8	M	The dictionary.
9	R	Okay, where else?
10	M	You could ask somebody.
11	R	Anywhere else you could look so you wouldn't have to ask a person?
12	M	Well, the dictionary last year, well they were all used up and so I went by the teacher's file and looked in it.
13	R	Oh okay, you sure were sneaky.
14	M	It was on the top of the desk anyways and it fell off, so I picked it up and glanced at it, but I realized it was what I was looking for.

(both second graders), responding to question #7, What do you do when you don't know how to spell a word? Lacey, who was not a very confident speller at the time, responded mainly by saying that she sounds words out (lines 2 & 10) or that she doesn't know (lines 4, 22, & 24). Most of her other answers were just agreement with the researcher's prompts. Mike, by contrast, also began with the conventional "sound it out," but then spontaneously mentioned using his knowledge of words to generate, monitor, and revise spellings (lines 4 & 6), and using resources, both the usual ones of the dictionary and other people (lines 8 & 10) and "living off the land" by spotting spellings in chance encounters with print (lines 12–14).

Gordon's response to the same question across four interviews in third and fourth grade (Table 9–4) shows a single learner changing in his use of strategies over time. In the first interview, he mentioned only the classic "sound it out," and in the second one expressed an awareness of internalized knowledge about spelling. In the third interview, he seemed to be thinking of specific episodes of using outside resources to find spellings, while by the fourth, he had a clearly defined set of strategies that he could state succinctly. Although any single inter-

TABLE 9–4
Interviews with Gordon

Question — How do you spell a word you don't know?
Interview #1 — Fall of third grade   G: I just sound it out.   R: Okay.   G: Sound it out then I see if I'm right.
Interview #2 — Spring of third grade   G: I just write it how I think it is.
Interview #3 — Fall of fourth grade   G: Sound it out.   R: Okay.   G: Or look it up in the dictionary.   R: Okay, anything else?   G: You can look in, look, if you have some, look in your desk and see if you spelled it already.   R: Okay, anything else?   G: Like if you have some, if you have it, like when you're writing up there like letters.   R: Oh, you mean if like Sister Susan has a thing on the wall with words. Yeah, that's somewhere else you can look. What else?   G: Ask somebody.   R: Okay, who might you ask?   G: Like, Anna or David.   R: Okay, do you ever ask a grown-up?   G: Yeah, sometimes when I used to write stories at my house, I used to ask my mother and my sister and my other sister.
Interview #4 — Spring of fourth grade   G: Look in the dictionary.   R: Oh, okay. what else?   G: Figure it out.   R: Okay, what else?   G: Sound it out.   R: Okay. What else?   G: Write on a piece of paper, then practice, then learn.   R: Like see if it looks right?   G: (nods)

view reflects the child's mood on that day and what is uppermost in his or her mind rather than being a definitive statement about the underlying knowledge base, interviews can certainly be combined with other information to provide a fuller picture of children's beliefs and feelings.

How can I assign grades for spelling?

Ken Goodman (personal communication, 1990) has said that giving a report card grade for spelling is like giving a separate grade for multiplication; it's a very small part of the larger writing process that's often blown up into something much bigger than it should be. But even if we believe a grade for spelling really shouldn't have to appear on report cards and know many teachers who are trying to change this in their own districts, it's still true that teachers don't always have the freedom to opt out of giving grades for spelling. Before suggesting some ways to meet this requirement honorably, we need to think about the purpose and practice of grading in general.

Three grading systems

There are three major ways to give grades to students; each one reflects a different philosophy of what grades are meant to do and be. The first of these is norm-referenced grading, often practiced and known colloquially as "grading on a curve." In such a system, learners are compared to each other; the average learner (as defined by a test score) is given an average grade and those with higher and lower scores get corresponding grades. In the purest form of a norm-referenced system, it doesn't matter what the actual average score is; a student scoring 70 percent on a test could still get an A if it was the highest score in the class. Also, in its purest form every A would be balanced out by an F. This form of grading is rarely used in elementary schools and only occasionally elsewhere. The second type of grading system is known as criterion-referenced; one's grade depends on how well one has mastered (again, as defined by a test score) a particular body of knowledge. If all students received high enough raw scores on a test, they would all receive A's. Criterion-referenced grading, in one form or another, is the most common method used in North American schools. A third model of grading doesn't, so far as I know, have a formal name; I'll refer to it as self-referenced grading. Under such a system, students receive grades based on how much they have learned, grown, or participated. Under such a system, a variety of students could all receive A's even though they had achieved differently since each student would have individual goals, rather than being compared to classmates or an external standard. Although my personal preference would be not to use grades at all in elementary school, I'd like to make a case for self-referenced grading in spelling and, by implication, throughout the curriculum.

My greatest concern about grading in elementary school is fairness; as we all know, children have different abilities and grow at different rates, in every area. Children also differ in the amount of commitment and effort they apply to learning. Grades can ultimately be based on natural ability, effort, or some combination of the two. Most teachers reject grading on a curve as largely unfair since effort can so easily go unrewarded. No matter how hard you study for a test, if other people study harder, you can end up with a poor grade. At first glance, criterion-referenced grading seems more equitable, yet in many ways it rewards pre-existing knowledge rather than effort, particularly in an area like spelling where children learn so much outside of formal curriculum and instruction. Consider a typical spelling book unit. On any pretest of 20 words, a large number of students in a class will know how to spell 10 to 15 or so of the words, a few will know all of them, and several students will know less than half, perhaps far less. Therefore, to get the same grade on the Friday spelling test (the one that counts), some students won't have to work at all, others will need to put forth

38 Spelling Celebration

Real word spellings

Anna, third grade: "Then he *TAKE* (*took*) HEM (*him*) there."
　　Rachel, third grade: I COLD (*could*) *SING* (*swing*) in the air."
　　Anna, third grade: "His *CAME* (*captain*) said, 'You are FRID (*fired*).'"

Often writers will come up with invented spellings that are real words. Some of them are easier to explain than others. Anna (with TAKE) used another tense of the word she had intended, and Rachel just left out a letter. But why would a writer produce CAME instead of *captain*? I have a few hunches as to what might be going on. These spellings might be the result of using common spelling patterns to create something that at least looks like a word, even if it's not the right one. They might be slips of the pen, produced below the level of conscious awareness, for words that writers know how to spell or could spell if they tried. Most adults have had the experience of writing quickly and coming up with the wrong word occasionally, only catching it when they proof-read. I think that real words, even if they're pretty far off the mark, are a high-level type of invented spelling since they at least show a concern for words' looking right. CAME for *captain* at least doesn't jar the eye the way a spelling like BEFXITST for *breakfast* does.

---

some effort, and others will work hard to learn perhaps more than they can manage. Some students are being sent a message that they don't need to put forth any effort to get A's, while others find that their efforts go unrewarded. Since learning to spell is a developmental process that's only somewhat within the individual's control, I feel that giving criterion-referenced grades through spelling tests is comparable to giving students grades based on how many inches they've grown in the past year; in practice, criterion-referenced tests in an area like spelling end up being norm-referenced tests in disguise. On the other hand, self-referenced grading for spelling is a fair system in which all students are capable of earning good grades and where no student can receive a good grade without working at it.

Writing, learning words, and spelling grades

The ultimate goal of spelling curriculum is, simply stated, for students to be able to produce written texts with appropriate spelling. It would seem, then, that grading should reflect this. I think that an appropriate way to determine spelling grades is to evaluate a number of students' final drafts or published pieces for spelling each marking period. (This, of course, assumes a classroom where regular writing takes place.) For older and more proficient students, the goal would be near-perfect spelling, while younger or less developmentally advanced students might merely be asked to show evidence that they had corrected a certain number of spellings from earlier drafts. If a student is able to produce a polished final draft that has been appropriately proofread and edited, using all the resources available, then certainly he or she deserves a good grade in spelling. The level of performance expected may, in the interests of fairness, vary from student to student, but the major focus is the same for everyone. Although in the upper elementary grades a perfectly spelled final draft may be quite effortless for some students, resulting in an "easy A" in spelling, at least everyone can agree that the grading criterion makes sense in terms of the real-life importance of spelling. If teachers feel it's important to have a spelling grade that at least partially reflects the learning of individual words, this is also easy enough to do in a fair way. If students are working individually on learning about five words a week (see Chapter 5), then they can be given a grade on their five-word, Friday test.

Strangely enough, the biggest objection to such a grading system might be that students' grades will be too good! It is, of course, necessary to explain to parents and administrators that a student's A in spelling in your class may not mean the same as an A from last year's or next year's teacher, but certainly a system where all students need to put forth effort to earn good grades, and succeed in doing so, has much to recommend it. The fact that expectations vary from student to student may be disturbing to some, but if grades are to be used at all, shouldn't they send a message that involvement in learning will be rewarded, rather than perpetuating differential recognition based on pre-existing variation in ability?

How will my students do on standardized tests?

A recent report by the National Commission on Testing and Public Policy (National Commission on Testing and Public Policy, 1990) has called for a major rethinking of the way standardized tests are used in the United States. One of this group's major criticisms of current practice is that the overemphasis on testing has led to a concern for high test scores that often drives the curriculum. In this discussion of standardized tests for spelling and punctuation, my major concern is not to suggest how students can be guaranteed to do well on such tests but rather to examine the premises and implications of the tests, with due consideration for the reality of teachers who may be feeling pressured about test scores.

What do standardized tests measure?

One of the underlying challenges in producing a standardized test that can evaluate large groups of learners in an easily scored format is to find a simple, direct way of measuring knowledge in an uncomplicated format. In the case of spelling and punctuation, the complex knowledge that we are trying to assess is whether students can produce written text that's correctly spelled and punctuated. But this cannot be measured directly in an easily scored (i.e., multiple-choice) format, so a supposedly related task is used instead.[4] For spelling, this

---

[4] The National Assessment of Educational Progress studies of student writing *have* examined spelling and punctuation directly in the context of writing (Applebee, Langer, & Mullis, 1987), but those tests, actually directed writing samples, are used with only a small sample of students to examine national trends and are far too time consuming to score to be used as a replacement for the usual standardized tests.

usually involves picking the one correctly (or incorrectly) spelled word in a group of four, while for punctuation, students are asked to flag and sometimes correct punctuation errors in sample sentences.

What's really being measured here? In the case of spelling, it would seem that a high score on such a task would reflect one's general visual awareness of spelling, which varies from one individual to another, as well as the particular words one has happened to learn, which is largely developmental. Since the misspellings on the tests are usually logical ones, one can't even say that knowledge of spelling rules and patterns is being measured, let alone the ability to spell appropriately when writing with dictionaries and other resources available. Although students will usually do better on these tests as they mature and become better spellers, this doesn't mean that low test scores show that they're not good spellers for their age. The link between what's supposedly being measured and the form the test takes is just too tenuous.[5] A similar argument can be made for punctuation. So I think that in one sense the appropriate answer to, How will my students do on standardized tests? is Does it matter? The forms of classroom-based evaluation discussed earlier give a complex, multi-dimensional picture of knowledge and development. Can a single, standardized, multiple-choice test add anything to this, other than a sense of students' ability to handle artificial test formats? If a test score contradicts the teacher's knowledge about a student, which measure is the more reliable and which should be discounted? The answer should be obvious.

How does testing distort instruction?

Many critics have spoken of how concern for test scores has distorted the goals and processes of education. The National Commission on Testing and Public Policy (1990) has stated that

> important rewards and sanctions directly linked to test results, efforts to align curricula with the tests, and direct teaching to the tests exist in virtually all the states. . . . The pressure to improve test scores has trickled down to kindergarten and first grade. Many early childhood programs and teachers emphasize rote academic learning at the expense of exploratory play and social learning. In the upper grades the pressure to show improved reading and math scores tends to turn teaching in these critical subjects into test preparation. For example, instead of reading books, students in many classrooms read isolated paragraphs and practice answering multiple-choice questions about them. (p. 19)

The proofreading exercises in spelling textbooks, like those on standardized tests, ask students to flag artificially misspelled words, rather than finding the invented spellings in their own writing. In some cases, textbooks even state that

---

[5] Although there appears to be evidence that these multiple-choice spelling tests measure the same knowledge as a dictated list of words (reported in Iowa Tests of Basic Skills, 1956, pp. 59–60), this is still more a measure of development than of knowledge directly acquired in school, and still differs from the ability to produce a correctly spelled final draft of one's own writing.

they're providing practice in the kinds of exercises students are likely to find on standardized tests, and will give students sets of four words, rather than paragraphs, to proofread, which follows the exact format of the tests.

What's wrong with these practices? In one sense, there's a legitimate case to be made for giving students enough familiarity with how standardized tests are set up that they won't receive low scores just because they don't understand what to do. But this could be accomplished with a brief mini-lesson shortly before the test. The problem comes when the curriculum starts being geared to the test. If such tests are to have any legitimacy, it's as an impartial measure of students' success in an independently established curriculum. Anyone who knows something about curriculum development realizes that standardized tests were never meant to determine curriculum goals. When students are given regular textbook proofreading exercises, rather than proofreading their own writing, or spend time learning words or rules because they might be on the test, they're wasting time, distorting the validity of the tests, or both. In the case of proofreading artificial spelling and punctuation errors, there's a further danger, discussed earlier in relation to spelling textbooks (Chapter 5). The more misspelled words one sees in print, the more likely one is to confuse them with the correct spellings. Since much of our spelling system is arbitrary as well as rule-governed, much of spelling knowledge has to come from remembering which of several reasonable spellings of a word is correct; this knowledge grows out of seeing words, particularly in books, correctly spelled. Children seeing a steady diet[6] of misspelled words in print (particularly in classrooms where they don't read much) are likely to become confused, mainly on an unconscious level, about the correct spelling of many of those words. This is a case where an instructional activity whose sole purpose is improving test scores, since it's only tangentially related to improving one's own writing, may well be counter productive of the presumed underlying goal of improving spelling itself.

What should teachers do about standardized tests in spelling and punctuation?

Standardized tests are at the present time an unfortunate fact of life in North American, particularly United States, schools. I think there are two ethically sound ways that whole-language teachers might choose to deal with them.

1. Generally ignore them.

A teacher holding this approach to standardized tests might say something like the following:

> I've planned a sound, meaningful curriculum in spelling and punctu-
> ation for my students, and I know from my own evaluative measures
> that they're growing and progressing in ways that are appropriate for
> each individual. If there's a standardized test that will confirm what
> I already know about my students, fine. If my students

---

[6] I'm suggesting that this particular problem arises from regular exercises where misspelled words are provided, not from seeing such words once a year on a test.

don't do well on standardized tests, this doesn't invalidate what I already know, and I would challenge the ability of a single, imperfect measure to provide more information than I can about children that I work with every day. If these tests have any validity at all, it's as a neutral measure of what I'm already doing; therefore, I won't attempt to inflate or distort my students' scores through any teaching to the test beyond a brief, general familiarization with test formats.

Although this approach takes a certain amount of courage, it is both intellectually and morally honest. Since principals and parents may see test scores as potential warning flags of teacher incompetence, whole-language teachers must be prepared to offer alternative evidence of program quality and student growth if test scores are low (relative, of course, to previous scores of the same students).

2. Fight to change them.

Although demands for more standardized tests continue to flourish, a counter-movement has been gathering force. For teachers who are interested in becoming more actively involved in this issue, the report of the National Commission on Testing and Public Policy (1990) is a good place to start.[7] Teachers and parents have formed lobbying groups to pressure for changes in testing policy. The *Whole Language Catalog* (Goodman, Bird, & Goodman, 1991, pp. 264–270, 273) describes some of these efforts, as well as discussing testing issues generally. Within one's own school, teachers can talk with colleagues and parents about testing concerns. Test scores are often used to pit teachers against each other, but this need not be the case. Teachers can work together to challenge a system that's harmful to their professionalism and to students.

How can I best communicate with parents and administrators about spelling?

Teachers have a responsibility to help their students' parents, as well as principals and other administrators, understand what is going on in their classrooms. In addition, although many parents and principals are supportive of curriculum innovation, some are not, and teachers may need to spend extra time and effort talking to them. In addition to some samples of general types of letters to send to parents informing them about invented spelling and a curriculum that grows out of it (Appendix B), I'll provide answers here to some typical, specific questions that might be asked by parents and principals. It might be helpful to keep in mind that when parents and administrators challenge a teacher's curriculum, what they might really be asking is (a) Are the children learning anything? and (b) Is this teacher competent? Responses that work at providing reassurance about these underlying questions can be helpful.

---

[7] This document can be ordered for $6.00 from the National Commission on Testing and Public Policy, McGuinn 529, Boston College, Chestnut Hill, MA 02167.

39 Spelling Celebration

The importance of observation

Gordon, fourth grade: "For the hole YAER (*year*) I was good . . ." (in a story about Santa Claus)

    In determining why Gordon reversed the vowel letters in *year*, we could consider a number of possibilities. First, we could begin by realizing that *r*-controlled vowels are tricky. Second, maybe *-er* looked better to Gordon at the end of a word than *-ar* would have. Third, those with a proclivity for neurological explanations might suggest that Gordon had a reversal problem. When we look at invented spellings, really all we can do is speculate, as we think about how English spelling works and look for patterns in any particular writer's work. If we observe and talk to children as they write, we often get a much more precise answer as to why a particular spelling was produced. As Gordon began to write *year*, first he wrote YER, changed it to YREN, erased that spelling, found the word in the dictionary, and transposed the two vowel letters as he copied it from the dictionary. Need I say more?

Why should kids be allowed to make mistakes in spelling? Won't they learn bad habits?

Learning and growth can't take place *without* making mistakes, and errors should be welcomed as signs of growth (Weaver, 1982). If infants were prevented from walking until they could do so without falling down, they'd never learn. In the area of language, parents can easily remember how imperfect their children's early attempts at speech were. Sometimes learners even seem to regress. A child might use the word *went*, then switch to *goed* for a while; this merely shows that she has learned something about how we put words in the past tense. Just as children outgrow less mature forms in their speech, they outgrow their early invented spellings. There has been a good deal of research over the years (see Henderson, 1981, for a summary of some of it) showing that spelling matures as children grow older and that particular invented spellings are, like baby talk, a stage that children pass through. Older children and even adults may consistently produce the same misspellings for particular words, but this is a different issue, a small, isolated problem that's easily corrected with some directed attention to the words involved. A good way for parents to monitor the change that occurs is to take a story written several months earlier by one's child and dictate the whole story, or several of the words spelled inventively in it, back to him to see how his spellings have changed over time. Even words that aren't correctly spelled yet are likely to have different, and perhaps more sophisticated, invented spellings.

Invented spelling may be fine for first drafts, but shouldn't kids eventually have to correct their spellings, at least on work that's going to go home or be displayed in the halls?

It depends. First of all, nobody proofreads *everything* they write; if a piece of writing isn't going to have a wide or long-term audience (e.g., shopping lists, diaries, notes on the refrigerator, unsent letters), there's no need to try to get them perfect, and few adults do so, unless they correct all misspellings almost by reflex. If children are spelling well already (85–90 percent or better), then it *is* appropriate to aim for 100% correctness in a polished, finished product, mainly because it's part of the pride of authorship to clean up such easily corrected imperfections. But for less accomplished writers, it should be acceptable, as mentioned in Chapter 5, to publish or display work that still has invented spellings, although some proofreading should still be a part of the process. (A typed version placed alongside the child's own writing can be used to assist the reader.) A principal who is unwilling to allow this is placing public relations above developmentally appropriate instruction; parents should be educated rather than pacified on this issue.

Why aren't you using the spelling books, written by experts, that the school district paid good money for?

The discussion in Chapter 5 of spelling books provides part of the answer to this question. But perhaps the most important point to emphasize is that textbooks provide a curriculum that is relatively impoverished in comparison to what a good teacher can do. At most, a spelling book helps students learn about five words a week that they didn't already know, as well as providing some awareness of spelling patterns, and it takes at least 15 minutes a day to do this. The curriculum described in Chapters 5 and 6 does all of this and much more (e.g., gearing word lists to the individual, developing strategies, providing interactive, exploratory lessons on spelling patterns) in a more interesting way, more efficiently, and without busywork. If a principal is insistent that the spelling book must be "covered," it may be useful to match up your own curriculum with the goals and objectives of the textbook and show how they're being met in a more active way. It's important to remember that textbooks are designed not as an ideal curriculum but as a least common denominator; they're planned so that they can be used by teachers with no writing curriculum as a context for spelling and punctuation, with children whom the textbook authors have never met.

Some final remarks

I'd like to conclude with some statements from children, taken from interviews, about spelling.

> Researcher: Can you think of anything else you would like to say about spelling?
> Alison: It's fun.

> Researcher: How do you feel about spelling? Do you like trying to figure out how to spell words?
> Mike: Well, I have most words that we have been working on down, but a couple of them, I like figuring them out and if they're wrong I just go look over them and if for some reason it looks wrong, I just go over it and try to get it the correct way.

Researcher: If you were to write the word *the,* would you know if you spelled it right?
Lacey: Yeah.
Researcher: How would you know?
Lacey: Because I already know how to spell it. I knew how to spell it when I was in kindergarten.

Researcher: How do people learn how to spell?
Sally: They go to school and then the teachers tell them and like you'll read books and you'll see them over a million times and you'll finally, the teacher will call you up to the board and then they'll totally know the word.

These children, from a whole language classroom, think of themselves as competent, active spellers who find the process of learning to spell to be interesting and fun. Let's hope that as teachers we can nourish and support such knowledge and attitudes in all students!

APPENDIX A

Symbols for Phonemes Used in This Book

Consonants		Vowels		
Symbol	Example	Type	Symbol	Example
b	buy	short	ă	had
ch	chew		ĕ	head
d	die		ĭ	hid
f	fee		ŏ	hot
g	guy		ŭ	hut
h	he	long	ā	hate
j	joy		ē	heed
k	key		ī	hide
l	lie		ō	hope
m	my		ū	huge
n	nigh	other	ŏŏ	hood
ng	sing		ōō	hoop
p	pie		ou	house
r	rye		oi	hoist
s	sigh		aw	hawk
sh	shy	schwa	ə	about
t	tie			
th	thigh			
TH	thy			
v	vie			
w	we			
y	ye			
z	zoo			
zh	azure			

APPENDIX B

Sample Letters to Parents About Spelling

For beginning writers (usually kindergarten and first-grade classrooms)

Dear Parents,

I'm writing to tell you a little about how I'll be helping your child to learn about spelling this year, and how this fits into our writing program.

You may have been surprised when your child came home from the first day of school this year saying that she'd written a story already, since you probably thought it would take a while before she'd know how to write. One of the exciting new areas that's been developing in early childhood education in the last several years is "invented spelling" (also known as developmental spelling). Researchers have discovered that when young children are encouraged to write words the way they sound, two exciting things happen: they're able to write independently at a much earlier age then we ever thought they could, and they also begin to figure out for themselves how words are spelled.

In the same way that children's speech makes more sense the older they get, invented spelling shows typical patterns of development over time. Some children are writing more than others when they enter school, because of differences in maturity, interest in language, and past experience. Children's writing may also show a blend of different kinds of invented spelling. You can watch for any or all of the following in your child:

1. Scribbling (lines and shapes but no real letters yet)
2. Letter strings (letters that aren't connected to sounds)
3. Letter-name spellings. Once children have learned the alphabet, they use the names of the letters to represent sounds. They might use the first letter only, just the consonants, or one letter for every sound, so that the word "like" could be spelled L, LK, or LIK.
4. More mature spellings (using 2 letters for long vowels, double consonants, more correct spellings, etc.)

As the year goes on, I'll keep you posted about what we're doing and about your child's writing development. I'd enjoy hearing from you about any spellings you think are interesting or can't figure out, as well as any interesting comments your child makes about spelling. You can be of tremendous help as your child grows as a writer and speller. Encouraging (but not requiring) her to write in a wide variety of situations (shopping lists, letters, stories, etc.) is the most important thing you can do. If she asks you how to spell a word, I'd suggest that rather than telling her, you ask her to figure it out for herself, with or without your help. You might enjoy saving writing samples throughout the year so that you can watch your child's growth.

In the past, some of my students' parents have been very concerned about the idea of invented spelling, since they know how important it is in our society to be a good speller. I want to make sure you realize that invented spelling isn't something children do *instead of* learning how to spell; it's an *avenue* to learning how to spell that carries the important advantage of allowing children to be writers from the very first day of school.

Please call or drop by if you have any questions.

Sincerely yours,

For developing spellers (roughly second through fourth grade)

Dear Parents,

I'd like to tell you a little about how our spelling program is working out this year. I'm focusing on 4 main areas with the class:

1. Reading and writing

   As you know, your child is doing a lot of reading and writing in school this year. One of the side benefits of this is for spelling; just like children can't learn to speak without hearing and using language every day, reading and writing are efficient and enjoyable ways to pick up both the meanings and spellings of many new words.

2. Learning words

   Rather than using a spelling textbook this year, I've asked each of my students to choose 5 words a week to learn. Although spelling books usually cover 20 words a week, children already know many of them, while my program helps children learn words that they don't already know but want to learn.

3. Learning about spelling patterns

   We have regular mini-lessons that help students discover and explore some common spelling patterns and rules in our language. They're then encouraged to be aware of these patterns in reading and writing. This is a more enriched, interactive replacement for many of the spelling book activities you may already be familiar with.

4. Spelling strategies

   This year, as my students get better at spelling, I'm encouraging them to proofread any writing that goes into a final draft (like a published book). As part of this, we've been talking a lot about how to use dictionaries, how to pick out your misspellings, when to trust your instincts that a spelling looks right, and so on.

One useful way you can support what we're doing is to expose your child to a lot of written words, particularly in informational books that relate to what we're doing in school. For instance, when we do our unit on plants and trees next month, you might look in your library or bookstore for reference books showing a large variety of trees, gardening books with a lot of pictures of flowers, and so on.

Please let me know if you have any questions or comments about our spelling program.

Sincerely yours,

For more mature spellers (upper elementary and above)

Dear Parents,

Although your child and the rest of my students are spelling well enough by now that we don't need much of a formal spelling program anymore, I'd like to let you know what we're doing to work towards the "100% correct" level that's so important for formal papers, job application letters, and so on.

As you probably know if you've ever misspelled a word and didn't realize it, proofreading can be tricky. Proofreading involves three processes:

1. Figuring out which words you didn't know the right spelling for;
2. Spotting misspellings, slips of the pen, and/or typos (since the eye often skips over them);
3. Determining the right spelling (through dictionaries and other strategies)

As part of our writing program this year, we're working on all 3 parts of this in the final editing process. For those students who are spelling at least 90% of words correctly in their first drafts, we're aiming for perfect final drafts of letters and published books, and all students are expected to do at least some proofreading for spelling.

You can also support this process at home, by helping your child edit rather than telling her how to spell words. I hope you're as excited as I am about all the writing your child is doing this year!

Sincerely,

APPENDIX C

Common Sound/Spelling Patterns[1]

Consonant Phonemes			
		Spellings	
Symbol	P[2]	Major	Minor
b	P	buy, robber	
ch		chew, watch	
d	P	die, madden	
f	P	fee, tiff	laugh, phone
g	P	guy, beggar	ghost, guide
h	P	he	who
j		joy, gene, badge	
k		key, cap, lock	quill, hiccup, chord
l	P	lie, wall	
m	P	my, hammer	comb, hymn
n	P	nigh, banner	knife, gnash
ng		sing, bank	
p	P	pie, happy	
r	P	rye, hurry	wrap
s		sigh, kiss, cent	scissors
sh		shy	notion
t	P	tie, button	
th	P	thigh	
TH	P	thy	
v	P	vie	
w	P	we, queen	
y		ye	
z		zoo, buzz, as	
zh		beige, usual	

continued on next page

Vowels			
		Spellings	
Type	Symbol	Major	Minor
short	ă	h<u>a</u>d	
	ĕ	b<u>e</u>t, h<u>ea</u>d	
	ĭ	h<u>i</u>d, g<u>y</u>m	
	ŏ	h<u>o</u>t, squ<u>a</u>d	
	ŭ	h<u>u</u>t, m<u>o</u>nth	
long[3]	ā	<u>a</u>corn, p<u>ai</u>n, m<u>ay</u>	r<u>ei</u>n, th<u>ey</u>, w<u>eigh</u>
	ē	b<u>e</u>, b<u>ee</u>, l<u>ea</u>k, happ<u>y</u>, pol<u>i</u>ce	ch<u>ie</u>f, c<u>ei</u>ling
	ī	<u>i</u>dol, m<u>y</u>, h<u>igh</u>	
	ō	g<u>o</u>, bl<u>ow</u>, t<u>oe</u>, s<u>oa</u>p	
	ū	m<u>u</u>sic, f<u>ew</u>, f<u>eu</u>d	
other	ŏŏ	h<u>oo</u>d, p<u>u</u>t	
	ōō	h<u>oo</u>p, t<u>u</u>na	d<u>o</u>, bl<u>ew</u>, c<u>ou</u>pon
	ou	h<u>ou</u>se, c<u>ow</u>	
	oi	h<u>oi</u>st, b<u>oy</u>	
	aw	r<u>aw</u>, f<u>au</u>n	l<u>o</u>ss, <u>a</u>ll, c<u>ou</u>gh
schwa	ə	any vowel letter or letters	
vowels before r[4]			

Notes

[1]The information in this table is based largely on Cummings (1988). *Major* spelling patterns are those defined as such by Cummings. *Minor* spelling patterns are those mentioned by Cummings that I see as useful for elementary school classrooms. Minor spelling patterns that are rare and/or occur mainly in more difficult words, such as the *c* for /ch/ found mainly in words of Italian origin like *cello*, haven't been included.

[2]Phonemes marked *P* are predictable enough that children will figure out how to spell them on their own, without formal instruction given appropriate experiences with written language.

[3]Many of the long and other vowel spellings also include variants with a silent final *e,*, such as the spelling *o–e* (as in bone) for long *o*.

[4]Vowels before *r* tend to be spelled like the regular vowels closest to them in pronunciation, with the exception of /ŭr/, which is spelled with more variation (h<u>e</u>r, s<u>i</u>r, w<u>o</u>rry, f<u>u</u>r), much like schwa.

APPENDIX D

Rule-Governed Spellings for Various Phonemes[1]

Phoneme	Spellings[2]	Rule
/ch/[3]	chew, watch	TCH appears at the ends of words after a single-letter short vowel spelling and CH elsewhere.
/j/	joy, gene, badge	J appears at the beginnings of words before a, o, and u, DG(E) appears at the ends of words after a single-letter short vowel spelling, and G appears elsewhere.
/k/	key, cap, lock, quill	Q appears before /w/, K appears before e and i, CK appears at the ends of words after a single-letter short vowel spelling, and C appears elsewhere.
/ng/	sing, bank	NG apears at the ends of words and N elsewhere (usually before k or g).
/s/	sigh, kiss cent	SS appears at the ends of words after a single-letter short vowel spelling, C appears frequently before e, i, and y, and S appears elsewhere.
/z/	zoo, buzz as	ZZ appears sometimes after a stressed short vowel (buzz, blizzard, dazzle), Z at the beginning of words, and S elsewhere.
/ā/	say	AY often appears at the ends of words
/ē/	slowly	Y often appears in suffixes
/ī/	fly	Y often appears at the end of words
/ū/	few	EW often appears at the ends of words
/ou/	house, cow	Each of these phonemes has one spelling at the ends of words or syllables (cow, boy, raw) and one (or more, in the case of /aw/) elsewhere (found, hoist, jaunt).
/oi/	hoist, boy	
/aw/	raw, faun	

---

[1]The information in this table has been derived from Cummings (1988).

[2]Only the spellings whose rules are described here are listed for each phoneme.

[3]/ch/, /j/, and /sh/ also have "palatalized" spellings, which exist because of historical changes in pronunciation. This can be seen in words like nature, gradual, and notion, which are related to native, grade, and note. Palatized spellings are probably too abstract to cover in elementary school other than as part of a general strategy of using a related word to help in spelling.

APPENDIX E

Students' open-ended spellings of mammal names
(A number appears next to spellings that occurred more than once, usually written by different children but sometimes including before and after spellings by the same child.)

AARDVARK
aardvark
addvark
adrverc
ardevarke
ardfark
ardvark (4)
ardvarke
ordvrk
rdvrk

ANT
ant

ANTEATER
anteetr

ANTELOPE
analope

APE
ape (2)
ayp

ARCTIC FOX
arctic fox

BABOON
baboo

BADGER
badger

BAT
bat (10)

BEAR
bare
bear (9)
ber
bera
borer

BEE
bee (2)

BIGHORN SHEEP
big horn sheep

BIRD
bird
brid (2)

BISON
bison

BUNNY
bune
bunny
buny

CALF
calf

CAMEL
camel (2)
caml

CARIBOU
caraboo

CAT
cat (25)

CATTLE
cattle

CHEETAH
ceto
cheatha
cheda
cheeda
cheeta (4)
cheetah
cheetasss

cheta
cheteh

CHIMPANZEE
chimp (2)
chimpazee
chimpanzee
cimp

CHIPMUNK
chipmunk (2)
cipmonk

COW
caw (2)
cow (6)
kaw

COYOTE
coyate

DEER
dear
deer (2)

DINOSAUR
dinosaur

DOG
dog (25)

DOLPHIN
dalfin
dalpfin
dolfin (4)
dolphan
dolphin (3)
doulfis

ELEPHANT
alufint (2)
elafint (3)

elaphant
elaphent
elefin
elephant (3)
elephent
elfent
elfot
elifint (2)

ELK
elk

FOX
fox (11)

FROG
frog

GERBIL
gerbal
gerble
jrbl

GIRAFFE
gerif
giraf
giraffe (5)
graf
grafe
graffe
jeraf
joraf
jraf
jrafe

GORILLA
goirlla
gorila (2)
gorilla (4)
gorrila
grila (3)

184
◆

grilo
groilla
gurilu

**GREAT HORN
SHEEP**
great horn sheep
grat hornd sheep

HARE
hare

**HIPPOPOT-
AMUS**
hipapadamiss
hipaponens
hipapotamas
hipo (4)
hipopotomus
hippo (4)
hippopotamus
(3)
hpo

HOG
hoog

HORSE
hore
hores
hors (3)
horse (5)
hours
hourse (2)

HUMAN
heumin
huemn
human
humen
humn
hyoms

HYENA
hyena

JACKAL
jakel

JACKASS
jack ass (2)
jackass

JAGUAR
jag weyr
jaguar (2)
jagur
jagure
jagwar
jagware
jagwire

KANGAROO
kagro
kanarar
kangara
kangaro
kangaroo (4)
kangroo
kangrow

KOALA BEAR
cwola bear
cwola
koala (2)
qolue

LAMB
lam

LEOPARD
leperd
leoperd

LION
lian (2)
lin (2)
line (4)
lion (9)
liyen
loin

LLAMA
lomaa
lomuh

MAN
man (4)
mane

MINK
mank
minks

MICE
mice (4)

MOLE
mole (2)

MONKEY
manke
mocee
moke
moky
monkey (4)
monky (3)
mucky

MOOSE
moese
moose (6)
mos
mose
mosse

**MOUNTAIN
GOAT**
mountaigoat

MOUSE
mouse (3)
mous

OCTOPUS
octopus
ogtpus

OPOSSUM
oposm

ORANGUTAN
orangatang

PANDA BEAR
panda (3)
panda bear
pandbera

PANTHER
panter
panther (5)

PENGUIN
panqen

PEOPLE
peopel (2)

people (2)
peple (3)
pipl
poepl

PIG
pig (12)

PLATYPUS
patpos
pladapews
pladapus
pladupus
platapus (2)
platopus
platrpoos
platupus

POLAR BEAR
polabear
poler bear
polerbare
polrbear
powler beir

PONY
boney
pony (2)

RABBIT
rabbit (4)
rabet
rabit (3)
rabt

RACOON
racon
racoon (2)

RAT
rat (17)

RHINOCEROS
rainosris
rhino (3)
rhinosaurus
rhinoserus
rhinosurrus
rinasaris
rino (3)
rinonosarus
rinosris

RODENT
roaden

SEA LION
sealian
sealion
sea lion (2)

SEA OTTER
odir
sea otter
seotra

SEAL
seal (5)
sel
sol

SHARK
shork

SHEEP
sheep (3)
shiep

SKUNK
skak
skunk (3)

SQUIRREL
scril
scweal
skerl
skrel
sor
sqorerl
sqorl
sqourle
squerl
squirl
squirrel
squirril (2)
srl

**TASMANIAN
DEVIL**
tasmanion devil
tasmnindavl

**TASMANIAN
FOX**
tasmanion fox

TIGER
tiger (7)
tigr (3)

WALRUS
elrus
walras
walrus

WHALE
wael
waiel
wail (2)
wal
wayle
wel (2)
wele
whale (6)
wheal

WOLF
wlofe
wofe
wolf (7)

**WOOLLY
MAMMOTH**
wolly mameth

WORM
worm

YAK
yak (2)

ZEBRA
zeba
zebera (2)
zebra (9)
zebrah
zibra

Appendix F

Books About Language for Teachers and Young Readers

Books and articles for teachers

This listing attempts to provide a little of everything: classic descriptions of English spelling, the most important spelling research studies, a few pieces of "ammunition" to share with parents and colleagues, and background reading on the English language in general. I haven't tried to include the many articles on invented spelling practice in the classroom, but many of them are mentioned in Chapter 2.

1. Applebee, Arthur W., Langer, Judith A., & Mullis, Ina V. (1987). *Grammar, punctuation, and spelling: Controlling the conventions of written English at ages 9, 13, and 17*. Princeton, NJ: Educational Testing Service. (ERIC Document Reproduction Service No. ED 282 928)

This little booklet, part of the National Assessment of Educational Progress, is a good summary of how well children spell and punctuate at three different ages; it might serve as a useful comparison point for your students.

2. Bissex, Glenda. (1980). *Gnys at wrk: A child learns to read and write*. Cambridge: Harvard.

This book, Bissex's case study of her young son, is an excellent longitudinal study of invented spelling (grounded in a much broader description of learning to read and write generally) that introduced many of the themes appearing in later spelling research.

3. Brengleman, Frederick H. (1970). Dialect and the teaching of spelling. *Research in the teaching of English, 4,* 129–138.

Although this article is somewhat difficult, it's an important discussion of how spelling reflects *all* dialects by representing a deeper level than that of pronunciation, so that it can't be assumed that Black and other minority dialect speakers will have particular problems with spelling.

4. Bryson, Bill. (1990). *The mother tongue: English and how it got that way*. New York: William Morrow.

This is one of the newest books written for lay readers about the English language. It's highly readable and puts topics like spelling, pronunciation, and swearing in historical context.

5. Calkins, Lucy M. (1980). When children want to punctuate: Basic skills belong in context. *Language Arts, 57,* 567–573.

A brief, classic article comparing punctuation in writing process and "skills" classrooms.

6. Chomsky, Carol. (1970). Reading, writing, and phonology. *Harvard Educational Review, 40,* 287–309.

7. Chomsky, Carol. (1971). Write now, read later. In Courtney B. Cazden (Ed.), *Language in early childhood education* (pp. 119–126). Washington, DC: Association for Education of Young Children.

Roughly contemporaneously with Charles Read's work, Carol Chomsky provided a theoretical basis for invented spelling and showed how children can begin writing through creating their own spellings. Like Read's, this is a groundbreaking work.

8. Clarke, Linda K. (1988). Invented versus traditional spelling in first graders' writings: Effects on learning to spell and read. *Research in the Teaching of English, 22,* 281–309.

This may be the first study to carry out a statistical comparison between writers in invented spelling and traditional spelling classrooms. The findings, which are complex and should be read in their entirety, show that invented spellers not only wrote more but spelled better.

9. Clay, Marie. (1975). *What did I write?* Portsmouth, NH: Heinemann.

Clay's book is especially valuable for teachers working with beginning writers—those who aren't using invented spelling as such yet but are still exploring principles like directionality and variety as they discover how letters are arranged on paper.

10. Cummings, D.W. (1988). *American English spelling: An informal description.* Baltimore: Johns Hopkins.

Although over 500 pages of detailed analysis of English spelling may not seem "informal" to the non-linguist reader, this is still an excellent, comprehensive description that's worth at least browsing in. If nothing else, look for this book at the library and read the introductory chapter, "Spelling as system," for an overview of why spelling is the way it is and how it's evolved over time.

11. Fitzsimmons, Robert J., & Loomer, Bradley M. (1978). *Spelling: Learning and instruction.* Des Moines: Iowa State Department of Public Instruction. (ERIC Document Reproduction Service No. ED 176 285).

This book, although it focuses on research findings about spelling largely in the context of a traditional textbook, word-list paradigm, can be useful ammunition for teachers who want to make a case that many of the practices typical of current practice (such as writing words ten times) aren't a good use of time.

12. Giacobbe, Mary Ellen. (1981). "Kids *can* write the first week of school." *Learning, 10,* 130–132.

This short and simple article provides convincing evidence that using invented spelling right from the very beginning of school is a solid practice that fosters both writing and learning to spell. It's an excellent choice for kindergarten and first-grade teachers to share with parents.

13. Grambs, David. (1989). *Death by spelling: A compendium of tests, super tests, and killer bees.* New York: Harper & Row.

This is a terrific book for browsing; it contains dozens of short essays on topics like spelling history, spelling reform, and proofreading, as well as about eight *really tough* spelling quizzes. This is an ideal resource for upper-grade teachers with students who can't find enough hard words to challenge themselves to learn; they could take on Grambs's list of American cities like Albuquerque and Winnemucca or gourmet cooking terms like cannelloni and radicchio!

14. Hanna, Paul R., Hanna, Jean S., Hodges, Richard E., & Rudorf, Erwin H., Jr. (1966). *Phoneme-grapheme correspondences as cues to spelling improvement.* Washington: U.S. Office of Education. (ERIC Document Reproduction Service No. ED 128 835)

For teachers who enjoy both linguistics and the history of our profession, this lengthy classic is a fascinating exploration of how our spelling system translates sound into written representations, and, by implication, the limitations of trying to reduce that system to a phonetic one. The number and complexity of the rules involved are a sobering reminder that learning to spell isn't just a matter of learning a few simple rules.

15. Hodges, Richard E. (1991). "The conventions of writing." In James Flood, Julie Jensen, Diane Lapp, & James R. Squire (Eds.), *Handbook of research on teaching the English language arts* (pp. 775–786). New York: Macmillan.

A concise, state-of-the-art review of literature about spelling, punctuation, and handwriting, focusing on both learning and instruction.

16. Horn, Ernest. (1929a). "The influence of past experiences upon spelling." *Journal of Educational Research, 19,* 283–288.

17. Horn, Ernest. (1929b). "A source of confusion in spelling." *Journal of Educational Research, 19,* 47–55.

18. Horn, Ernest. (1929c). "The child's early experience with the letter *a.*" *Journal of Educational Psychology, 20,* 161–168.

These three pieces, although more than sixty years old, are still fun to read as Horn provides exhaustive evidence of how complicated our spelling system is: children see 47 different sound associations for the letter *a* (alone or with other letters) in first grade (1929c), and any word can be spelled many, many different ways if we just look at sound/spelling relationships. (1929b see Spelling Celebration #6.) He also shows dozens of invented spellings of the words *circus, tease,* and *miscellaneous* (1929a), thereby proving that invented spelling didn't suddenly evolve in the 1970s!

19. Lederer, Richard. (1989). *Crazy English: The ultimate joy ride through our language.* New York: Pocket Books.

Lederer has established a small cottage industry producing books like this one about little oddities and interesting tidbits of our language. The pieces are short and make easy reading; this book includes a discussion of contenders for the longest word in English, a list of words about words, and some new eponyms (words derived from people—or quasi-people) like "mickey mouse" used as an adjective.

20. McCrum, Robert, Cran, William, & MacNeil, Robert. (1986). *The story of English.* New York: Viking Penguin.

This companion book to the PBS television series is an excellent overview of the history of English in a global context, with excellent sections on the varieties of English found in many countries around the world. A teacher who read this book for background knowledge would have many, many ideas for developing a thematic unit on language.

21. Moats, Louisa C. (1983). A comparison of the spelling errors of older dyslexic and second-grade normal children. *Annals of Dyslexia, 33,* 121–140.

This is a valuable reference source to show to parents or colleagues who insist that dyslexic children produce bizarre spellings that probably indicate visual/perceptual problems. Moats provides convincing evidence that children labeled dyslexic produce the same kinds of invented spellings as other children (with, if anything, *fewer* reversal problems), which have been misinterpreted by researchers without adequate knowledge about developmental spelling.

22. Read, Charles. (1971). Pre-school children's knowledge of English phonology. *Harvard Educational Review, 41,* 1–34.
23. Read, Charles. (1975). *Children's categorizations of speech sounds in English.* Urbana, IL: National Council of Teachers of English.

These two pieces, the second one an expanded version of the first, laid the groundwork for invented spelling as an area of research. *The* classic work explaining why young children spell the way that they do, and showing that their spellings are phonetically based rather than random. Along with Carol Chomsky's work, these should be read by anyone with an interest in the original foundations of invented spelling in the classroom.

24. Rice, J.M.. (1897). The futility of the spelling grind. *The Forum, 23,* 163–172, 409–419.

Another piece of terrific historical interest. Rice conducted a large-scale survey of spelling in schools throughout the United States, and found both a good deal of variety and quite a bit of tedious practice (as his title indicates!).

25. Tuleja, Tad. (1987). *Namesakes: An entertaining guide to the origins of more than 300 words named for people.* New York: McGraw-Hill.

An interesting resource book, arranged in a variety of categories. Did you know, for instance, that the flowers begonia, fuchsia, and poinsettia were all named after people?

26. Venezky, Richard L. (1970). *The structure of English orthography.* The Hague: Mouton.

This book, like Cummings', is a very useful background reference about how the spelling system itself actually works.

27. Villiers, Una. (1989). *Luk mume luke dade I kan rit.* New York: Scholastic.

An easy-to-read journey through some early writing samples, arranged in the form of children's texts and commentary on them.

Books for young readers

As with the books for teachers, I've tried to be suggestive rather than exhaustive, providing information about a range of different kinds of books that are available. The picture books listed are often at least as valuable for upper elementary children as for younger ones, while the informational books will in many cases be good reference books for teachers of all grades as well as for upper elementary and middle school children who are their target audience.

Picture books

1. Ameny, Heather. (1979). *The first 1,000 words: A picture word book*. London: Usborne.

This is an excellent resource book for young writers, particularly for finding concrete nouns, since the words are arranged categorically rather than alphabetically and are all illustrated.

2. Charlip, Remy, Beth, Mary, & Ancona, George. (1974). *Handtalk: An ABC of finger spelling and sign language*. New York: Macmillan.

This alphabet book uses photographs of sign language and finger spelling to illustrate every letter of the alphabet. Part of the fun is guessing what words are being illustrated.

3. Civardi, Anne, & King, Colin. (1984). *Usborne children's wordfinder*. London: Usborne.

This excellent picture dictionary contains double-page spreads with headings like "On the farm," "Food," and "At the airport," each one with about a hundred words as labels for things in the picture. There are some Britishisms, but not as many as one would expect; for instance, the words *headlamp* and *number plate* [license plate] appear, but *trunk* and *truck* are used instead of *boot* and *lorry*. Other books in the series include *Animals* and *Around the world*. (In the latter, do keep an eye out for the use of insensitive words like *squaw* and *papoose*.)

4. Gwynne, Fred. (1970). *The king who rained*. New York: Simon & Schuster.
5. Gwynne, Fred. (1976). *A chocolate moose for dinner*. New York: Simon & Schuster.

These two very well-known books contain vivid illustrations of how homophones can suggest funny misinterpretations. Imagine having a literal "frog" in your throat, or waiting to see the "blue prince" for your new house!

6. Heller, Ruth. (1988). *Kites sail high: A book about verbs*. New York: Grosset & Dunlap.

Heller's vibrantly illustrated series of picture books on parts of speech (also including *A cache of jewels and other collective nouns* and *Many luscious lollipops: A book about adjectives*) shows that even the driest topic can be made interesting if done well. What I like best about these books is the double-page spreads that simply illustrate parts of speech (such as the three pictures for "Pelicans FLY, kites SAIL high, and rabbits quickly MULTIPLY"). In using these with children, I'd play down the more didactic sections ("The SUBJUNCTIVE MOOD expresses a wish . . . or uses the words 'as though' or 'if' "). Although this series does not address spelling and punctuation directly, it will support a more generalized interest in language.

7. Maestro, Giulio. (1984). *What's a frank frank? Tasty homograph riddles*. New York: Clarion.

A lot of the fun of this book is in the pictures that bring together sometimes unlikely combinations of words that happen to be spelled and pronounced the same. For instance, a fish lying next to a shoe at the bottom of the ocean illustrates "How is a sole sole like a sole?" ("One [single] flat fish is like the bottom of a shoe.")

8. McMillan, Bruce. (1990). *One sun: A book of terse verse*. New York: Holiday House.

Bruce McMillan's photographs of people at the beach illustrate a collection of two-word poems. These are an excellent way to create awareness of the patterned variability of our spelling system, since some of the rhyming pairs have parallel spellings (snail trail, sand hand) while others don't (six sticks, whale pail). Children might enjoy creating their own books of terse verse.

9. Obligado, Lilian. (1983). *Faint frogs feeling feverish & other terrifically tantalizing tongue twisters*. New York: Puffin.

Since the phrases in this book (which are less tongue twisters than alliterations, like "rhinoceros racing roadrunner" and "cat cooking codfish") are arranged alphabetically, they'd be especially useful to use with beginners who are still getting familiar with the alphabet. Since they are all about animals, they could fit into an animal unit in science or literature.

10. Spier, Peter. (1971). *Gobble growl grunt*. Garden City, NY: Doubleday.

Spier's book of words for animal "speech" includes common words like "neigh" and "oink" but also invents spellings for sounds that we haven't conventionalized an expression for, like a flamingo's "hoong-hoong" and a camel's "sffit."

11. Steig, William. (1968). *CDB!*. New York: Simon & Schuster.

12. Steig, William. (1970). *The bad speller*. New York: Simon & Schuster.

Steig's classic *CDB!* uses letters as rebuses, with pictures to help the reader figure out (for instance) that the child pointing to a panel of buttons, captioned "I M N D L-F-8-R," is probably in a high-rise building. This would be fun for older readers to use to reflect back on their own earlier letter-name spelling. *The bad speller*, made up of what the jacket copy calls "inspired misspellings" uses the same format but higher-level invented spellings, like "KIDZ COUGHT IN A HEVY DOUNPOR OV RANE."

Informational books

1. Espy, Willard R. (1982). *A children's almanac of words at play*. New York: Clarkson N. Potter.

Like his similar books for adults, Espy's almanac is arranged with an entry for every day of the year, and includes poems, puns, jokes, and word puzzles. Two examples: February 16 asks the reader to guess the English versions of various place names written in their own language (*Po* is Tibetans' name for their country, while *Lydveldid Island* is Iceland's "real" name), while July 2 has spoonerisms like "Coffee always weeps me a cake."

2. Greenfeld, Howard. (1978). *Sumer is icumen in: Our ever-changing language*. New York: Crown.

This history of the English language focuses mostly on meaning, but also has some examples of how our spelling system has changed over time, such as Chaucer's "*condiciun, seyd, contree,* and *armee*, spellings no less logical than our own."

3. Hackwell, W. John. (1987). *Signs, letters, words: Archaeology discovers writing*. New York: Scribner's.

Although a more accurate title for this book might be *The genealogy of the alphabet,* since it deals primarily with the precursors of our own writing system, it is still a fascinating introduction for upper elementary and middle school students who wonder how our writing system came to be.

4. Kaye, Cathryn B. (1985). *Word works: Why the alphabet is a kid's best friend.*
   Boston: Little, Brown.

This book, from the "Brown Paper School" series, may be the liveliest, most diverse informational book on language for children available. It deals with words in the larger context of writing, with sections not only on word origins and sign language but on newspapers and diaries.

5. Kohn, Bernice. (1974). *What a funny thing to say!* New York: Dial.

A good general book with chapters on topics like word origins, cliches, and wordplay.

6. Kraske, Robert. (1975). *The story of the dictionary.* New York: Harcourt
Brace Jovanovich.

This description of the history of dictionaries and the process of compiling them is surprisingly interesting, even for teachers, and could inspire a class dictionary-writing project (perhaps of local slang). The procedures described are largely pre-computerization, and there are many photographs of index cards and other paraphernalia for manual word-arranging. Another class project might be to research how dictionaries are written today.

7. Meltzer, Milton. (1984). *A book about names.* New York: Crowell.

A fascinating collection of short takes on various aspects of names and naming: historical vignettes, cultural diversity in naming, pet names and nicknames, and so on. One passage talks about what names were like before the standardization of spelling: "George Washington's half brother, Lawrence, was known as Wasshington when a student at Oxford. Jefferson was once Jeffeson and Giffersonne."

8. Nurnberg, Maxwell. (1968). *Wonders in words.* Englewood Cliffs, NJ: Prentice-Hall.

This book focuses on word origins, and is arranged categorically, with chapters on flower names (e.g., *dandelion* comes from a phrase meaning "lion's tooth" in French), eponyms (words derived from people's names), and words based on animal names (*muscle* comes from the Latin for "little mouse," which described the look of rippling biceps!).

9. Schiller, Andrew, & Jenkins, William A. (1977). *In other words: A beginning
   thesaurus.* New York: Lothrop, Lee & Shepard.

Unlike adult thesauruses, this version for children not only provides synonyms but defines them in informal language so that they'll be used appropriately.

10. Schwartz, Alvin. (1982). *The cat's elbow and other secret languages.* New York: Farrar Straus Giroux.

Schwartz's look at Pig Latin and its less familiar cousins like Iggity, Ziph, and Thief Talk (including Cockney rhyming slang) are fascinating descriptions of the secret languages that children are often fascinated with. My favorite is Boontling, a secret language with no particular rules used in Boonville, California, from the 1880s to the 1930s.

11. Silverstein, Alvin & Virginia. (1988). *Wonders of speech.* New York: Morrow.

This is an excellent introduction to linguistics for young adult readers; although it doesn't deal with spelling or indeed with written language at all, it does help readers learn about the sounds of language, its history, how children learn it, and the controversy over animal language research.

12. Sperling, Susan K. (1985). *Murfles and wink-a-peeps: Funny old words for kids.*
    New York: Clarkson N. Potter.

Sperling has written several books about obsolete words (including *Poplollies and bellibones*, 1977, for adults). Children are likely to enjoy learning words like *murfles* (freckles) and *lip-claps* (kisses) to drop into their conversation.

13. Steckler, Arthur. (1979). *101 words and how they began*. Garden City, NY: Doubleday.

14. Steckler, Arthur. (1980). *101 more words and how they began*. Garden City, NY: Doubleday.

The titles of these books are self-explanatory. They would be useful both as browsing resources for children and for teacher background knowledge in helping children explore word origins.

15. Sullivan, Mary B., & Bourke, Linda. (1980). *A show of hands: Say it in sign language*. New York: Lippincott.

An excellent introduction to another form of language, this book is written largely in cartoon style in order to show sign language in context. Many children enjoy using finger spelling, which is described and illustrated here.

16. Terban, Marvin. (1988). *Guppies in tuxedos: Funny eponyms*. New York: Clarion.

Terban has created a whole series of books focusing on interesting words, where they came from, and how they work. Others in the series include: *Eight ate: A feast of homonym riddles*; *In a pickle: And other funny idioms*; *I think I thought: And other tricky verbs*; *Too hot to hoot: Funny palindrome riddles*; and *Your foot's on my feet!: And other tricky nouns*. The whole series is available in paperback and would be an excellent resource for learning about words though browsing.

REFERENCES

Allington, Richard. (1983). The reading instruction provided readers of differing reading ability. *Elementary School Journal, 83,* 548–559.

Andrews, Robert M. (1991, May 31). Spelling bee winner, 13, shows no inappetence for her subject. *Arizona Daily Star.* p. A8.

Applebee, Arthur W., Langer, Judith A., & Mullis, Ina V. (1987). *Grammar, punctuation, and spelling: Controlling the conventions of written English at ages 9, 13, and 17.* Princeton, NJ: Educational Testing Service. (ERIC Document Reproduction Service No. ED 282 928).

Baghban, Marcia. (1984). *Our daughter learns to read and write: A case study from birth to three.* Newark, DL: International Reading Association.

Baldwin, R. Scott, & Coady, James M. (1978). Psycholinguistic approaches to a theory of punctuation. *Journal of Reading Behavior, 10,* 363–375.

Barron, Roderick W. (1980). Visual and phonological strategies in reading and spelling. In Uta Frith (Ed.), *Cognitive processes in spelling* (pp. 195–213). London: Academic Press.

Base, Graeme. (1986). *Animalia.* New York: Abrams.

Beers, James W., & Henderson, Edmund H. (1977). A study of developing orthographic concepts among first graders. *Research in the Teaching of English, 11,* 133–148.

Bissex, Glenda. (1980). *Gnys at wrk: A child learns to read and write.* Cambridge, MA: Harvard.

Boiarsky, Carolyn. (1969). Consistency of spelling and pronunciation deviations of Appalachian students. *The Modern Language Journal, 53,* 347–350.

Boitani, Luigi, & Bartoli, Stefania. (1983). *Simon & Schuster's guide to mammals.* New York: Simon & Schuster.

Brown, T. Julian. (1985). Punctuation. *Encyclopedia Britannica* (Vol. 29) 1006–1008.

Bryant, Peter E., & Bradley, Lynette. (1980). Why children sometimes write words which they do not read. In Uta Frith (Ed.), *Cognitive processes in spelling* (pp. 355–370). London: Academic Press.

Bryant, Peter E., & Bradley, Lynette. (1983). Psychological strategies and the development of reading and writing. In Margaret Martlew (Ed.), *The psychology of written language* (pp. 163–178). Chichester, England: John Wiley.

Calkins, Lucy M. (1980). When children want to punctuate: basic skills belong in context. *Language Arts, 57,* 567–573.

Calkins, Lucy M. (1986). *The art of teaching writing.* Portsmouth, NH: Heinemann.

Chomsky, Carol. (1970). Reading, writing, and phonology. *Harvard Educational Review, 40,* 287–309.

Chomsky, Carol. (1971). Invented spelling in the open classroom. *Word, 27,* 499–518.

Chomsky, Carol. (1972). Write now, read later. In Courtney B. Cazden (Ed.), *Language in early childhood education* (pp. 119–126). Washington, DC: Association for Education of Young Children.

Chomsky, Carol. (1979). Approaching reading through invented spelling. In Lauren B. Resnick & Phyllis A. Weaver (Eds.), *Theory and practice of early reading* (Vol. 2) (pp. 43–65). Hillsdale, NJ: Lawrence Erlbaum.

Clay, Marie. (1975). *What did I write?* Portsmouth, NH: Heinemann.

Clifton, Lucille. (1973). *All us come cross the water*. New York: Holt, Rinehart, & Winston.

Cordeiro, Patricia, Giacobbe, Mary Ellen, & Cazden, Courtney. (1983). Apostrophes, quotation marks, and periods: Learning punctuation in the first grade. *Language Arts, 60,* 323–332.

Cronnell, Bruce. (1980). *Punctuation and capitalization: A review of the literature.* Los Alamitos, CA: Southwest Regional Laboratory for Educational Research and Development. (ERIC Document Reproduction Service No. ED 208 404).

Cummings, D. W. (1988). American English spelling: An informal description. Baltimore: Johns Hopkins.

deGoes, Cecilia, & Martlew, Margaret. (1983). Young children's approach to literacy. In Margaret Martlew (Ed.), *The psychology of written language* (pp. 217–236). Chichester, England: John Wiley.

DeVilliers, Jill G., & DeVilliers, Peter A. (1978). *Language Acquisition.* Cambridge, MA: Harvard.

Dolch, E.W. (1941). *Teaching primary reading.* Champaign, IL: Garrard.

Durham, Robert. (1987). *333 word book: Animals everywhere.* N.p.: Children's Press Choice.

Durkin, Dolores. (1978–9). What classroom observations reveal about reading comprehension instruction. *Reading Research Quarterly, 4,* 481–538.

Edelsky, Carole. (1983). Segmentation and punctuation: Developmental data from young writers in a bilingual program. *Research in the Teaching of English, 17,* 135–156.

Ferreiro, Emilia, & Teberosky, Ana. (1982). *Literacy before schooling.* Portsmouth, NH: Heinemann.

Fillion, Bryant. (1983). Let me see you learn. *Language Arts, 60,* 702–710.

Finnegan, William. (1986). *Crossing the line: A year in the land of apartheid.* New York: Harper & Row.

Fitzsimmons, Robert J., & Loomer, Bradley M. (1978). *Spelling: Learning and instruction.* Des Moines: Iowa State Department of Public Instruction. (ERIC Document Reproduction Service No. ED 176 285).

Frith, Uta. (1979). Reading by eye and writing by ear. In Paul A. Kolers, Merald E. Wrolstad, & Herman Bouma (Eds.), *Processing of visible language* (Vol. 1) (pp. 379–390). New York: Plenum Press.

Frith, Uta (Ed.). (1980a). *Cognitive processes in spelling.* London: Academic Press.

Frith, Uta. (1980b). Unexpected spelling problems. In Uta Frith (Ed.), *Cognitive processes in spelling* (pp. 495–515). London: Academic Press.

Frumkes, Lewis B. (1983). *How to raise your I.Q. by eating gifted children.* New York: McGraw-Hill.

Gelb, I. J. (1952). *A study of writing.* Chicago: University of Chicago Press.

Geller, Linda G. (1985). *Wordplay and language learning for children.* Urbana, IL: National Council of Teachers of English.

Gerber, Michael M. (1984). Orthographic problem-solving abilities of learning disabled and normally achieving students. *Learning Disability Quarterly, 7,* 157–164.

Giacobbe, Mary Ellen. (1981). Kids *can* write the first week of school. *Learning, 10,* 130–132.

Gibson, Eleanor J., & Levin, Harry. (1975). *The psychology of reading.* Cambridge, MA: MIT Press.

Golick, Margie. (1987). *Playing with words.* Markham, Ontario: Pembroke. (Distributed in the United States by Heinemann, Portsmouth, NH.)

Goodman, Kenneth S. (1982). *Language and literacy: The selected writings of Kenneth S. Goodman* (Vol. 1). Boston: Routledge & Kegan Paul.

Goodman, Kenneth S. (1984). Unity in reading. In Alan C. Purves & Olive Niles (Eds.), *Becoming readers in a complex society* (Eighty-third yearbook of the National Society for the Study of Education) (pp. 79–114). Chicago: National Society for the Study of Education.

Goodman, Kenneth S. (1985). Growing into literacy. *Prospects: Quarterly Review of Education, 15,* 57–65.

Goodman, Kenneth. (1986). *What's whole in whole language?.* Portsmouth, NH: Heinemann.

Goodman, Kenneth S. (1988, July). *Language and learning: Toward a social-personal view.* Paper presented at Brisbane (Australia) Conference on Language and Learning.

Goodman, Kenneth S., & Goodman, Yetta M. (1963). Spelling ability of a self-taught reader. *The Elementary School Journal, 64,* 149–154.

Goodman, Kenneth S., Bird, Lois B., & Goodman, Yetta M. (1991). *The whole language catalog.* Santa Rosa, CA: American School Publishers.

Goodman, Yetta. (1978). Kidwatching: An alternative to testing. *National Elementary School Principal, 57,* 41–45.

Goodman, Yetta. (1979). The sadlamation point [Letter to the editor]. *Language Arts, 56,* 482.

Goodman, Yetta. (1984). *A two-year case study observing the development of third and fourth grade Native American children's writing processes.* Final report, National Institute of Education Grant No. NIE-G-81–0127. Tucson, AZ: Program in Language and Literacy, College of Education, University of Arizona.

Gordon, Karen. (1983). *The well-tempered sentence: A punctuation handbook for the innocent, the eager, and the doomed.* New York: Ticknor & Fields.

Graham, Richard T., & Rudorf, E. Hugh. (1970). Dialect and spelling. *Elementary English, 47,* 363–376.

Graves, Donald. (1983). *Writing: Teachers and children at work.* Portsmouth, NH: Heinemann.

Groff, Patrick. (1978). Children's spelling of features of Black English. *Research in the Teaching of English, 12,* 21–28.

Gwynne, Fred. (1970). *The king who rained.* New York: Simon & Schuster.

Gwynne, Fred. (1975). *A chocolate moose for dinner.* New York: Simon & Schuster.

Hanna, Paul R., Hanna, Jean S., Hodges, Richard E., & Rudorf, Erwin H., Jr. (1966). *Phoneme-grapheme correspondences as cues to spelling improvement.* Washington DC: U.S. Office of Education. (ERIC Document Reproduction Service No. ED 128 835)

Hansen, Jane. (1987). *When writers read*. Portsmouth, NH: Heinemann.

Harste, Jerome C., Woodward, Virginia A., & Burke, Carolyn L. (1984). *Language stories and literacy lessons*. Portsmouth, NH: Heinemann.

Heald-Taylor, B. Gail. (1984). Scribble in first grade writing. *Reading Teacher, 38*, 4–8.

Henderson, Edmund. (1981). *Learning to read and spell: The child's knowledge of words*. DeKalb, IL: Northern Illinois University.

Henderson, Edmund. (1985). *Teaching spelling*. Boston: Houghton Mifflin.

Henderson, Edmund H., & Beers, James W. (Eds.). (1980). *Developmental and cognitive aspects of learning to spell: A reflection of word knowledge*. Newark, DL: International Reading Association.

Hildreth, Gertrude. (1936). Developmental sequences in name writing. *Child Development, 7*, 291–303.

Hildreth, Gertrude. (1947). Spelling as a language tool. *Elementary School Journal, 48*, 33–40.

Hildreth, Gertrude. (1948). Word frequency as a factor in learning to read and spell. *Journal of Educational Research, 41*, 467–471.

Hodges, Richard E. (1981). The language base of spelling. In Victor Froese & Stanley B. Straw (Eds.), *Research in the language arts: Language and schooling* (pp. 203–226). Baltimore: University Park Press.

Hodges, Richard E. (1982). *Improving spelling and vocabulary in the secondary school*. Urbana, IL: ERIC Clearinghouse on Reading and Communication Skills and National Council of Teachers of English. (ERIC Document Reproduction Service No. ED 218 645).

Hodges, Richard E. (1987). American spelling instruction: Retrospect and prospect. *Visible Language, 21*, 215–234.

Holmes, Deborah Lott, & Peper, Richard J. (1977). An evaluation of the use of spelling error analysis in the diagnosis of reading difficulties. *Child Development, 48*, 1708–1711.

Horn, Ernest. (1929a). The influence of past experiences upon spelling. *Journal of Educational Research, 19*, 283–288.

Horn, Ernest. (1929b). A source of confusion in spelling. *Journal of Educational Research, 19*, 47–55.

Horn, Ernest. (1954). *Teaching spelling*. Washington: National Education Association.

Iowa Tests of Basic Skills. (1956). *Manual for administrators, supervisors, and counselors*. Boston: Houghton Mifflin.

Jimenez, Robert. (forthcoming). *The strategic reading processes of expert Hispanic bilingual readers*. Doctoral dissertation, University of Illinois.

Kamii, Constance. (1984). *Young children reinvent arithmetic: Implications of Piaget's theory*. New York: Teachers College Press.

Kirk, Ursula. (1983). Introduction: Toward an understanding of the neuropsychology of language, reading, and spelling. In Ursula Kirk (Ed.), *Neuropsychology of language, reading and spelling* (pp. 3–31). New York: Academic Press.

Kligman, Donna S., Cronnell, Bruce A., & Verna, Gary B. (1972). Black English pronunciation and spelling performance. *Elementary English, 49*, 1247–1253.

Labov, William. (1970). The logic of nonstandard English. *Georgetown Monographs of Language and Linguistics, 22,* 1–22.

Lashley, K. S. (1951). The problem of serial order in behavior. In L. A. Jeffress (Ed.), *Cerebral mechanisms in behavior.* New York: John Wiley.

Lindfors, Judith W. (1987). *Children's language and learning* (2nd ed.). Englewood Cliffs, NJ: Prentice-Hall.

Little, Greta D. (1984). Punctuation. In Michael Moran & Ronald Lunsford (Eds.), *Research in rhetoric and composition* (pp. 371–398). Westport, CT: Greenwood Press.

Manolakes, George. (1975). The teaching of spelling: A pilot study. *Elementary English, 52,* 243–247.

Marek, Ann. (1989). Using evaluation as an instructional strategy for adult readers. In Kenneth Goodman, Yetta Goodman, & Wendy Hood (Eds.), *The whole language evaluation book* (pp. 213–226). Portsmouth, NH: Heinemann.

Marino, Jacqueline L. (1980). What makes a good speller? *Language Arts, 53,* 173–177.

Marsh, George, Friedman, Morton, Welch, Veronica, & Desberg, Peter. (1980). The development of strategies in spelling. In Uta Frith (Ed.), *Cognitive processes in spelling* (pp. 339–353). London: Academic Press.

Martin, Bill, Jr. (1983). *Brown bear, brown bear, what do you see?* New York: Holt.

Masters, Harry. (1927). A study of errors in common difficult words. *The Elementary English Review, 4,* 113–116.

McCardle, Peggy. (1980). *Vernacular Black English and underlying phonological form: Evidence from child spelling.* Paper presented at the annual meeting of the Linguistic Society of America, San Antonio. (ERIC Document Reproduction Service No. ED 211 614).

McCrum, Robert, Cran, William, & MacNeil, Robert. (1986). *The story of English.* New York: Viking.

McGee, Lea M., & Richgels, Donald J. (1989). "*K* is Kristen's": Learning the alphabet from a child's perspective. *The reading teacher, 43,* 216–225.

Miller, Lynne D. and Woodley, John W. (1983). Retrospective miscue analysis: procedures for research and instruction. *Research on reading in secondary schools.* (College of Education, University of Arizona), 10–11, 53–67.

Milz, Vera E. (1983). A psycholinguistic description of the development of writing in selected first grade students. (Doctoral dissertation, University of Arizona). *Dissertation Abstracts International, 44,* 3279A.

Moats, Louisa C. (1983). A comparison of the spelling errors of older dyslexic and second-grade normal children. *Annals of Dyslexia, 33,* 121–140.

Nagy, William E., Herman, Patricia A., & Anderson, Richard C. (1985). Learning words from context. *Reading Research Quarterly, 20,* 233-253.

National Commission on Testing and Public Policy. (1990). *From gatekeeper to gateway: Transforming testing in America.* Chestnut Hill, MA: National Commission on Testing and Public Policy, Boston College.

National Council of Teachers of English. (1974, special fall issue). Students' right to their own language. *College composition and communication, 25,* 1–32.

Neisser, Ulric. (1976). *Cognition and reality.* San Francisco: W. H. Freeman.

Noble, Trinka H. (1984). *The day Jimmy's boa ate the wash.* New York: Dial.

Nolen, Patricia, & McCartin, Rosemarie. (1984). Spelling strategies on the Wide Range Achievement Test. *The Reading Teacher, 38,* 148–157.

O'Neal, Verley, & Trabasso, Tom. (1976). Is there a correspondence between sound and spelling? In Deborah S. Harrison & Tom Trabasso (Eds.), *Black English: A seminar* (pp. 171–190). Hillsdale, NJ: Lawrence Erlbaum.

Odom, Robert R. (1962). Growth of a language skill: Capitalization. *California Journal of Educational Research, 13,* 3–8.

Parker, Steve. (1989). *Mammal* (Eyewitness Books). New York: Knopf.

Polanyi, Michael. (1966). *The tacit dimension.* Garden City, NY: Doubleday.

Radebaugh, Muriel R. (1985). Children's perceptions of their spelling strategies. *Reading Teacher, 38,* 532–536.

Read, Charles. (1971). Pre-school children's knowledge of English phonology. *Harvard Educational Review, 41,* 1–34.

Read, Charles. (1975). *Children's categorizations of speech sounds in English.* Urbana, IL: National Council of Teachers of English.

Read, Charles. (1981). Writing is not the inverse of reading for young children. In Carl H. Frederickson & Joseph F. Dominic (Eds.), *Writing: The nature, development, and teaching of written communication* (Vol. 2). (pp. 105–118). Hillsdale, NJ: Lawrence Erlbaum.

Rice, J.M.. (1897). The futility of the spelling grind. *The Forum, 23,* 163–172, 409–419.

Rinsland, Henry D. (1945). *A basic vocabulary of elementary school children.* New York: Macmillan.

Rosinski, Richard R., & Wheeler, Kirk E. (1972). Children's use of orthographic structure in word discrimination. *Psychonomic Sciences, 26,* 97–98.

Shaughnessy, Mina P. (1977). *Errors and expectations.* New York: Oxford.

Shaw, Harry. (1963). *Punctuate it right!* New York: Barnes & Noble.

Simon, Dorothea P., & Simon, Herbert A. (1973). Alternative uses of phonemic information in spelling. *Review of Educational Research, 43,* 115–137.

Sloboda, John A. (1980). Visual imagery and individual differences in spelling. In Uta Frith (Ed.), *Cognitive processes in spelling* (pp. 231–248). London: Academic Press.

Smith, Frank. (1982). *Writing and the writer.* New York: Holt, Rinehart, & Winston.

Smith, Frank. (1988). *Joining the literacy club.* Portsmouth, NH: Heinemann.

Smith, Madorah. (1926). An investigation of the development of the sentence and the extent of vocabulary in young children. *University of Iowa Studies in Child Welfare, 3* (5).

Smith, Philip T. (1980). In defence of conservatism in English orthography. *Visible Language, 14,* 122–136.

Stetson, Elton G., & Boutin, Frances. (1980). *Spelling instruction: Diagnostic-prescriptive minus the diagnostic.* Unpublished paper. (ERIC Document Reproduction Service No. ED 205 980).

Stever, Elizabeth F. (1980). Dialect and spelling. In Edmund H. Henderson & James W. Beers (Eds.), *Developmental and cognitive aspects of learning to spell* (pp. 46–51). Newark, DL: International Reading Association.

Templin, Mildred C. (1957). *Language skills in children: Their development and interrelationships*. Minneapolis: University of Minnesota.

Tompkins, Gail E., & Yaden, David B., Jr. (1986). *Answering students' questions about words*. Urbana, IL: ERIC Clearinghouse on Reading and Communication Skills and National Council of Teachers of English.

Tovey, Duane R. (1978). "Sound-it-out": A reasonable approach to spelling? *Reading World, 17*, 220–233.

Twain, Mark. (1959). *The adventures of Huckleberry Finn*. New York: New American Library. (originally published 1884).

Valmont, William J. (1972). Spelling consciousness: A long neglected area. *Elementary English, 49*, 1219–1221.

Venezky, Richard L. (1979). Orthographic regularities in English words. In Paul A. Kolers, Merald Wrolstad, & Herman Bouma (Eds.), *Processing of visible language* (Vol. 1) (pp. 283–293). New York: Plenum Press.

Villiers, Una. (1989). *Luk mume luke dade I kan rit*. New York: Scholastic.

Vygotsky, L. S. (1978). *Mind in society*. Cambridge: Harvard University Press.

Walker, Laurence. (1979). Newfoundland dialect interference in fourth grade spelling. *The Alberta Journal of Educational Research, 25*, 221–233.

Watt, W. C., & Jacobs, David. (1975). The child's conception of the alphabet. *Proceedings of the Claremont Reading Conference*, 131–137.

Weaver, Constance, (1982). Welcoming errors as signs of growth. *Language Arts, 49* 438–444.

Weaver, Constance. (1988). *Reading process and practice*. Portsmouth, NH: Heinemann.

Webster's ninth new collegiate dictionary. (1983). Springfield, MA: Merriam-Webster.

Wheat, Leonard B. (1932). Four spelling rules. *Elementary School Journal, 32*, 697–706.

Why not Earth? (1989, June 12). *Time*, p. 6.

Wilde, Sandra. (1987). An analysis of the development of spelling and punctuation in selected third and fourth grade children. (Doctoral dissertation, University of Arizona, 1986). *Dissertation Abstracts International, 47*, 2452A.

Wilde, Sandra. (1988). Learning to spell and punctuate: A study of eight- and nine-year-old children. *Language and Education: An International Journal, 2*, 35–59.

Wilde, Sandra. (1989a) Looking at invented spelling: A kid-watcher's guide to spelling, part 1. In Kenneth Goodman, Yetta Goodman, & Wendy Hood (Eds.), *The whole language evaluation book* (pp. 213–226). Portsmouth, NH: Heinemann.

Wilde, Sandra. (1989b) Understanding spelling strategies: A kid-watcher's guide to spelling, part 2. In Kenneth Goodman, Yetta Goodman, & Wendy Hood (Eds.), *The whole language evaluation book* (pp. 227–236). Portsmouth, NH: Heinemann.

Wilde, Sandra. (1990a). A proposal for a new spelling curriculum. *Elementary School Journal, 90*, 275–289.

Wilde, Sandra. (1990b). Spelling textbooks: A critical review. *Linguistics and Education, 2*, 259–280.

Wilde, Sandra. (1990c). *Will children learn to spell in whole-language classrooms?.* Unpublished paper.

Zutell, Jerry. (1978). Some psycholinguistic perspectives on children's spelling. *Language Arts, 55,* 844–850.

Zutell, Jerry. (1979). Spelling strategies of primary school children and their relationship to Piaget's concept of decentration. *Research in the teaching of English, 13,* 69–80.

INDEX